Contemp

CONTEMPORARY ARCHITECTURE
in Washington, D.C.

Claudia D. Kousoulas • George W. Kousoulas
Photography by George W. Kousoulas

The Preservation Press
National Trust for Historic Preservation

John Wiley & Sons, Inc.
New York • Chichester • Brisbane • Toronto • Singapore

The Preservation Press

John Wiley & Sons, Inc.

The National Trust for Historic Preservation is the only private, nonprofit organization chartered by Congress to encourage public participation in the preservation of sites, buildings, and objects significant in American history and culture. In carrying out this mission, the National Trust fosters an appreciation of the diverse character and meaning of our American cultural heritage and preserves and revitalizes the livability of our communities by leading the nation in saving America's historic environments.

Support for the National Trust is provided by membership dues, contributions, and a matching grant from the National Park Service, U.S. Department of the Interior, under provisions of the National Historic Preservation Act of 1966. The opinions expressed here do not necessarily reflect the views or policies of the Interior Department.

Printed in the United States of America
97 96 95   5 4 3 2

Library of Congress Cataloging-in-Publication Data

Kousoulas, Claudia D.
          Contemporary architecture of Washington, D.C. / Claudia D.
Kousoulas, George W. Kousoulas.
               p. cm.
          Includes bibliographical references (p.   -   ) and index.
          ISBN 0-471-14374-X
          1. Architecture, Modern—20th century—Washington Region.
2. Architecture—Washington Region. 3. Washington (D.C.)—
Buildings, structures, etc.   I. Kousoulas, George W.   II. Title
NA735.W3K68   1994
720'.9753' 09045—dc20

                                                              94-32132

Design by Viviane Silverman, Quicksilver Design
Produced by Watermark Design Office

Foreword

Cities have personalities. They talk to you in special ways; most through their physicality, others through people. Some tell you their history, others their geography or topography. There are cities that project an image before you visit them; Beijing and Shanghai are exotic; New Orleans is sultry. My city, New York, is raucous, aggressive, and without manners, but with a unique and compelling energy.

Washington is a special city. A symbolic city. It is what we want our city to be. It speaks softly and with an overlay of green. Except for the obvious symbols of civic architecture and monuments, Washington is a city that is about space, trees, and green. It manages to possess a civic urbanity without feeling urban. Over time and through transformation it has come to symbolize the country it serves. Try as the planners will to keep the classical organization of the L'Enfant plan, there is a persistent resistance to any form of submission to the plan's axis and rigidity. Like Americans, each building and space strives for its own individuality in spite of rule and order. As hard as they tried to make Pennsylvania Avenue the Champs Elysees, it ends up as the nation's Main Street—an aggregation of disparate buildings and spaces. We like to visit our European antecedents, yet resist the plaza or piazza in favor of the mall, the courthouse square, or the central park. The more we aspire for monumentality and coherence, the more individualistic are the results. This contradiction defines us as a people and is appropriate. Washington communicates our values in its expression of our fierce egalitarianism and individualism.

Washington is clearly about us, as Americans. It is a city of places not connected; I've never felt crowded or pressured there. I enjoy having the honor of dressing up a small segment of this languid, cool lady, and telling my friends and visitors that if it's beauty you wish to see, it's Washington D.C. No other American city equals it nor is like it.

M. Paul Friedberg

Table of Contents

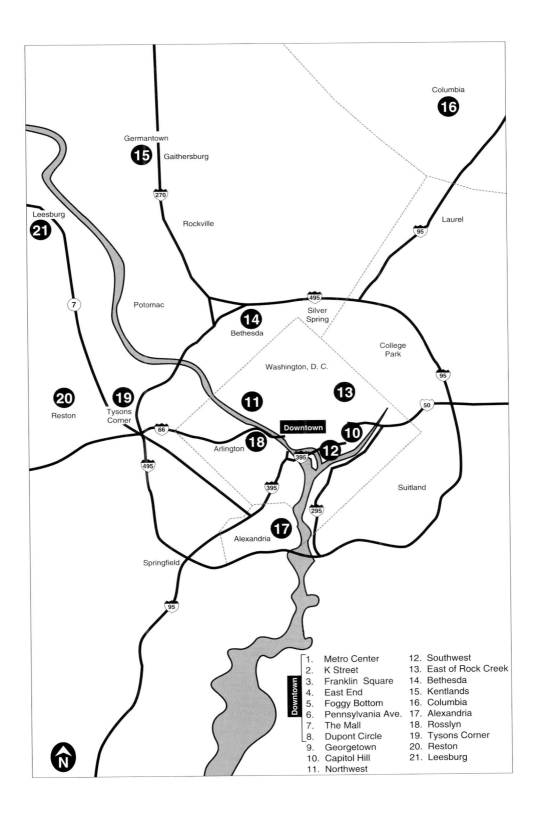

Columbia
16

Germantown
15   Gaithersburg

〔270〕

Leesburg
21

Rockville

〔95〕   Laurel

⑦

Potomac

〔495〕

Silver Spring

14
Bethesda

College Park

〔95〕

Washington, D. C.

20   **19**   **11**   **13**

Reston   Tysons Corner   〔50〕

〔66〕   **Downtown**   **10**

〔495〕   **18**   **12**
Arlington   〔395〕

                〔395〕
                                        Suitland

                        〔295〕

                17
            Alexandria

Springfield

〔95〕

N

Downtown	1. Metro Center	12. Southwest
	2. K Street	13. East of Rock Creek
	3. Franklin Square	14. Bethesda
	4. East End	15. Kentlands
	5. Foggy Bottom	16. Columbia
	6. Pennsylvania Ave.	17. Alexandria
	7. The Mall	18. Rosslyn
	8. Dupont Circle	19. Tysons Corner
	9. Georgetown	20. Reston
	10. Capitol Hill	21. Leesburg
	11. Northwest	

Introduction

Americans must ever see in their National Capital the 'Soul of America'.
Looking for the ideal in their Capital City, they must never see the
smoke and industrial litter of the average factory town. Washington must ever
wear good clothes.

CALVIN COOLIDGE

lanned cities in the New World are not unusual. The Spanish Crown
established rule over its New World colonies by formally laying out towns
that replicated the seats of power in Spain. In young Philadelphia, city
founders planned public squares for the citizenry, signaling new opportunities for colonial settlers. But Washington was the first community
planned in the consciousness of a new nation that spread its avenues wide
for history to fill in. Its name, plan, and buildings place it both in history
and in the future. As Coolidge's words point out, Washington is more than
an urban agglomeration of buildings; it is the ideal of polis, the record of
our glory and goals.

L'Enfant's plan drew on baroque models, on their anchored axes that
clarified the power of popes and princes. His genius was in reconfiguring
this autocratic model to democratic purpose. His siting of the "President's
House," "Congress House," and "Judiciary Court" displays a fine understanding of both this new type of governance and old architectural meanings. The city's founders and financiers complained about his expensive,
wide streets. Visitors, most notably Charles Dickens, ridiculed the empty
lots as a city of magnificent intentions. But the wisdom of L'Enfant's vision
is evident today. His primary axis, Pennsylvania Avenue, strikes a balance
between comfortably scaled walkability and monumental grandeur. Later
plans, the McMillan Plan and the plan of the Pennsylvania Avenue
Development Corporation (PADC), respected L'Enfant's plan and solidified
the extent and nature of the monumental core. The images of postcards
and the evening news are the conscious creations of these plans.

Washington remains dressed in its good clothes. Even for private commercial buildings, monumental images are the designer's stock. Has there
ever been an architect with a Washington commission who has not looked

at L'Enfant's plan and driven the curving parkways past monuments to dead presidents, wondering about context and history? It is a sometimes simplistic equation: noble ideas expressed by white buildings equal good clothes.

But good clothes can be as banal as a navy blazer or as sublime as an Armani suit. Many Washington buildings ascend to sublimity, many are banal, most are good background architecture. They stand, serve their purpose, and add to our enjoyment of the city. The most interesting of them challenge monumental metaphors and mine history for new images relevant to the community and durable into the future.

Long before the 1980s, when CEOs sought famous or infamous architects to create corporate images for new headquarters,, buildings have sent messages. "This is the house of the King," or "Here is where we worship God." In their shape, siting, and materials we define our buildings and ourselves. Buildings send the community's most significant message: "This is where we choose to spend our time, our energy, and our money." Without a prince or pope the meaning may be less direct, but every building sends a message about its builder and the community in which it is built.

Washington's buildings speak in two languages that meld into a unique patois. The monumental city, planned and built to express the power and purpose of nationhood, meets the mercantile city of offices, stores, and lifelong residents. This local city thrives on government, perseveres beyond politics, and picks up a few monumental metaphors for itself. Even in the era of modernism, architects have responded to Washington's unique historical role and developed a classical attitude without columns.

Two elements of the capital city influence the entire city: the height limit and allegorical classicism. The height limit, established by statute in 1910, restricts buildings to roughly 10 stories—a bit higher on the wider streets. It is a requirement that has contributed to Washington's unique feeling of open sky and parklike setting. It has also frustrated architects by limiting their palette in an age of skyscraper aesthetics.

As for allegory, even the commonest office building allows itself a flourish of white marble or columns. Pennsylvania Avenue has always been the dividing line between the local and the federal city. Most recently, however, Market Square has picked up the columns and hemicycles of the Federal Triangle and moved them to the north side of the street, into the local realm.

In this context of moumentality, where history is a constant reference, how does the modern architect proceed with an aesthetic that deliberately erases history? Likewise, how does the postmodern architect proceed with punctured pediments and bright colors in a city where white marble classicism is taken very seriously? These two shifts in architectural styles and the building boom of the 1980s added new buildings to the city's stock and renovated old ones, offering designers a variety of opportunities to develop a new language for Washington architecture.

The L'Enfant Plan and the buildings of every era in both the local and federal cities give Washington layers of meaning. Every block has its unique expression, but at the same time fits into the larger image of Washington. Atop those layers is one more, our own perception of the city—the meaning we give to its places simply by using them. We adopt buildings, streets, parks, and places as personal landmarks to mark events and times in our lives. Memories of success, failure, pain, and joy make the city resonate for each of us beyond the history lesson intended by the designer. The rich variety of these personal associations makes Washington more than a sterile assemblage of marble; they make it a place of life. The favorite buildings and places of notable locals show the depth of the community. Maureen Dowd remembers the Lincoln Memorial as a place for high school dates, and Richard Moe remembers the inspiration he took from the setting of his first Washington job in the Russell Office Building. It is perhaps for this same reason that the Vietnam Memorial is so successful; it is a design that invites our emotions and adopts them as its own.

We imagine that cities just are, that we arrive and they have been here long before us, that they are something we inherit. Their size, noise, and gravitational pull are overwhelming. Their force is such that we cannot imagine what came before paved streets and buildings. Only in small isolated pockets do we get a glimpse of the past—a wooded view that obscures all that is man-made, or a small clapboard building set alone on its site.

But cities—though they take on a force of their own—are our own creations. What we invest, emotionally and monetarily, are the foundations of the city. It is our actions and goals that come together to create a city that will, in turn, explain us as individuals and as a society.

As has every city, Washington has changed. Streets have been paved and lighted, streetcars have come and gone, columns have been erased in favor of sleek steel and have returned again. But more than any other city, Washington remains timeless and perfect, the expression of our ideal. ∎

Chronology of Planning and Development in Washington, D.C.

1749 Alexandria established by the Virginia Assembly; George Washington, working as a surveyor's assistant, helps lay out the town

1789 Georgetown incorporated

George Washington inaugurated as president

1790 Residence Act, passed by Congress meeting in Philadelphia, establishes a permanent home for the federal government within 10 years in the area between the eastern branch of the Potomac and the mouth of Conogocheague Creek (Williamsport, Md.)

Population of Alexandria is 5,000

1791 Pierre L'Enfant submits his plan, "A Map of the City of Washington in the Territory of Columbia"

1792 L'Enfant dismissed

Architect James Hoban begins work on the White House

1793 Construction begins on the Capitol building, designed by William Thornton

1797 Chain Bridge is the first bridge to be built across the Potomac

1799 George Washington dies in December

1800 City population is 14,000

Congress leaves Philadelphia to settle in Washington

1801 Alexandria included within the federal boundaries

A public market established on the south side of Pennsylvania Avenue at Eighth Street becomes the focus of downtown commercial activity

Thomas Jefferson inaugurated as president

1802 Congress authorizes city government of a mayor and 12 council members

1803	President Jefferson makes the first improvements along Pennsylvania Avenue, planting a double row of poplars
1812	U.S. declares war on Britain
1814	British burn capital city, including the White House
1826	Ordinance passed banning cattle from the center of the city
1828	President John Quincy Adams breaks ground for the C&O Canal at Great Falls
1840	City population is 44,000
1842	Pennsylvania Avenue illuminated by oil lights
1844	Samuel Morse sends the first telegram between Baltimore and Washington
1846-1847	Alexandria ceded back to Virginia, reducing the District of Columbia to an area of 68 square miles
	Smithsonian Institution founded
1848	Washington Monument begun with private financing
1850	City population is 50,000
	Representatives of the Union's 31 states begin to cause crowding in the Capitol building; Congress authorizes expansion
1854	Depleted funds temporarily halt construction of the Washington Monument
1860	City population is 75,000
1861	Civil War begins
1862	Horse-drawn streetcars begin running on Washington streets
1863	Capitol dome completed
1867	City experiences a post–Civil War building boom; downtown landmarks built include the Masonic Temple (Lansburgh's Furniture Store) (1867), Franklin School (1868), LeDroit Building (1875), Pension Building (1883), Riggs Building (1891) and Old Post Office (1899)

1870   City population is 132,000

Washington contains 200 miles of unpaved streets; more without sewers or drainage

1871   Territorial Act replaces local city government with a congressionally appointed governor, council, and Board of Public Works (overseen by Alexander "Boss" Shepard)

Georgetown becomes part of the District of Columbia

C&O Canal has its peak year, carrying 900,000 tons of cargo

1872   Over 1,200 new structures built in Washington

1874   Territorial government replaced by three presidentially appointed commissioners

1879   City population is 150,000

1880   Federal government employs 7,800 people

1882   Army Corps of Engineers dredges the Potomac River channel and uses the fill to construct East and West Potomac Parks out of former tidal basins

1884   Capstone of the Washington Monument, the largest piece of aluminum then cast, set in place

1887   2,500 new buildings constructed in the city

1888   Steam elevator installed in the Washington Monument, making it a perennially popular tourist attraction

City Highway Plan prepared by District of Columbia commissioners extends the essence and pattern of L'Enfant's grid and avenues—Congress requires subdivision in conformance with the Plan, citing sprawl of "suburban" expansion

Electric streetcars begin to replace horse and cable cars on city streets

1890   Congress acquires Rock Creek Park

Chevy Chase Land Company established to develop community of Chevy Chase

First entirely steel-framed building constructed in Chicago

1893 World's Columbian Exposition held in Chicago

Federal Highway Act creates streets and parkways designed by landscape architects

1898 The District's first car dealership is established on 14th Street, N.W.

1899 Congress enacts Height of Buildings Act, prompted by the 14-story, 160-foot tall Cairo Hotel

1900 City population is 280,000

1901 Report of the Senate's McMillan Commission outlines the elements of monumental Washington, including Union Station, the Federal Triangle, the Mall museums, and the Lincoln Memorial

1908 Congress authorizes the construction of Union Station, the District Building, Central Library, House and Senate Office Buildings, Department of Agriculture, National Museum (of Natural History), and Army War College

1909 Train station and tracks removed from the Mall

Frank Lloyd Wright builds the Robie House in Chicago; Charles McKim of McKim, Mead and White dies

1910 City population is 330,000

Congress further limits building heights to width of frontage street plus 20 feet

Commission of Fine Arts established to review art, location of statues, fountains, monuments, and buildings in the Federal district

1918 Federal government employs 120,000 people

1919 The Bauhaus founded by Walter Gropius in Weimar, Germany

1920 City zoning ordinance adopted governing land use and building height and bulk, exempting federal buildings

City population is 440,000

1922 Lincoln Memorial completed

1923 Le Corbusier publishes *Towards a New Architecture*

1924   National Capital Park and Planning Commission (NCPC) established

1925   NCPC creates a City Planning Committee

1926   Congress passes Public Buildings Act, authorizing construction of the Federal Triangle, to cover 70 acres

Capital Garage opens at 13th Street and New York Avenue, N.W. At 10 stories, holding 1,300 cars, it is the largest in the world

1927   Maryland National Capital Park and Planning Commission established

1928   Pennsylvania Avenue Market, established in 1801, torn down

1930   City population is 487,000; 72 percent of metropolitan area population, which is 724,000

Shipstead-Luce Act gives Commission of Fine Arts authority to review public and private development adjoining federal buildings or parks

1931   New York City's Empire State Building completed

1932   Arlington Memorial Bridge completed

Philip Johnson and Henry-Russell Hitchcock introduce modern architecture to America with a show at the Museum of Modern Art, New York

1933   Home Owners Loan Corporation set up with federal money to finance long-term, low-interest mortgages

1934   Alley Dwelling Act passed by Congress as a slum clearance measure

1940   City population is 663,000; metropolitan area population reaches 1 million

1941   Staggered hours instituted for federal workers to reduce traffic congestion

First flights at National Airport

National Gallery of Art opens

1943 Jefferson Memorial completed

The Pentagon, the largest office building in the world with 3.7 million square feet of space, completed after a construction period of 16 months

1945 D.C. Redevelopment Act authorizes NCPC to designate renewal areas and adopt plans

1949 National Housing Act finances redevelopment and public housing, authorizing slum clearance

1950 City population is 800,000; metropolitan area population is 1.5 million

Decentralization of federal agencies to the suburbs (CIA, NRC) started by a declaration of national emergency based on vulnerability to attack

40 percent of area's workers employed by the federal government

1955 NCPC conducts mass-transit survey

1960 President Dwight Eisenhower signs National Capital Transportation Act authorizing creation of a rapid-rail system

34 percent of the area's workers employed by the federal government

City population is 764,000; metropolitan area population is 2.1 million

1961 NCPC Year 2000 Policies Plan focuses regional growth in a radial corridor pattern

John F. Kennedy notices the shabby state of the street on his inaugural ride down Pennsylvania Avenue

1962 President's Council on Pennsylvania Avenue is formed, starting the effort to rehabilitate the "grand avenue"

Washington's last streetcar makes its final trip

Dulles Airport completed

1964 Capital Beltway opens

1965   President Johnson asks Congress to authorize a 25-mile, $431 million regional rapid transit system (Metro)

1966   Federal legislation establishes historic preservation in the District of Columbia

1968   Martin Luther King, Jr., assassinated, precipitating riots in commercial centers along H Street N.E., and 7th and 14th Streets, N.W.—Property damage is eventually estimated at $57 million, affecting 1,300 businesses and leaving an impression of downtown as an unsafe place

1969   Metro breaks ground at Judiciary Square

   72 percent of the metropolitan area population lives in the suburbs, a reversal from 1930, when 72 percent lived within the District's boundaries

1970   30 percent of area's workers employed by the federal government

   Metropolitan area population is 2.9 million

1971   Don't Tear It Down, a historic preservation action group, is formed in response to threatened razing of the Old Post Office

   Kennedy Center for the Performing Arts opens

1972   Pennsylvania Avenue Development Corporation is established

1973   Congress grants the District limited home rule under a mayor and council system

1975   United States begins the Bicentennial of the Revolution festivities with ceremonies at the Old North Church in Boston

1976   On March 27, Metro opening day, 51,000 people take free rides over 4.6 miles of completed track

1978   District enacts its Historic Preservation Act

1979   U.S. Department of the Interior files suit against Arlington County, Virginia, claiming that three high-rise buildings planned for Rosslyn "would compete with the Mall memorials and Capitol dome, thus marring their symbolism"

   Metropolitan area population is 3.1 million

1984 21 percent of area's workers employed by the federal government

1985 City planning department completes a comprehensive plan that focuses on economic development in the "city beyond the monuments"

1990 Downtown Washington adds 15.2 million square feet of office space, 408,000 square feet of retail space, and more than 4,000 hotel rooms since 1980

Metro area population is 3.9 million

1991 City population is 598,000, the lowest number since the 1930s

1993 Disney proposes American history theme park

1994 Disney withdraws proposal

Architecture and Urbanism

"The physician can bury his mistakes, but the architect can only advise his client to plant vines."

FRANK LLOYD WRIGHT, 1953

How we experience our cities largely depends on their qualities of architecture and urbanism. Look quickly at a building or a city block and you will have an immediate reaction. Your reaction may be buried deep under concerns about getting to work on time, looking for a bank machine, or catching the next subway train, but it will be there. Look again more closely and you will be able to identify what you are reacting to: light, noise, shape, color, pattern, and activity.

The relationship between architecture and urbanism is a complicated one. Architecture defines buildings: how buildings come together as resolutions of specific problems and how they respond to their setting. Urbanism defines the city: what identifies the public realm and what is expected of the private one. It is difficult to appreciate one without the other. Urbanism cannot exist without architecture; it is the buildings that give form to cities. On the other hand, urbanism is best when architecture recognizes it.

Visual components of buildings—scale, massing, rooflines, windows, materials, entrances, color, and decoration—are the elements of architecture. Architects compose these elements with techniques such as repetition, rhythm, and emphasis to create their buildings. Each period has its own style and accentuates these elements to reflect that style. The boxlike massing and classical symmetry of the Georgian style reflected a formal society. The International Style eschewed color and decoration, but pursued the machine ethic in an age that was transformed by technology. The elements and emphasis may change with style, but they send messages of use and importance. The church steeple is a clear signal of faith and purpose, a glass skyscraper sends a message of progressive success.

Architects manipulate the elements to respond to their own vision, the

CLASSICISM

ANY EXAMINATION OF Washington's architecture must acknowledge the influence of classicism in the city. Architectural styles derived from true classical architecture dominate the monumental buildings of Washington. Whether it is the Georgian and Palladian influenced White House, the early 19th-century Classical Revival Treasury Building, or the 1930s neo-classical Federal Triangle, these styles build upon the Greco-Roman tradition. A number of buildings designed in the 1930s went so far as to combine classical facade organization with the Art Deco style then popular, flattening and graphically stylizing familiar classical details to produce what has been called "Greco-Deco."

The city's and the nation's early growth coincided with an evolving appreciation of the classical cultures of Greece and Rome. At the heart of classical architecture are the orders:

Doric, Ionic, and Corinthian, and two Roman variations, Tuscan and Composite. Each has its own system of organization, composition, and proportion. During the Renaissance, architects rediscovered these systems, rigorously documented them, and carefully applied them in new ways to all types of Renaissance buildings. Andrea Palladio, one of the most influential of the architects of the Italian Renaissance, took the basic language of classical orders and inventively used scale, rhythm, and new elements in his famous villas. Palladio's work and ideas were introduced to England in the 17th century by Inigo Jones, William Kent, and other architects. Their adaptations led to the style we know as Georgian.

Toward the end of the 18th century in America, Thomas Jefferson, in his role as architect and tastemaker, promoted a direct return to the

architectural principles of republican Rome as the true course for a new democracy—a classical revival. Georgian architecture was seen as a style of colonialism and English oppression; the United States instead should look to the architecture of the political cultures of Greece and Rome for inspiration. Ironically, both Georgian and Classical Revival have the same roots.

In the 19th century a French architectural school, the Ecole des Beaux-Arts, dominated architectural education. The school promoted a rigorous yet eclectic application of classical design. Students were schooled in an architectural language that was symmetrical, formal, and hierarchical, but that used elaborate decoration. Beaux-Arts design was a more exuberant excursion into classicism than the earlier revival had been. It also coincided with a technological revolution in building construction, notably steel, which allowed unprecedented ease in spanning great distances. Any space that could be framed in steel could then be clad in a classical veneer.

By the end of the century, American practitioners were mesmerized by the Beaux-Arts aesthetic, and noted architects of the time, including Daniel Burnham and McKim, Mead and White designed some of America's greatest civic buildings using Beaux-Arts principles. The McMillan Plan, which reinterpreted the L'Enfant Plan, is a product of these ideas, as are Union Station, the West Building of the National Gallery, and the Federal Triangle. Beaux-Arts design provided a comprehensive approach to the internal organization, facade treatment, and detailing of buildings of any size. Its influence over American architects held until the end of World War II, when the power of expatriate European modern architects took over.

In Washington the architects of the Federal Triangle organized and published a newsletter to defend their classicism against the new International Style. Paul Cret, architect of the Folger Shakespeare Library and the Organization of American States building, described their work as "the Moderne traditionalized, the Traditional modernized."

Classicism can be a visual reminder of Periclean Athens, but it is also a way of thinking about design: rationality, logic, beauty, order, and balance. As a design approach, classicism is not about columns, entablatures, and peristyles, but about the organization and essence of buildings. Going beyond visual style, it provides an entire basis for design, similar to that of modern architecture.

Superficially, much mainstream postmodernism in Washington appears to be trying to resurrect classicism, but postmodernism and classicism are not the same. Postmodernism makes references to classical details ironically and obliquely, and deliberately tries to subvert the classical position that buildings can be rational and clear. Modern architecture, with its faith in reason, is actually closer to classicism.

Classicism has, more than other styles, become ageless. Unlike a Victorian pile, which looks dark and antique, or a modern building, which can be dated by the design of its wall panels, classicism can be built over centuries and successfully blend with itself. In Washington, one might have a hard time placing classically detailed buildings on a time line, but their construction spans from the White House in the late 1700s to the Jefferson Memorial just before World War II. It is this timeless quality that contributes to Washington's monumental character.

demands of the client, and the character of the surrounding community. They also use these elements to meet our expectations of what a building should be, or to surprise us into a second look. Can you imagine the Capitol building painted like a circus tent? Or a day-care center in columned white marble? The architect may be telling us that government is for clowns and that our children are our most important asset, but clearly the buildings send messages. Whether they fit in or stick out may be the whole point.

The elements of urbanism, the bits and pieces that make up a city or town, are assembled in the same manner, but by a large number of interests acting independently or in concert, guided or unguided. Buildings, squares, ceremonial streets, landscaping, sidewalks, paths, landmarks, and districts take shape when public and private landowners build. In Washington, the L'Enfant Plan and its later interpretations have given strong guidance to the development of the city. L'Enfant assembled elements to create grand distances and link buildings reflecting the goals of a new democracy. Even though the plan took more than a century to complete and was altered over time, it created a shared vision of what Washington should be.

As with architectural patterns, patterns of urbanism can also be used to send messages. Elegant brownstones around a green square and soaring skyscrapers hard by a city street each create their own environment and image. Cities can also send mixed messages. A downtown parking garage is there because we love our cars, but its blank walls and wide driveways leave us cold as soon as we get out and walk on the sidewalk.

Regardless of the prevailing style, there are underlying patterns and structures that are the architect's creative tools. Our visceral response will vary with our expectations and environment. After decades of modernistic boxes and concrete freeways, ornate Victorian townhouses on tree-lined streets look good to us. To someone who grew up in those houses and is tired of the inconveniences of old plumbing and small closets, a sleek high-rise looks pretty good. The eye is fickle, and we seek change and variety from year to year. But underneath the surface are eternal structures and patterns that create pleasing buildings and cordial cities.

Patterns of Architecture

Scale is one of the most misunderstood architectural characteristics. It is often substituted for size, as in "the scale of that [obviously large] building is too big." Scale is not size, but how we come to appreciate size. Familiar features—steps, windowpanes, doorknobs, even bricks—give scale to other objects by transferring what we know about human dimensions like stride, height, and hand size. In this way, some buildings have no scale because they provide no clues by which to judge their size.

Skyscrapers can have a human scale and small buildings can have an overbearing scale. Some buildings, such as a Doric temple or a Renaissance church, play a deliberate game with scale. From a distance features like the steps of the Parthenon or the windows of St. Peters lend an appealing, apparent lessening of the buildings' sizes. Near the Parthenon, we can see the steps, we believe we know the size of a step, and we can imagine ourselves next to the building. Moving next to the building we find that each step is really about 18 inches tall. We shrink in awe next to this monumental structure.

In Washington, scale has been the Achilles' heel of many building designs. Monumental scale in buildings is most effective when used sparingly, because it communicates what is truly important and sets aside the smaller scales that make a city livable in favor of impact. Washington's downtown is filled with the monumental, both in buildings that warrant it and those that do not.

One of the greatest criticisms of modern architecture is that architects often have deleted scale-giving detail. This is why we feel uncomfortable in downtowns dominated by modern buildings. One only has to see a modern building infused with scale-giving detail—like the German Chancery—to see how good modern architecture can be.

Massing is the shaping of the large parts of a building and their arrangement in relation to each other. Is the building a simple box? Is the box broken up with projections and recesses? Do many boxes fit together to make up the building? Massing can be simple or complex. Massing is driven by the building's interior organization, by property lines, or by shared notions of what a particular style should look like. Massing can be symmetrical or asymmetrical, formal or informal. On a street lined with buildings of similar and simple massing the effect can be either rhythmic and comforting, or dull. On the other hand, buildings of complex and varied massing can create an environment that is engaging and exciting, or jarring. The

MODERNISM

MODERNISM WAS THE primary movement of 20th-century architecture. It was an umbrella for a number of substyles that shared a common view of the relationship between what architecture should be and what it should do. It was a powerful movement that shaped our buildings as well as our cities. In all its variations, modern architecture has influenced more construction than all other architectural styles combined.

Generally, modern architects believed that buildings should strip themselves of pretense and honestly reveal their purpose, their construction, and their organization. They believed that buildings were meant to be experienced not only in space but also in time. To appreciate a building fully, they thought, one should move through its spaces, which are shaped simply by light and massing. The construction and material capabilities of a new age could be shown, not hidden behind ornamentation. The arbitrary decoration of the building was no longer necessary or desirable. In the search for a universal building language, context and symbolism became unimportant. Without a cultural or social framework for understanding the building, modernism could became a style for the whole world. A submovement would be called the International Style.

Modern architecture was partly a natural reaction to the extreme ornamentation of buildings in the late 19th century. It was also a political and social statement by Europeans divorcing Europe and its architecture from the images of aristocracy. If anything was implied by the movement, it was that the past was out. New ways of thinking about buildings and cities were in.

The impulse towards modern architecture began in Europe and America before the turn of the century. In the United States, architects like Louis Sullivan and Frank Lloyd Wright began to break with the past. Sullivan coined the now infamous phrase "form follows function," meaning not that a building's appearance should derive solely from its use, but, more subtly, should grow from its purpose. Buildings should look like what they are. A bank should look like a bank, a solid and secure place to keep your life savings. A bank should not look like a house or a factory, or a gas station. Though taken as a battle cry by modernists, his phrase and idea have very little to do with style and everything to do with a shared cultural building language.

The work of Frank Lloyd Wright, who was a student of Sullivan, moved in a very individual direction, but along modern lines, away from strict facade hierarchies and toward a more dynamic expression of the building's site and interior. His work was a far cry from the austere white buildings of later modernists. He was noted for his use of organic materials and decorations, not as a screen on the building, but to complement the building's shape.

After World War I, Germany's Bauhaus became a focal point for modern design. The designers and artists of this school wanted to break with symbols of European aristocracy, including the Beaux-Arts, and used the machine as a basis for their aesthetic. They designed products that used the simple beauty of mass-produced forms. They also used the machine itself as a motif. Ocean liners, trains, and skyscrapers fascinated them as harbingers of a new age of speed and movement. Many Bauhaus architects later fled Hitler and immigrated to the United States. An important exhibition of their work was organized by Henry-Russell Hitchcock and Philip Johnson and published as The International Style. This exhibition established the International Style as the preeminent thread of modern architecture; in fact, to many it became synonymous with modern architecture.

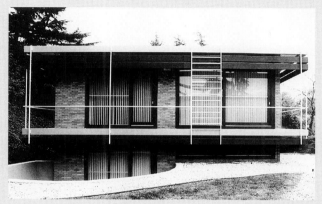

Modern buildings are characterized by unadorned surfaces and a massing that reflects the internal uses. Visual excitement is usually provided by structural bravado, or dramatic asymmetries. Typical materials include glass, steel, aluminum, and precast and poured-in-place concrete. Shadows from changes in massing and recesses in the materials are used to provide visual play in the facade. Ornament is all but banished. Roofs are flat. Featureless windows repeat across the facade.

Buildings by modern masters are starkly beautiful, and rare. As the movement matured (and just about every architect practiced it) the quality of modern buildings suffered. For every Seagram Building—Ludwig Mies van der Rohe's elegant New York City glass tower—there are hundreds of banal knock-offs.

A weakness of modern architec-

ture was that it did not make good background architecture or urban fabric. A walk down Washington's K Street is sad proof. Modern buildings lack the texture and ornament that relieve the otherwise plain facades of traditional buildings. Discarding scale-defining detail for visual clarity and omitting symbolism and contextualism for universality left people without the visual references to understand unfamiliar buildings. What was meant to be clean and minimally beautiful, was seen as cold and sterile. Simplicity became dullness.

In Washington, the liabilities of modern architecture are compounded by the city's height limit. By eschewing ornament and picturesque articulation, the style had to rely on form to provide aesthetic interest. In Washington, modulating form is not an option, as zoning and the height limit force buildings to conform to simple, boxlike massing. These restrictions further force each building up against the next so that downtown streets are lined by flat and tiresome facades.

Like unruly though intellectual teenagers, each generation of architects must turn away from its elders. Postmodernism has libraries full of history to play with, and deconstructivism is already taking buildings apart at their seams. But the ideals and standards of modern architecture have been absorbed and endure. Beautiful modern buildings are fine, elegant, hopeful things that deserve to be the historic landmarks of the next generation.

massing's similarity or complexity determines how pleasant the effect is in concert with the other elements of architecture that relate the buildings to each other.

In Washington, the height limit has restricted massing options. Buildings tend to be boxes of about 10 stories that reflect the shapes of their lots. As architects have moved away from the modernist box, they have experimented with massing to animate a building facade, while staying within the limits of zoning.

Roofs shape the tops of buildings. Residentially, roofs are often pitched in a variety of gables, hips, and sheds that we expect on a house. On larger buildings, roof shapes have more varied patterns. They can reach up in a pinnacle, like the top of a New York skyscraper, or they can be flat, like the roofs of most modern office buildings. The tops of large commercial buildings must accommodate a forest of mechanical equipment. The equipment is enclosed in the skyscraper's pinnacle or a plain box on top of the larger plain box of the modern building. How to deal with this rooftop box has been a major preoccupation for contemporary architects. Even a flat roof offers a variety of alternatives. Roof and facade can meet at a straight edge, with no hint of the intersection revealed in the repetition of the facade. Or the facade can make a gesture to the intersection with a cornice line. Finally, the facade and roof can meet, not at a line, but at a third element, like the inclined plane of a mansard roof.

Fenestration refers to the openings—usually windows—that punctuate a building facade. Traditionally, openings have been distinct rectangles. This is because the space between windows was a structural support for the building. Modern architecture and steel-frame construction allowed exploration of a building structure independent from its outer wall. Without the need for intervening supports, openings could be gathered horizontally to create the ribbon window, or vertically to form the continuous glass window wall common in modern buildings.

Materials in a city vary from the omnipresent asphalt and concrete of sidewalks and streets, to the steel, concrete, masonry, glass, brick, and stone of buildings. Each material sends a different message of wealth and importance. Brick was originally a grand material; it was a manufactured product that required cash to purchase. In our time brick has become a homey material, a way to create instant history. Modern architects were enamored of the lightness and flexibility of glass and steel, a reaction to heavy masonry. Limestone is often used on buildings looking for a combination of stature and fine detail, and marble is invariably used to stress quality and importance, as when a developer brags that the lobby of a "spec" office building is paved in it.

Entrances to a building can be obvious or obscure; the front door might be framed and decorated while the entire facade defers to it, or it might be one in a series of recesses. Traditionally, buildings have had entrances clearly marked with ornate surrounds. Modern buildings, with their reliance on form and light instead of decoration, often treated the door as an abstract plane, deeply recessed in a simple pocket. Sometimes this recess can be powerful; yet it is often obscure, a dark shadow at the base of the building.

Ornament is the surface decoration of a building's facade. Ornament can be applied to send messages as literal as the inscriptions carved into Union Station. It can be arbitrary, as in a grand apartment building that

POSTMODERNISM

A CASUAL GLANCE AT *buildings erected in the 1980s reveals a clear difference from those "modern" buildings that came before. The new buildings, loosely called "postmodern," use overt historical references and blunt symbolism in a break from the flat facades of modern architecture. Thus office buildings routinely display pediments at their rooflines, overscaled arches for entrances, robust masonry details, and plenty of facade articulation. The subtleties or starkness of modern architecture faded next to postmodern buildings that demanded attention with visual gyrations.*

Postmodernism in architecture began as an academic movement in the 1960s and reached maturity by the mid-1970s. Architectural theorists held

that the messages sent by buildings should be complex, inherently contradictory, and that history and symbolism could not be ignored. They declared that because modern architecture did not value these notions it left us feeling miserable about our cities. Robert Venturi, one of the first to break from modernist dogma, found his inspiration in the kitsch and glitz of Las Vegas; the Bauhaus seemed puritanical by comparison. Irony and metaphor were important to these architects. How does a building express irony? An early postmodernist, Michael Graves, put a statue of Portlandia, a reinterpreted historical figure, atop his Portland Building. While a few of these architects received actual commissions, most of them wrote articles and drew pictures.

The academics came down from their ivory tower with two important buildings. In 1978, Philip Johnson, who had helped introduce America to modern architecture almost 50 years earlier, designed the AT&T headquarters building in New York. It looked like a 500-foot-tall, granite Chippendale highboy. Corporate America, until then wedded to the glass skyscraper, had bought its first postmodern building. In 1981 Michael Graves's postmodern design for the Portland Building won a competition.

could easily exchange a French motif for an Egyptian one. Or ornament can be integral to the building's purpose and attitude, as is the carved stone of a Gothic cathedral.

While we think of ornament as being simply decorative, architects use it to address the mundane issues of construction. Carrying water off a roof, spreading out structural loads, and camouflaging awkward joints are all difficult conditions resolved by pieces added to a building's facade. It is the architect's choice to make a rain gutter out of a simple scupper or a

The completed building was both lauded and detested by architects around the country, but it was too late: postmodernism had become the style.

By the mid-1980s, mainstream development appropriated postmodernism. The avant-garde became acceptable as well-financed developers adopted the movement and distilled it. To make a building look up-to-date it was clad in granite and stonelike precast concrete. The historical references and ornamentation became more literal but seldom had the finesse and beauty of the original. The influence of postmodernism was strongest in urban areas where it allowed architects to relate to context and urban scale. In the suburbs it usually led to a superscaled faux-traditionalism that was cartoonlike. A criticism of postmodern architecture often voiced is that it is merely a slipcover over a modern building. This is largely true for office buildings, which have the same plan requirements, whether modern or postmodern.

Much of postmodernism's message of irony and metaphor was lost when it became a mainstream style, used for everything from libraries to shopping malls. Perhaps the final irony is that the historical language used by postmodernists has been so well learned that columns and pediments are applied seriously, rather than with tongue in cheek. Washington architect Mark McInturf calls this rather

humorless approach "precast classicism."

In Washington, postmodernism was met by a receptive community. Washington has always been a city uncomfortable with modern architecture. Low-end modernism produced banal K Street. High-end modernism produced some of the city's most bombastic civic buildings. Too avant-garde to have much effect in its academic form, postmodernism in its mainstream sense was influenced by and reaffirmed the city's neoclassical character.

Modern architecture made a powerful break with the past. Walter Gropius, when he came from the Bauhaus to teach at Harvard, threw out all the Beaux-Arts treatises; they simply would not be needed. Given this education and experience, postmodernists were reluctant to return so literally to the past. To do so would appear naive. Many architects today are uncomfortable with such a literal recitation of history. Instead they want to synthesize the stance of modern architecture with the wealth of historical and cultural knowledge we have available. The postmodern message was about taking off where premodern architecture left off, not recapturing it. The better postmodernists applied the old in a way that told us that their architecture was not about artistic truth, but about our shared notion of culture and history.

gargoyle. Even the modernists who banished ornament arranged steel beams and carefully tinted concrete to subtly emphasize details of a building facade.

Color historically has been strongly linked to style. Classically styled buildings, mimicking the bleached marble of their antecedents, were made of white marble, or its lesser relation, limestone. Victorian buildings, not tied to a specific palette, often expressed the material in use: painted wood on simple houses, red brick and brownstone on more substantial buildings and very large industrial buildings, and white stone for the grandest buildings. This distinction is easy to see in Washington, where the monumental core is dominated by white buildings juxtaposed with the local city's brick and darker stone buildings.

In the early years of modern architecture, while colors were used graphically to accent specific features, most architects relied on light playing on a monochrome surface to provide definition. As the range of materials broadened through the century, architects added subtle color, from the turquoise panels of the early 1960s to the bronze mirrored glass of the 1970s. More often color was looked at warily and, without color, bland buildings became blander still. Postmodernists reintroduced color, lavishly applied to emphasize features that their flat detailing could not.

Patterns of Urbanism

Our impressions of urbanism range from the literal and figurative concrete of buildings, squares, and streets to our individual perceptions of the city which, over time, become personal landmarks. Urbanism is the composition of elements used to shape a community.

Buildings are the fundamental pieces of a community. Our impressions of a place are affected by both the building's placement in space and its details. Regular brownstones lining a square define a space; the details of their stonework, windows, and rooflines engage our eye and interest. A skyscraper set amid a plaza can be equally engaging, its size and simplicity appealing to our sense of drama. In a baroque city plan like Washington's, buildings also define outdoor public space. L'Enfant and his contemporaries viewed streets and squares as rooms, and building facades were the walls of those rooms.

Streets are both functional and aesthetic. They are lines that become an organizing system around which communities grow. The Romans used the intersection and divisions of the cardo and decumanus, the cardinal axes, to establish their colonies. L'Enfant used his diagonal boulevards to connect the two most important points in the center of a new American government, the Capitol and White House. His roads are functional, but their width and route have symbolic meaning and their space is neatly defined by building walls. Streets have been compared to veins and

arteries, rivers and streams, that allow a city to work. It is almost impossible to imagine a city without streets. As much as we complain about traffic, it is profoundly satisfying to drive a sinuous parkway or prowl infinitely varied city blocks.

Squares, whether green with landscaping or marked with paving, are both meeting places and resting places. By interrupting the street pattern, the open space of the square creates a defining landmark that pulls together views and travel routes, while creating a space that is a rest from the repetition. As streets converge at a square they open up views and set off building facades.

In Washington, squares are legacies of L'Enfant's elegant tradition of 18th-century city planning that set aside land not only for roads and development, but simply for aesthetic enjoyment as well. They become outdoor rooms, elegantly walled with appropriately scaled building facades. Ironically, this seemingly useless land, which generates no product or taxes, adds immeasurable value to surrounding properties. In every city, lots on a park or square, from Central Park West to Louisburg Square, are desirable addresses.

Streetscaping is all the pieces that furnish a street—lampposts, mailboxes, pavers, trees, benches. Urban designers may page through endless catalogs to find just the right wastebasket, but people still throw their fast-food wrappers on the ground. Pleasant as is the environment this furniture can create, we tend to notice it only subconsciously. And if traffic creates an unsafe crossing or if storefronts are vacant or nonexistent, street furniture can have little impact. Streetscaping is perhaps most effective as a signal of public investment. A city spends money in the public domain in hopes that the private sector will ante up as well. In Washington, the

Pennsylvania Avenue Development Corporation made street improvements to signal the avenue's rebirth as a prestigious address and to express the street's ceremonial and historic role.

Paths are the formal and informal routes we take in our travels on foot or in a car, including sidewalks, back alleys, and freeways. A good path is safe, interesting, and convenient, taking us where we want to go. Some paths are well established by unspoken consensus, others require the weight of bureaucratic decision. The gargantuan effort of building a freeway takes the actions of thousands of individuals from planners and politicians to construction workers and commuters. Paths are also personal, our own routes from home to school, work, and shopping that reflect the ways we run our lives and organize our image of a place.

Nodes take us deep into what is perceptual. For a mother a node may be the park where she and her toddler meet other children and parents. For a downtown worker a node may be the busy intersection near the office that is always backed up, but where you can pick up a newspaper and a cup of coffee. Some nodes are easy to agree on: Times Square, Union Station. Washington seems to be a city of many nodes. Downtown stretches for blocks without culmination at a port or riverside, and even government, the central business of Washington, is dispersed among Capitol Hill, the Federal Triangle and Foggy Bottom.

Landmarks in Washington are for the entire nation, but the city also has smaller landmarks by which residents define the city. Certainly the

Lincoln Memorial from Arlington Memorial Bridge is a clear gateway to the city, but the drop from MacArthur Boulevard to Canal Road at Georgetown also marks an entrance. Even in an environment seemingly devoid of markers we define perceptual high points from positions along our routes; early mail routes were marked by notches in trees, and old deeds defined property lines by boulders, trees, and hills.

Edges are positive and negative, barriers and boundaries, natural or man-made. Edges signal change. A freeway that isolates a city neighborhood may also protect its residents from redevelopment and displacement. The river that stops expansion of city blocks can also be vaulted with bridges to create new links. Pennsylvania Avenue is an edge between the federal city and the local city.

Districts are areas defined by a common activity or appearance. They may have fuzzy perceptual edges or legal boundaries, like those of a historic district. Neighborhoods and districts expand and contract, helping us define a part of the city with a simple image. Desirable city and suburban districts have a way of spreading beyond their initial boundaries. In New York, as Soho (South of Houston Street) became a popular and economic success, it spawned Tribeca (Triangle Below Canal) and Soso (South of Soho). And the tony Washington suburb of Potomac seems to cover half of Montgomery County, according to some real estate agents.

The elements of architecture and urbanism—some formally established by government or development, others by our own point of view—help us navigate, understand, and use the city. The elements remain constant, though their scale may shift in different communities. Urban, suburban, and rural communities are all built with the same elements but at different scales, with more or less of the natural environment, manicured or wild, in between. Regardless of style, there are underlying patterns and structures in both architecture and urbanism. Our visceral response varies only with our social or perhaps anthropological position. When "modern" was new and progressive it was positive. With the return of historical styles, we see it as barren. As postmodernism becomes top-heavy with historical illusion, architects are returning to a more stripped down aesthetic. But beneath the shift of preference and style, the patterns and structures of architecture and urbanism remain as tools to express our community goals and values. ∎

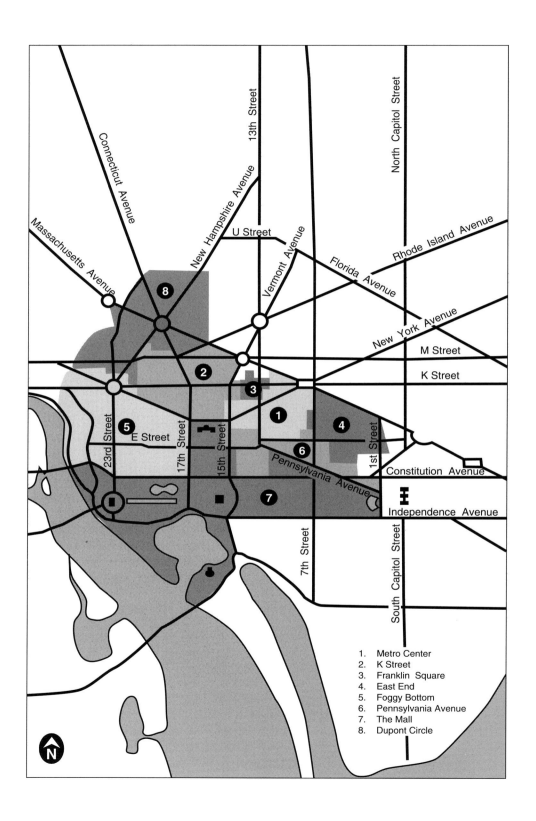

1. Metro Center
2. K Street
3. Franklin Square
4. East End
5. Foggy Bottom
6. Pennsylvania Avenue
7. The Mall
8. Dupont Circle

Downtown

Uncle Sam is never idle; and pay days occur with unfailing regularity.

FROM *WASHINGTON PAST AND PRESENT,*

J. C. PROCTOR, ED., 1930

Washington is the only American city whose downtown seems incidental to the image and identity of the city. For visitors, suburbanites, or new residents the blocks north of Pennsylvania Avenue and the Mall are a shadowy area of images that run together. School field trips and nightly newcasts have established an image of monumental Washington in our national consciousness; the sprawling blocks of offices and stores beyond barely register.

The federal city was the formative concept that brought Washington into being. In this era of entrenched bureaucracy and beltway bandits, it is hard to imagine a time when the capital's fortunes were completely dependent on the comings and goings of Congress. A history of the city completed in 1930 described Washington's struggle to become an independent economy and "not a mere appendage of Baltimore." The federal government has become a steady customer of the local city. The "Three As"— accountants, attorneys, and associations—have become so ubiquitous downtown that city planning efforts are focused on providing a variety of uses, including housing, arts and culture, restaurants, and entertainment.

Washington's downtown is neither a single place nor a static place, but a conglomeration of neighborhoods each reflecting a character bestowed by history. K Street was transformed from a neighborhood of rowhouses and corner streets to block after block of sterile office buildings. Foggy Bottom began life as a waterfront industrial area, later became an enclave of modest downtown housing, and is now disappearing beneath institutional expansion. Franklin Square, once noted for the variety of its porno shops and theaters, is now a prestigious office location.

The increased foot traffic resulting when the Metrorail system opened in 1976, combined with the Pennsylvania Avenue Development

HEIGHT LIMIT

WASHINGTON, THAT MOST American of cities, has none of that most American of buildings, the skyscraper. American cities reflect the expediency of business; development tears down and rebuilds, rewriting history daily. In Washington the city of commerce is subordinate to the city of monuments, a relationship guaranteed by a strictly enforced height limit.

The height limit was enacted by the city commissioners in 1899 in response to the 14-story Cairo apartment building on Q Street east of Dupont Circle. As in many cities at the time, the commissioners were concerned about the impacts of height on fire safety, light, and air. In the era when the technology to build taller— elevators and steel framing—was developed, city governments were not equipped to douse a skyscraper fire. As tenement slums generated public health problems it became important for light and air to reach city streets. In 1910 Congress amended the Height of Buildings Act, limiting buildings in Washington to 120 feet or about 10 stories. It has not changed since.

What began as a common urban reaction to a new building type became an aesthetic cause. The Commission of Fine Arts, established in 1910 as a design review commission for the federal district, supported the height limit as a way to protect the visual dominance of the Capitol. It became a patriotic stance and, over time, a matter of tradition. In other cities the economic pressure of demand for expensive downtown land would have overridden the statute decades ago, but in Washington, despite an occasional debate in the editorial pages, the height limit is insurmountable.

The benefit of the height limit is obvious—a postcard city with a park-like setting that is the perfect complement to national monuments. The Washington Monument and the Capitol dome jutting above a uniform base of low buildings and trees is Washington's most prominent visual characteristic, the one that sticks in your memory.

At the same time, however, the height limit forces the city to spread out. Washington's office district rambles for dozens of blocks, while in

most cities it is focused on a few blocks, like Wall Street in New York or the Loop in Chicago. As the buildings spread out, so does the traffic and activity they generate. In Washington, proportionately fewer people hit the pavement around each building in a workday than in Boston, New York, or Chicago. Fewer people mean less activity and support for businesses that thrive on foot traffic. Design guidelines may promote shops and restaurants, but the customers are not there to support them. The height limit cheats the city out of the density that could give it vitality.

As the office buildings spread out, they also move beyond the traditional boundaries of downtown, supplanting other interesting uses and buildings. The spreading office district consumes the diverse city fabric that has built up over time. The houses in nearby Foggy Bottom are being replaced by offices; those of K Street disappeared long ago. Ironically, skyscrapers, seen by many as the bane of urban environments, can conserve adjacent urban fabric.

Office buildings must use their building sites to the fullest for economic return. The height limit pushes Washington buildings out to the property lines on all sides, presenting tough aesthetic problems for modern

architects, whose only option is to sheathe a squat box with a plain skin. K Street is synonymous with this type of building. By the mid-1970s, architects were beginning to sculpt the boxes to relieve the tedium. They subtracted a wedge here and a notch there, all to give the flat box three-dimensional qualities. The sheathing remained the typical modern mix of glass, metal, and concrete.

By the 1980s postmodern architecture gave designers a long list of features to enliven buildings. The plain modern wall was replaced by sculpted facades with stonelike facing, classical organization of openings, and emphatic entrances. The squat box was reshaped through jutting roofs and towers that exploited a loophole in the height limit. The new buildings seemed more lively and appealing than their recent predecessors.

Design variety was not enough to create a lively environment. Postmodern facades cannot create activity on the street the way shops and restaurants can. A change in architectural appearance cannot alter the way people behave in a city. This is determined by more fundamental patterns of urbanism. Architecture can only reinforce existing patterns, not change them.

Corporation's (PADC) revitalization efforts, the appeal of festival markets at the Old Post Office and the Shops at National Place, and the real estate boom of the 1980s gave downtown new life. An appreciation of urbanity, of the historical forms of buildings and city planning that have made cities walkable and appealing, is being reestablished in Washington to create the "living downtown" sought by planners. ■

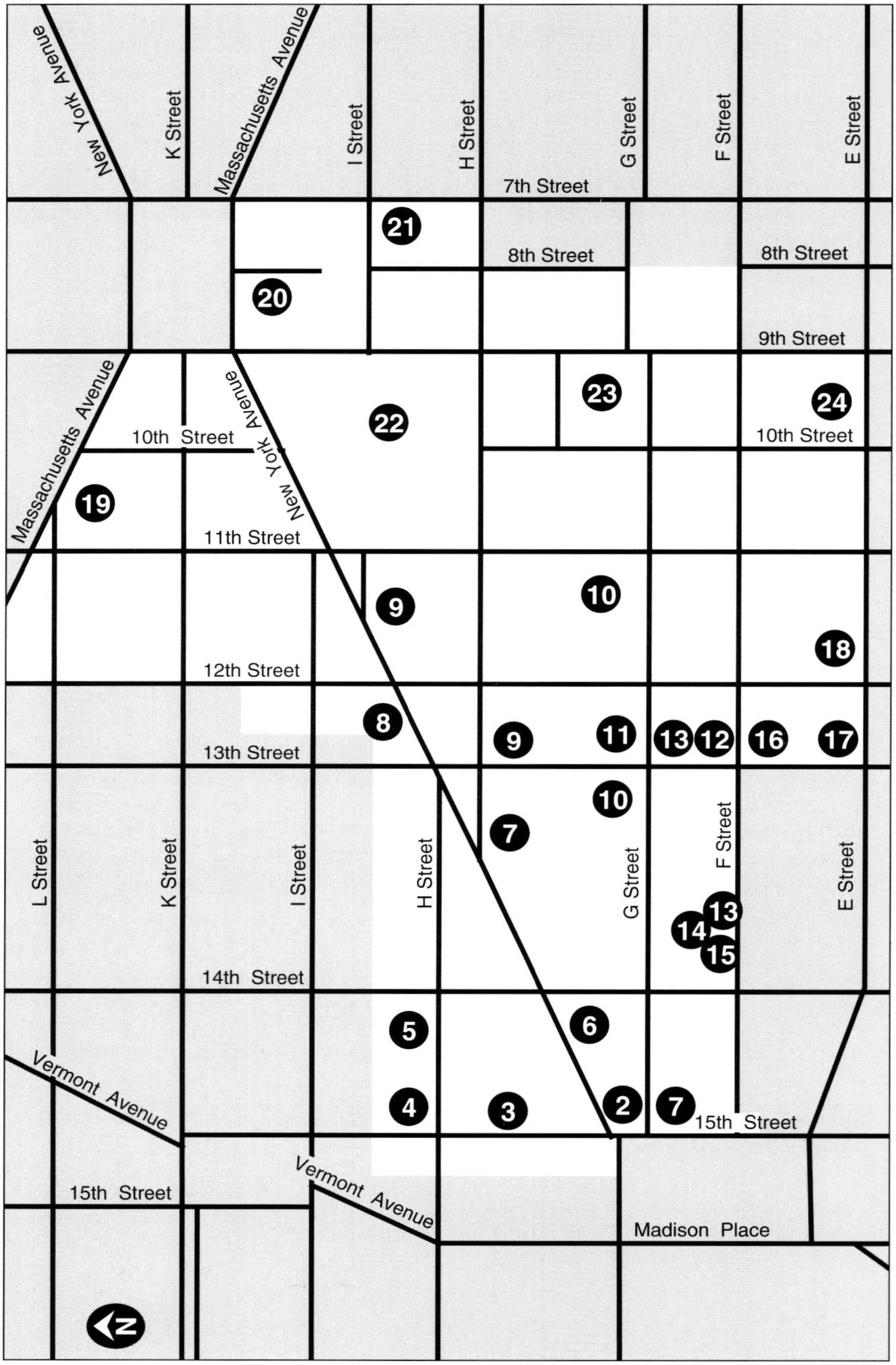

New York Avenue

K Street

Massachusetts Avenue

I Street

H Street

G Street

F Street

E Street

7th Street

21

8th Street

8th Street

20

9th Street

Massachusetts Avenue

New York Avenue

23

24

10th Street

10th Street

22

19

11th Street

11th Street

9

10

12th Street

12th Street

18

8

13th Street

9

11

13 **12**

16

17

13th Street

10

L Street

K Street

I Street

H Street

G Street

F Street

E Street

7

13

14

15

14th Street

14th Street

5

6

Vermont Avenue

4

3

2

7

15th Street

15th Street

Vermont Avenue

Madison Place

N

Metro Center

Americans have to an extraordinary degree, the power to retain in our minds diametrically opposed ideas. A trained capacity for dutiful self-deception sustains our religion, our politics, and our patriotism. Why should it not also enter into our art, particularly here at Washington, the busiest market for this kind of thought, in all its branches?

ELBERT PEETS, 1937

Metro Center is the traditional downtown of Washington. Just east of 15th Street, it is home to most of the city's great 19th- and early 20th-century commercial architecture. It is the location of Washington's once great retail street—F Street—and department stores. It also contains landmarks like Ford's Theater and two historic districts. Its southern edge has always been Pennsylvania Avenue, potentially the city's premier street. If the Mall and its monuments have come to represent the capital city, Metro Center has been the city's commercial heart for decades.

L'Enfant envisioned a commercial downtown east of the Capitol, but the market on Pennsylvania Avenue at the end of the Tiber Creek established a commercial hub just west of the Capitol. Businesses eventually moved north to escape floods from Tiber Creek, and department stores clustered around the intersection of streetcar lines that brought customers in from surrounding neighborhoods. F Street's department stores, streetcars, and shops served a regional market.

This changed after World War II as development shifted westward. The postwar spirit of newness and optimism caused people to look for easily developable land, which was found along K Street, north and west of the White House. There, houses and small structures were easier to replace than the larger buildings east of 15th Street. This land was also closer to residential development, which was spreading farther to the northwest. The urban riots of 1968 seemed to kill off the old downtown forever.

About 10 years later, however, the old downtown began to attract investment. By the mid-1970s the "new" downtown along K Street was reaching its capacity for office space. Also, an appreciation of historic preservation was taking hold, not only in the renovation of old buildings, but in an understanding of the ambiance and value they add to a neighborhood. The 15th Street Historic District was established to preserve the financial buildings that clustered around the Treasury. Perhaps most importantly, the Metro Center station for Washington's striking new subway opened up directly beneath the old downtown area: an intersection of two lines that draws in riders from Maryland and Virginia. By the mid-1980s, the redevelopment of Pennsylvania Avenue's north side bolstered the area's commercial prestige.

Today the Metro Center area is the focal point of the city's most interesting commercial development. Grand turn-of-the-century office buildings like the Bond Building have been renovated. Other fine old buildings like the Greyhound Terminal and the Homer Building have been added onto in significant, if sometimes controversial, ways. Many of the city's best new commercial buildings are located in this renewed old downtown. The area is enlivened by cultural and historical places such as the National Portrait Gallery and the Martin Luther King Memorial Library. Planners are trying to further animate the neighborhood with mixed uses by encouraging housing and by creating the Downtown Arts District. Development in this district between 6th and 14th Streets, Pennsylvania Avenue, and G Place can use zoning incentives that encourage the arts and arts-related uses.

Because of the amount and character of redevelopment, Metro Center has been the greatest opportunity to reshape downtown as an appealing place to be. As Benjamin Forgey of *The Washington Post* has observed, development in the area exemplifies most of the issues confronting urban architecture in the 1980s: regulation, preservation, postmodernism, contextualism, infill, and retail and residential infusion. ∎

1. Metropolitan Square
655 15th Street, N.W.
Skidmore, Owings and Merrill/Vlastimil Koubek *1986*

The development of Metropolitan Square will live in Washington's history because it removed a piece of Washington's history. By the 1980s, The Rhodes Tavern, at the corner of 15th and F streets, was Washington's oldest continuously operating commer-cial establishment. It had been the British headquarters during the burning of the White House, and had served as a polling place, an auction house, and home to the Orphans' Court. Though altered and deteriorated, it was clearly a building of local and national significance. A 1970 survey of District landmarks noted, "If it were properly restored, it would be of great tourist interest and a fine example of civic responsibility on the part of the developers."

The tavern was bulldozed for this project, although three historic buildings are incorporated into the new project: the Metropolitan Bank, the Keith-Albee Theater, and the interior of the Old Ebbitt Grill behind the theater facade.

The new building meets the street where the tavern used to stand with a considerably larger eight-story building tricked out in classical details. The pattern of rusticated base, central portion of windows divided by pilasters, and mansard roof with dormers picks up details of the theater facade and sets the pattern for the facade along G Street.

2. Washington Building
710 15th Street, N.W.
Coolidge Shepley Bulfinch Abbott
1927
Keyes Condon Florance *1987*

As development shifted from K Street into the old downtown to the east, investors reexamined every site and building for development opportunities. Like many downtown, this building was not originally built to the maximum allowed by the height limit. The demand for downtown office space made an upper story addition economically profitable, which in turn helped finance the building's renovation.

The original building delicately adapted Beaux-Arts formality to a modern office use. The building's organizing features—a base, shaft, and cornice line marked by frieze and beltcourse—are decorated with modern motifs like

telephones. A 1964 renovation hid much of the original detail and altered the ground floor with projecting storefronts. The 1987 renovation restored historical detail and built to the allowed floor area ratio by infilling the building's courtyard and a one-story addition above the existing cornice line.

The materials and details of the original are composed into an attic addition that doesn't merely cap the building but has its own rhythm and hierarchy. The addition is faced with the polished brown granite of the base, and its details are picked out in the limestone of the original facade. The facade of the attic story is articulated with a series of arched windows that echo the arched openings at the building's base. Its corners are marked with oversized, incised limestone acroteria which echo the finely etched bas-reliefs of the original facade.

At this visible corner in the 15th Street Historic District, the renovation returns the building's dignity while meeting economic demands.

and texture to the marble of the original, so that the entire upper facade seems to slide behind the ornate columns and cornice. The upper stories of the addition step back behind balustrades of plain vertical shafts. The addition neatly fills a gap in the streetscape.

4. Southern Building
1425 H Street, N.W.
Daniel Burnham *1912*
Shalom Baranes Associates *1990*

The Southern Building is part of the 15th Street Historic District, an area of financial buildings from the turn of the century that cluster around the Treasury Building and the White House.

The strong, simple profile of the Southern Building is a frame for ornate and delightful terra-cotta decoration. The two blocks of the building are separated by a large light well, but connected at ground level by a three-story facade. The facade is organized in the classical style with base, shaft, and capital, with lone rectangular lines of paired windows running up the facade. The building's sharp corners and rectilinearity contrast nicely with the florid curves and deep molding of the terra-cotta banding around the windows, in

3. Playhouse Theater
727 15th Street, N.W.
Paul Pelz *1908*
Mariani and Associates *1985*

The original one-story building that has, over time, housed a brokerage firm, a restaurant, and a movie theater, is so heavily ornate it seems like a base waiting for its shaft. Paired Corinthian columns flank a flight of stairs and support a built-up cornice with a central marble escutcheon held in place by two figures. Built a few years after the neighboring Folger Building, it picks up that building's details of vertical banding, a central entrance, and strong cornice line.

Just as the one-story original complements the Folger Building, so does the addition of seven stories. It is formed with a five-story projecting oriel composed of black glass and white marble. The marble is similar in color

the spandrels, and at the cornice. Its strong, unornamented corners and division of the building into two wings emphasizes the building's vertical profile.

The addition is a two-story penthouse that continues the facade's strong linear character above the deeply molded cornice of the original. As on the original, three bays of windows are grouped in pairs divided by a pilaster topped with simplified acroteria. While not attempting the rich detail of the original, the addition continues within the building's framework of rhythm and pattern.

5. City Center
1401 H Street, N.W.
Sikes, Jennings, Kelly and Brewer *1992*

Planners and designers often assume that ground-floor shops are the only way to create an interesting streetscape, but poorly located and designed retail space that does not thrive can be just as deadening as a blank wall. Even though this corner building has only one small storefront, it contributes to a pleasant streetscape with a variety of materials applied at a human scale.

The narrow granite base is broken by molding lines and metal-grilled basement windows. The building's base is completed with an area of beige precast concrete that contrasts with the brighter white precast concrete of the building's facade. The classical organization of the facade continues to the heavy cornice line and two-story penthouse. The rhythm and details echo the Southern Building to the west, and the building completes another urbane city block in the rebuilding of Washington's downtown.

6. Bond Building
14th Street and New York Avenue, N.W.
George Cooper *1902*
Shalom Baranes Associates *1987*

Part of what makes the Metro Center neighborhood so appealing are the blocks of old buildings that were saved by neglect as development and investment moved west to K Street. Even those buildings that are not formally designated as historic landmarks have a human scale and appealing detail. An aesthetic principle that values history and the economics of building makes them worth saving.

Here, as elsewhere, the architect

has designed a penthouse and two corner bay additions that respond sensitively to the original building. There is nothing blunt about the meeting of the two buildings. The penthouse mimics the original's hierarchy of rhythms with a tall lower story and shorter top story. Although the double columns on the penthouse do not occur in the main building, they follow a similar rhythm of breaks in the facade and are analogous to the pilasters on lower floors. The penthouse also follows the facade pattern of the original that gradually lightens as it moves up. The original structure's heavy base with small windows and lighter walls and larger windows on upper floors are repeated in the penthouse's columned facade.

The corner additions are identical to each other but different from the original building and the penthouse addition. On their own, they appear to be independent, slender townhouses, but viewed from the corner they look like bookends.

7. Inter-American Development Bank Building
1300 New York Avenue, N.W.
Skidmore, Owings and Merrill (David Childs) *1983*

To someone looking southwest on New York Avenue, this building defines a large intersection. Its massive wall edges the south side of New York Avenue as it curves at its intersection with 13th Street. The building's facade curves to follow the street.

In comparison with more recent buildings, the precast concrete and stone details look stripped down, but this was one of Wasington's first buildings to return to the classical organization of base, shaft, and capital articulated with ornament. The architect, David Childs, was at the forefront of Washington's plunge into mainstream postmodernism in the mid-1980s.

The facade is organized with a vertical and horizontal hierarchy. The center six stories of repeated windows are separated from the heavier three-story base and the recessed upper floors by a slightly lighter color. The solid corners anchor a lighter and glassier facade in between. A large, arched entry breaks the sweep of the curve at the middle.

The building is built around an internal atrium that pushes the structure out to its lot lines and creates the feeling of tremendous bulk.

8. 1225 New York Avenue, N.W.
Clark, Tribble, Harris and Li/Vlastimil Koubek *1993*

Many of the new buildings in the Metro Center neighborhood are additions to existing historic buildings and continue the patterns and details of the originals. Even much new construction turns to historic neighbors for influence. The muscular classicism of the National Museum of Women in the Arts (originally the Masonic Temple; Wood, Donn and Deming, 1908) has estab-

lished an aesthetic standard for this end of New York Avenue. The building immediately to the east of the museum and 1225 New York Avenue both echo the museum's columns and raised basement first story.

This new office building on a triangular lot is classically organized. It meets the street with a two-story arched base and a third story of square-punched windows divides the base from the rest of the building. The most notable features of the facade are massive grouped columns inset into the wall. Their scale and placement echo the museum across the street, but as unadorned cylinders placed in front of green ribbon windows they mark this as a modern building.

The facade is capped with a cornice line built up of elements on three stories: a one-story band of paired windows divided by metope–like ornaments and two windowed stories above that. The building is finished with a standing seam, green metal mansard roof.

Despite the formal organization and vaguely antique details, the building is uncomfortable with classicism and is a sometimes awkward meeting of two schools of architectural thought. On the edge of this downtown neighborhood the building further defines the emerging character of New York Avenue.

9. 1100 New York Avenue, N.W.
Keyes Condon Florance *1992*

The original Greyhound Terminal is one of Washington's best Art Moderne buildings. Its streamlined mass buttressing a central finial with the word GREYHOUND was a prominent landmark on New York Avenue. The facade's front curves swept around to the circular rear of the building, where buses were once splayed out in a pinwheel. It was a dynamic building in a city renowned for static architectural compositions.

Today the terminal has been renovated. The buses have been removed and a new office building rises above and behind it. The new building is colored in varying shades of gray and beige stone that play off the limestone

of the original. The office building's stepped profile, softened corners, and subtle Art Deco motifs are evocative of the terminal's massing and decoration. The most intriguing new details are the fluted metal spandrel panels between windows that recall the sheet metal sides of older buses.

The renovation left the terminal essentially intact, unlike earlier facade preservation projects that awkwardly severed building parts. But the new 1100 New York Avenue has nearly swallowed the Greyhound Terminal whole; the terminal serves as an ornamental entry to the dominant office building. Some may see this as a victory for the older building, others may consider the historic facade reduced to a doorway.

Aside from design questions, the building raises the question of what downtowns should be. It seems that offices are the only remunerative structures in cities, and that even the bus station is shifted to a less central location.

10. 700 13th Street, N.W.
700 11th Street, N.W.
Skidmore, Owings and Merrill *1989*

These buildings play a contextual game with the neighboring Hecht Company

Department Store, mirroring its curved cornice line and plinth, square punched openings with banded borders, and circular insets. They also achieve the illusion of verticality and an animated roofscape by careful arrangement of receding planes, broken cornice lines, and projecting penthouses.

The two buildings were developed at the same time and form bookends for the Hecht Company. The 11th Street building pulls back from the corner to create a plaza for a Metro entrance. The 13th Street building has a through lobby that connects to the landmark Epiphany Church. A small, elaborately paved courtyard garden creates a pleasant space, but one that seems a bit sterile, edged by blank building walls and not immediately accessible from the street.

11. Hecht Company Department Store
G Street between 12th and 13th Streets, N.W.
Skidmore, Owings and Merrill *1985*

Historically, department stores have been downtown focal points, anchoring the main shopping street just as they do in a suburban shopping mall. In that ancient era before malls, downtown was the retail center for surround-

ing communities, and downtown department stores were ornate palaces. They had bit parts in movie classics and sponsored community entertainment; just think of Macy's every Thanksgiving. With a rash of department store bankruptcies and buy-outs, and the relocation of shoppers and their money, downtown department stores are losing out to their suburban siblings. It is a significant event when a new one is built. The Hecht Company left its 6th Street store, not for the suburbs, but for a location directly above the Metro Center subway station.

Traditionally, department stores have looked like large, squat ornate office buildings—since they were really multilevel warehouses with an outer layer of offices. In Washington, the height limit forced office buildings into the same profile, so the architect had to differentiate this store from neighboring offices.

The Hecht Company's massive, windowless facade is topped by a heavy cornice etched with the company name and broken by entrances and show windows. The almost museum-like solidity of the building contrasts with adjacent office buildings and reflects confidence and a significant investment in downtown retailing.

12. Homer Building
13th and G Streets, N.W.
Appleton P. Clarke *1915*
Shalom Baranes Associates *1990*

Land values and high office rents make older, smaller buildings prime targets for renovation. At the same time, the established ethic of historic preservation finds value in old structures. These two positions combined in the case of this building, which is small by downtown standards, to make addition

13. Metro Center Station
12th and G Streets, N.W.
Harry Weese and Associates *1976*

The Metro Center Station is the hub of a 103-mile system that serves downtown and suburban commuters. The system opened in 1976 on a limited downtown route and is still under construction in the farther reaches of the metropolitan area.

The basis of the system's design is an engineering solution—coffered barrel vaults. As in the best engineering, the design takes its elegance not from trendy details, but from simplicity. The vaulted spaces are timeless; they worked for the Romans and they work here. At Metro Center and other transfer stations the barrel vaults intersect at the junction of two train lines to create unobstructed platforms on a par with Washington's grand monumental spaces.

inevitable. Eight stories were added on top of the original four. In his research and design, the architect discovered original plans for expanding the building to approximately the height of the new structure.

In this extreme example of a penthouse addition, Baranes skillfully extracts important features of the original and extrapolates them up through the new facade. Vertical panels between the window bays pick up the vertical emphasis of the ground level pilasters. Rectangular windows in both the old and new facades are arranged in groups of three. Both buildings share a simple, rectilinear incised detailing.

The corners of the added stories project slightly to emphasize the new character of the original building; once a complete structure, it is now the base of a larger building. When it was built, the Homer was heralded for its sensitive addition to a rejuvenating downtown and for its spectacular girdered atrium.

The Metro system's commitment to design resulted in a palette of details and materials that were used as a kit of parts to design every station, both above and below ground. The coffered concrete vaults, tile floors with granite edging, and indirect lighting come together with the most impact at the Metro Center station.

Such high-quality design is unusual in municipal architecture, and the time, money, and effort have paid off in creating stations that are safe, appealing, and sturdy. The simple design has a timeless quality that will serve the system well in years to come.

14. 1331 F Street, N.W.
Kress-Cox *1988*

Washington architects, their dreams of New York-style skyscrapers frustrated by the city's height limit, always seem to be striving to create vertical buildings, or at least images of them. The inset, curved central tower of this building is flanked by two lower wings, stepping up to a tall profile. Verticality is further emphasized by long spandrels between the window bays in which vertical mullions are heavier than the horizontal mullions.

Although its layering of classical details—a quoined base, pilasters, and cornice lines—lacks the sleekness of its smaller modern neighbor to the west, the building's storefronts and ground-floor scale make it street friendly.

15. The Westory
607 14th Street, N.W.
Henry L. A. Jeckel *1908*
Shalom Baranes Associates *1991*

This building goes beyond facadism with the addition of two larger wings and a penthouse to the original building on a corner site. Adjacent sites have been added to this project, expanding the building's footprint from its original 2,500 square feet to 18,000 square feet.

Baranes, a master of contextual additions, has picked up the original building's slender, delicate detailing. The additions are successful because he avoids the heavy precast classicism of the 1980s and uses metal to replicate a more elegant Art Deco style . In truth, the detail of the original building

is not reproducible today. The factories that made it are no longer in business, and custom work is prohibitively expensive. Nonetheless, Baranes found a comfortable alternative that is appropriate to its time and budget.

The attic-story addition of structural steel and glass cubes is clearly a contemporary construct. The entire facade is refocused to the northern corner with an arched metal structure at the roofline. The two additions to the side of the original rigorously follow its rhythm and details. Cornice lines are matched, the paired window groups continue, and the lion's heads on the original are echoed with a square concrete detail on the addition. While the size of the additions tend to overwhelm the older building, the crisp modern lines and materials have a sketchy character that defers to the original.

16. Columbia Square
F Street between 12th and 13th Streets, N.W.
I. M. Pei and Partners *1987*

This building was one of the first downtown to be designed by a renowned architect and to use high-grade materials and finishes. It set a new standard for downtown construction. The building's design goals were to provide as much prime office space as possible, while also helping to revitalize F Street, once Washington's primary retail corridor. These types of individual decisions and investments have accumulated to change the character of downtown.

The architect chose to create a planar facade that is ornamented not by sculptural manipulations but by an overall pattern of inset squares cut into solids and voids. Surface decoration with finely scaled pattern is unusual in Washington, where the "magnificent

distances" described by Charles Dickens in 1842 often require grand architectural statements. Also, compared to typical Washington facades of buff limestone and pale marble, this rose and blue-gray building is rich, deep, and colorful.

In this typical urban street of narrow width, closely lined with shopfronts, the building's street edge contributes to our first impression. Here, as in other Washington buildings, the base is carved out to accommodate a Metro entrance and retail facades. Even when a stated goal is to animate the street, retail space is hidden, and the public domain is slighted in favor of an internal atrium.

17. Warner Theater
1299 Pennsylvania Avenue, N.W.
(E Street between 12th and 13th)
Pei Cobb Freed and Partners/Shalom Baranes Associates *1992*

Warner Office Building
1299 Pennsylvania Avenue, N.W.
(E Street between 12th and 13th)
Pei Cobb Freed and Partners (James
Ingo Freed) *1992*

This project renovated an existing theater, adding three floors of offices at its
top, and added a new office building
along E Street. The design of the additions—their scale and details—are

METRO

THE CAPITOL DOME is stunning at night and the words of Jefferson and Lincoln, carved on their memorials, still inspire, but visitors are equally impressed by Metro, Washington's rapid-rail transit system. Clean, quiet cars that run swiftly between safe, handsome stations is not what most riders expect from an urban subway system.

Even though the planning and legislative action to create Metro began 40 years ago, the system is young compared to those in other cities. In New York the first section of the IRT opened in 1904, linking Brooklyn Bridge with City Hall. In Boston, laborers tunneled for two years, beginning in 1895, to create the nation's first subway. Streetcar development has always led to expanded community development. In Washington, the developers of Chevy Chase built a streetcar line up Connecticut Avenue to connect potential homeowners with their downtown jobs. Metro planners knew their history and used the system's design to reinforce existing communities and create new ones.

After studies and plans, recommendations and referenda, impasses and appropriations, Metro broke ground in 1969 at Judiciary Square. All through this process, Metro planners worked with local municipalities to determine where commercial and residential communities existed or where they should be created. Significant concentrations of people warranted a stop. After determining these points they drew lines on maps and tested the potential routes for cost, ridership, and revenue. The system finally adopted, with its 86 stations over 97.2 miles of track, is nearly complete and reaches out from the monumental core to the surrounding communities, expanding the metropolitan area and creating new suburban downtowns.

By planning for future growth, Metro created new centers that had a variety and vitality previously unseen in the suburbs. After what seemed like endless construction, suburban downtowns like Bethesda and Clarendon are generating restaurants, jobs, and shopping that were once the purview of the traditional downtown. Metro stations are designed to link with auto and bus commuter routes, making regional transportation potentially more efficient.

But Metro planners made one assumption that has proven to be wrong. The system's radial pattern assumes that downtown Washington is the single center generating jobs and shopping. In fact, Metro and the Beltway together have created a ring of edge cities and smaller centers that have increased the number of people commuting between suburbs. A looped Metro route that would link edge cities and smaller centers seems logical but because of cost, virtually unachievable.

What is perhaps most extraordinary about Metro is its architectural design. For the first time on a project of this scale the architect and engineer were given equal authority, to ensure that aesthetics would not be set aside in favor of engineering expediency. The Commission of Fine Arts participated in station design discussions between 1965 and 1971. In searching for a new approach they determined that the stations should be consistently designed. A palette of materials was arranged in consistent patterns for above- and below-ground stations, a simple design approach that gives Metro a distinctive image throughout the region.

Regular riders may complain about the low light levels, and visitors perennially fumble with their farecards, but extraordinary design and meticulous maintenance has made Metro a model transit system.

carefully related to their context, an unusual approach for this noted modernist firm.

Rather than overwhelming the original theater building and its landmark corner tower with new construction, the top three office floors are set back. For consistency, the top three floors of the addition are also set back. To give the original and its tower further precedence, the facade of the new building plays a visual trick. It is divided in half, giving the illusion of being two smaller buildings. A less prominent tower at its east end echoes the theater tower.

The movie theater, built as the Earle in the 1920s, had lavish interiors based on the Hall of Mirrors at Versailles. Such delicious excess was typical of the fantasy architecture of old movie palaces. The film house has been remodeled to accommodate live performances and renovation required finding space for all the backstage activities of live theater. The restoration costs were offset by a federal downtown revitalization grant and by the increased revenue from added office space. Earlier owners tried to get the landmark theater removed from the protection of the District's historic preservation laws, but the developer saw the value of not only saving the old building, but adding to the vitality of the neighborhood.

It is a tribute to the success of the PADC that although the building is on E Street it takes a Pennsylvania Avenue address.

18. 555 12th Street, N.W.
Florance Eichbaum Esocoff King Architects *1994*

In their return to historic detail, contemporary Washington architects first used the columns and capitals of

classical architecture. As these trained modernists became more comfortable with ornament, they applied the Victorian embellishments of mercantile Washington. Most recently, Washington architects have experimented with the streamlined machine ethic of Art Deco. Perhaps it is only a matter of time before we come full circle to neo-modernism.

The stacked metal panels that create the window bays on this building's facade evoke New York's Art Deco skyscrapers in providing both a decorative sheath and a vertical emphasis. The architects have returned to a heroic skyscraper past that Washington never had.

Unlike Columbia Square, across 12th Street, which pulls its shop windows beneath a deep overhang, this building meets the street in the same way as its older neighbors. Woodward and Lothrop and the Homer Building both have windowed bases that add visual interest to the street. This building has a two-story base of windows and doors framed with geometric patterns that echo the circles and cylinders of the bays above. The facade returns urbanity to what was once Washington's premier shopping street.

19. Cato Institute
1000 Massachusetts Avenue, N.W.
Hellmuth, Obata and Kassabaum
(Charles George) *1993*

This building responds to L'Enfant's
plan of diagonals intersecting a grid in
an almost literal and certainly graceful
way. The building's plan and facade
are composed of a series of grids intersecting at different angles. The masonry
block that makes up most of the building parallels the gridded streets of
L'Enfant's plan. A steel-frame and glass
winter garden encasing the front of the
building parallels the diagonal of
Massachusetts Avenue.

The building's facade further
explores the intersection of grids. The
surface of the split-face block building
is articulated with varying square and
rectangular openings. At the base is a
line of large, rectangular windows. The
building's midsection is a series of
square windows grouped in fours,
topped by a cornice line of small,
incised squares. The facade of the winter garden along Massachusetts Avenue

is fronted by a white steel frame. The square windows it creates are broken into smaller squares by mullions, and the whole is underlain by a diagonal lateral bracing.

Rather than an authentic historical approach that would recreate the baroque walls of monumental Washington, this crisp, dynamic facade responds in a contemporary way to the L'Enfant Plan.

20. Techworld Plaza
800 K Street, N.W.
999 9th Street, N.W.
Smith-Williams Group *1989*

What makes Washington so extraordinary is its plan. While it has been tweaked and altered over time, the plan provides a framework against which every generation can check its work. Along 8th Street, the north-south axis halfway between the White House and the Capitol, L'Enfant envisioned a series of squares, fountains and monuments. While only some of his vision has been realized, it has always been respected. The site between F and G Streets that he proposed for the National Church is instead occupied by the National Archives, and Federal Triangle planners shifted the Archives facade to respond to 8th Street rather

than the diagonal of Pennsylvania Avenue.

Techworld Plaza, the pair of buildings flanking 8th Street opposite Mount Vernon Square was touted as a merchandise mart for the information age, an economic savior for downtown. In return for such investment, the city allowed development of a bridge across 8th Street between the building's sixth and eighth stories. While the promised economic revival did not materialize, the bridge did, and, while a thoughtfully designed span could have framed an important vista, this singularly awkward building steps into the picture like a thumb in a camera lens.

The glassy facade makes a bleak streetscape and, rather than respond to Mount Vernon Square, leaves its Beaux-Arts library stranded.

21. 810 7th Street, N.W.
Original architect and date unknown
Weihe Partnership *1992*

The demand for more downtown office space has changed the character of the Metro Center neighborhood. The small buildings that served downtown are no longer razed but now serve as bases for new construction filling in up to the height limit.

Here the details and materials of a two-story brick corner building and a three-bay, white terra-cotta facade along 7th Street set a physical and aesthetic base for new office space above. The added floors step back as they rise up from the original buildings. The new facades are brick with Chinese-style gables and decorative panels. The gable ends are marked with shallow, ribbed urns.

The renovation of the original buildings retains the full length of streetfront retail space. If the stores are successfully leased, the project could add activity to this out-of-the-way corner of the neighborhood.

22. Washington Convention Center
11th and H Streets, N.W.
Welton Beckett Associates *1983*

Convention centers seem to be the most sought after and the most disposable buildings of our time. Cities compete fiercely for convention business and a newer and larger center is the only answer. Washington's convention center was the third largest in the country when it opened, but ten years later it had dropped to twenty-fifth. The call went out for a $.5 billion replacement before the mortgages were paid off on other buildings of the same age.

Convention centers also are probably the most difficult buildings to fit into an urban setting. They are vast exhibition halls with daunting loading and staging requirements. Their featureless bulk obliterates city blocks. Sized for the largest conventions, they are used as huge containers only a half-dozen weeks a year. The balance is made up of multiple functions that could have been held at smaller facilities.

It is within this pattern that the Washington Convention Center was built. Its large, featureless facade is vacuous even by convention center standards. It is essentially a blank concrete block set atop a base of dark glass. Occasional folds and recesses in the building provide no relief. The large rooftop trusses that provide column-free interior space cannot provide any structural bravado on the exterior.

Because the building is so large and blocks some cross streets, it is very visible. From certain streets, the "C" logo on the concrete facade is visible, a feeble attempt at contextual decoration and a gesture to the importance of axial views in Washington.

The alternatives to convention center design are few. One is a design so dramatic in its modernist daring that it recalls the great exhibition halls of an earlier time. The best location for such centers is at the edges of downtowns. Another approach, for some reason rarely used, is to disguise the center behind appealing, urbane streetfronts.

23. Martin Luther King, Jr., Memorial Library
901 G Street, N.W.
Ludwig Mies van der Rohe *1972*

The austere lines of Mies's minimalist modernism need to be sited like sculpture to have the most impact. His most effective buildings, including the Seagram Building in midtown Manhattan, stand apart from the street—on a podium or behind a plaza. They become perfectly placed objets d'art.

In Washington, the library is set into the street and feels crowded by its more ornate neighbors. From some views it is in pleasing contrast to their details, but from others it seems bleak and cramped.

The building displays typical features of Mies's work: simple block massing, a monochrome facade, and glass walls articulated with steel girders. Here the building is set up on pilotis and its ground-floor entry is recessed.

Although this is one of the architect's last buildings, it was the first modern building approved by the Commission of Fine Arts. Even today it forces a reexamination of what civic architecture should be. The intention here was to make knowledge open and accessible, rather than to hide it inside a masonry temple.

24. 901 E Street, N.W.
RTKL Associates *1989*

This building introduces a welcome variety into the neighborhood, particularly behind the brutal box of the FBI Headquarters. But next to the simple Richardsonian bank building to the north, the building seems almost tortured in its architectural effort.

The facade is composed of projecting bays that step down to a central entrance. The building's Chicago-style windows—a central pane flanked by smaller double-hung windows—add more linear pattern to the facade. Further embellishments come from the balustrades atop the bays.

By contrast, the Riggs Bank building next door (originally Washington Loan and Trust Company, James G. Hill, 1891) is a simple box that takes its impact from the texture of its rusticated stone walls pierced by windows set in deep reveals that build up a facade of complementary elements. The result is simple, but visually arresting.

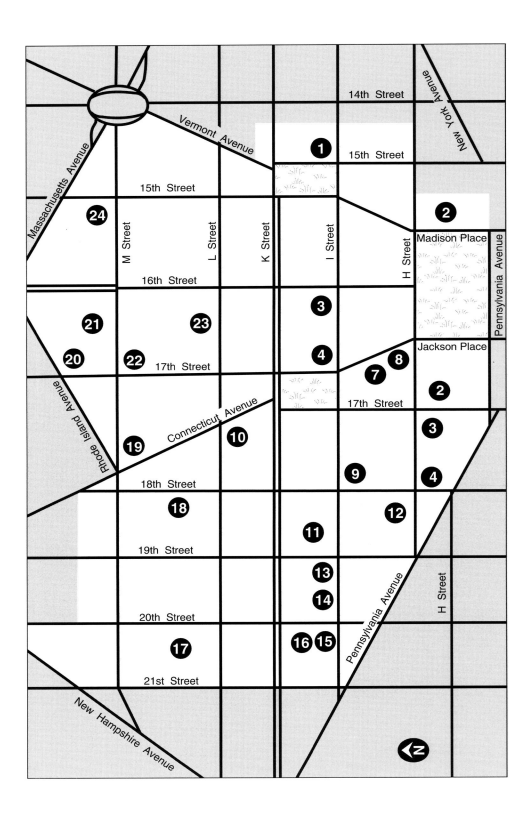

K Street

Washington has inexhaustible resources for those who have the gift of fashioning dramatic experiences out of architecture.

ELBERT PEETS, 1942

K Street was once a residential area of town houses and mansions, punctuated by corner stores. Like Dupont Circle to the north it was an area of architectural variety at a human scale. Out of the shifting sands of real estate have risen block after block of poor imitations of modern masterpieces. The area is tomblike after dark, when its office workers clear out to more exciting urban neighborhoods like Dupont Circle, Adams Morgan, or Georgetown. As the sands shift again toward redeveloping Metro Center, K Street has become an architectural and planning object lesson.

Early development clustered around the White House. Lafayette Square, Washington's second most desirable address, has been home to Dolley Madison; financier and cofounder of the Riggs Bank, William W. Corcoran; and John Hay and Henry Adams (whose houses, designed by Henry Hobson Richardson in 1884, were razed in 1927 by developer Henry Wardman, who replaced them with the Hay-Adams Hotel). Around the corner from Lafayette Square is the Blair-Lee House, now an official residence for state visitors. In 1872, Alexander "Boss" Shepard, who, as the District's public works czar, did much to modernize 19th-century Washington, lived nearby at Connecticut and K Street. More modest homes filled in the blocks farther away from the White House.

After World War II, pent-up demand for office space, the expanded needs of the federal government, and an obsolete downtown drew investors' attention from the area of Metro Center, between 6th and 15th Streets, to the area west of the White House. First the town houses and small commercial buildings were renovated for commercial and office use. As commercial demand increased, the old buildings were razed and replaced.

At the time, the office buildings must have seemed sleek and modern, framed in steel and sheathed in glass. By comparison, the old downtown's Victorian and Art Deco masonry must have looked dowdy. Soon there were just a few older buildings left, and K Street was lined with squat steel-and-glass boxes that have been described as eggcrates and crackerboxes. By the late 1970s, architects beginning their break from the strictures of modernism began to scoop out corners and create interior atriums, but the result was negligible, adding little visual variety and further removing life from the street.

Even historic Lafayette Square was threatened by spreading office development. As early as 1902 the McMillan Plan proposed a vast executive branch office
complex for the area. In the 1940s, the General Services Administration picked up
the proposal. But the public soon realized what would be lost, and a congressional lobby succeeded in blocking construction funds for one year. The project
forged ahead, however, with bureaucratic momentum; by 1961 the GSA had spent
$4 million on the design of the buildings and construction drawings were com-
plete. Yet Washington's Committee of 100, a group of influential citizens concerned with the city's development, persevered, and through personal connections
and meetings at state dinners and lectures, the possible destruction of the square
was brought to the attention of Jacqueline Kennedy. The first lady was intrigued,
and her attention stopped the bureaucratic juggernaut.

During the same period, Connecticut Avenue between K Street and Dupont
Circle developed into a high-end retail street with shops like Cartier, Polo, and
Burberrys. The atmosphere was buttressed by older luxury hotels that have never
lost their panache—the Jefferson, the Mayflower, and the Hay-Adams. This street
of fur salons and dress boutiques thrived through the boom years of the 1980s. In
the 1990s, retail concentration and competition in the suburbs and department
store bankruptcies may shift the retail profile of Connecticut Avenue. Many older
retailers have closed their stores, and Filene's Basement has moved in to replace
the defunct Raleigh's, a one-time legend among upper-crust retailers.

Downtown Washington seems an unwieldy thing. It shifts according to
economic tides as investors seek opportunity; the height limit flattens its buildings,
spreading and diluting their impact for blocks; and it must always compete with
the Mall's history theme park for tourist and even resident dollars and attention.
As the old downtown to the east, with its stock of historic buildings, regenerates
itself into a lively and attractive environment, planners are reexamining K Street's
architecture and the retail character of Connecticut Avenue. ■

1. McPherson Building
901 15th Street, N.W.
Clark, Tribble, Harris and Li *1987*

Though the facade of this building is
classically organized according to a
vertical hierarchy, the planes created
by the formal divisions are filled in
with modern details.

The building's granite base is
pierced with round and square window
openings. Their size and simplicity
make them a graphic device rather
than an incremental contribution to the
facade. Above the base, central
recessed porches at each level are

topped by projecting glass canopies and pierced by pilotis. The simple tubes of the pilotis rise through the facade, emphasizing that this is not a classical load-bearing wall, but a modern screen. The screening character of the curtain wall is further emphasized by wrapped corner windows, a standard modern device. The interplay between modern and classical motifs continues on the building's roof, where a brick gable rises in front of a mechanical penthouse sheathed in glass.

What the overall composition lacks in subtlety it makes up by being a lively, well-scaled edge to McPherson Square.

2. New Executive Office Building and Court of Claims Building
722 Jackson Place, N.W.
717 Madison Place, N.W.
John Carl Warnecke *1969*

Although today these buildings seem uninspired compared with the confidence of the neighboring Renwick Gallery and Old Executive Office Building and the simple dignity of the buildings surrounding Lafayette Square, at the time they were built they represented a significant change in attitude toward Washington's historic buildings.

When the McMilan Plan's grandiose view of an executive branch office complex on Lafayette Square was dropped, the need for office space remained. Warnecke was charged with creating a building scheme that would preserve this elegant forefront to the White House.

His buildings are among the first that recognize and reflect the scale and materials of historic fabric: They rise from the center of the block, preserving the historic streetscape; they are made

of brick, a popular historic material and complementary in tone to the Renwick's brownstone; they reach 10 stories, a height comparable to that of the Old Executive Office Building; and their details, including mansard roofs and domestically scaled oriel windows, relate the office buildings to their residential neighbors and to the Second Empire details of the Renwick.

Heins and La Farge *1908*
Keyes Condon Florance *1989*

1775 Pennsylvania Avenue, N.W.
Hartman-Cox Architects *1976*

The firm of Keyes Condon Florance, like others in Washington, has made a gentle move from modernism to historicism. Without designing literal recreations, their buildings incorporate visually interesting and urban-appropriate details.

Of a different scale and era, this building nevertheless extends the materials and details of the adjacent Metropolitan Club. Both have a simple rectilinearity marked with more or less elaborate classical details. The windowframes, lintels, and balustrades of the office building are less ornate than those of the club.

In deference to the original, the office building steps back as it rises from the street, creating an interesting facade. The office building connects to the club and brings itself down to street scale with a two-story limestone base marked by an arched entrance and retail shopfronts.

4. National Permanent Building

In the continuum of Hartman-Cox's work, which has moved from modern to historical in appearance, this building combines modern details classically organized to create a distinctive yet cost-effective speculative office building.

Unadorned concrete pilotis decrease in circumference and height as they ascend the building, a classical device that reflects the structural necessity of a base broadened to carry weight. A glass wall slides behind the columns, giving the facade a visually interesting depth. The recessed windows are in shade, lowering the cost of air conditioning.

A mansard roof is formed by utility ducts, finished in black and sloped to the roof's shape. By putting the utility ducts on the building's exterior the architects freed up more leasable space on the inside and used structure as architectural ornament on the outside.

5. Third Church of Christ Scientist

5. Third Church of Christ Scientist
900–910 16th Street, N.W.
I. M. Pei and Partners *1972*

This complex of office and church
buildings is formed, like much of Pei's
work, by simple, bold shapes. The
church is reminiscent of a faceted
Renaissance baptistry, sited here adjacent to an office tower rather than a
bell tower. This spare building has
none of the riveting sculpture and

paintings that were integral to Renaissance buildings. Instead, its pink-tinted, poured-in-place concrete is decorated primarily with the impressions of its wood and fiberglass pouring molds.

From 16th Street, the building's facade opens with two rectangular windows and peels away to form a carillon. Minimalism is difficult to achieve in the K Street neighborhood, where every office building is stripped down. In a more richly detailed environment this sculptural simplicity would be an effective offset to surrounding architectural cacophony or a lush natural setting, but in this location it becomes just another box.

prescribed by the zoning ordinance. The added space is turned over to offices.

The penthouse addition is one of the architect's earlier additions to a downtown building. Like his other successful designs of this type, this one expands details of the original in a subtle way that avoids direct mimicry. The addition picks up the rhythm of the original structure, in which articulated corners flank a central bay. The five pedimented windows of the addition mirror the five arched windows of the ballroom, and iron balconies on the original facade are repeated on the upper stories.

This addition is less refined than the architect's later work, but still builds up a handsome facade on a very visible site on McPherson Square.

6. Army Navy Club
901 17th Street, N.W.
Hornblower and Marshall *1911*
Shalom Baranes Associates *1987*

This club started as a six-story building and was first expanded in the 1950s with a single bay and upper story. This latest penthouse addition brings the building up to the height limit

7. 816 Connecticut Avenue, N.W.
Shalom Baranes Associates *1987*

In a city and time when megadevelopments covering a full block are the rule, a single bay facade is the exception. Here a simple treatment achieves a sophisticated result.

The most striking feature of this granite and glass facade is a triangular oriel that runs down the center of the building, stopping just above the first two stories. Crisp, simple details highlight the shape and allow this dramatic element to dominate. The variety created by this bold treatment is a refreshing change from the monumental scale of many public and private Washington buildings.

8. Lafayette Square
800 Connecticut Avenue, N.W.
Keyes Condon Florance *1991*

The public space known as Lafayette Square is a small gem in the Washington streetscape. While no longer residential, its town houses remain elegant reminders of the past. The park and buildings create a graceful transition between the White House and the rest of the city. It is fitting that a new office building incorporate some of this inherent elegance.

The building's curved entrance is centered on the corner, marked with a cable-hung steel canopy, and set in a four-story base that is scaled to Lafayette Square's historic town houses. From the base, the building steps back, the corner marked by a curved bay of windows, the whole rising to a series of stepped, flat roofs. The building's setbacks are articulated with what the architects call "power porches"—balconies offering a view of the White House. Unlike Warnecke, who chose brick to blend in with the historic material of the square, the architects here created a white, glassy facade that is noticeable but not intrusive.

With the abandonment of

modernism, history has opened its paintbox to architects. This building combines elements of Art Deco and Viennese modernism to create a friendly, contextual building.

9. Republic Place
1776 I Street, N.W.
Keyes Condon Florance *1987*

Washington's height limit combines with economic imperatives to create boxy buildings expanded to lot lines and filled with atria that create a second interior facade. Architects constantly experiment with ways to enliven this formula, and postmodernism's

return to historicist details has opened
new opportunities.

Here the architects articulate the
corner with an inset tower topped by
an open belvedere. The corner tower,
not counted in building height, exploits
a loophole in the zoning law. It is also
a way to distinguish a building, particularly in a grid streetscape. Other details
include a cornice line lightly topped
with urns, globes, and globular lamps.
The building's facade is spotted with
brick patterns.

This is a basic Washington office
building in its height, massing, and
window patterns, but it is given a slipcover of vaguely historical decoration.

10. Washington Square
1050 Connecticut Avenue, N.W.
Chloethiel Woodard Smith and
Associates *1984*

This is a power building for a power
town. It commands its block with a
sleek profile and high-rent tenants.
Upscale clothing stores and Duke
Zeibert's, a venerable Washington
restaurant, add to the posh retail atmosphere along Connecticut Avenue.

Cloethial Woodard Smith's work in
the metropolitan Washington area, particularly in Southwest Washington and
Reston, is in the modernist vein of
clean lines and simple massing, but she
adds elements of warmth and visual
interest through her siting and choice
of materials. Here, she has taken the
standard Washington office box and
varied the massing with two faceted
corner atria, rather than the usual central atrium. The sparkling glassy facade
has a transparency not usually seen in
Washington's solid monuments or even
its modern office buildings.

11. International Square
1850 K Street, N.W.
Vlastimil Koubek *1974–81*

When it was built, this building took some first steps away from the ortho-dox modernism that had plagued K Street, but they were small steps. The project covers most of a city block and makes connections with a Metro sta-tion. The concrete and ribbon-win-dowed facade is cut out at ground-floor corner entrances and stepped back on upper levels. Its offices are arranged around an interior atrium of shops and restaurants. Both the Metro connection and the atrium make it a busy place, but the activity is absorbed off the street and hidden within the building. Even the K Street storefronts are turned inward. The building is a plain brown wrapper with all its goodies on the inside.

The building creates the kind of controlled environment that city-wary users like and that developers can eas-ily offer within limited budgets. The design and uses set up a formula for large-lot downtown development in Washington.

12. MCI World Headquarters
Pennsylvania Avenue and 18th Streets, N.W.
Skidmore, Owings and Merrill (Craig Hartman) *1992*

With the return to historicist details allowed by postmodernism, many architects have taken the standard Washington office box and elaborated it with tacked-on towers and turrets to create an image of verticality. This building takes a more structural approach to creating a tower, building up the facade through elements that create a vertical profile.

The facade's two corners flank a curved, recessed central bay topped by a projecting domed drum. Vertically proportioned windows rising up the facade add to the illusion of height. There are no overt historical references here, such as turrets or cupolas, but perhaps the most emphatic introduc-tion of an office tower into Washington to date.

The building's vertical profile is emphasized by its siting on a slight rise above Pennsylvania Avenue and H Street. Also, the intersection of these streets creates a small traffic triangle that affords a wider view of the building.

In such a determinedly horizontal city as Washington, this vertical building may reflect an aesthetic shift in the way we view the city.

13. Presidential Plaza
900 19th Street, N.W.
Keyes Condon Florance *1986*

As architects moved away from the formulaic central atrium ringed with offices and clad in a plain modern facade, they discovered another loophole in the zoning ordinance that was a comfortable fit with a return to historicist detail. The corner tower, as unleasable space, could rise above the 10-story height limit and distinguish the newest office building from its neigh-

bors. Clad in any variety of historical details, a new device was created. This same firm used corner towers at nearby Republic Place (see number 9, above). Other firms and buildings in Metro Center and Franklin Square use paired towers and central towers.

This building chooses an Art Deco image and expands the palette of acceptable colors, using the ribbon windows that curve around the corners to create a smooth, banded facade of polished pink granite. The projecting tower contains a clock.

14. 1915 I Street, N.W.
Swaney, Kearns (Robert Barber Anderson) *1983*

This office building addition is a clever and lively variation on facadism. The facade is bound by its narrow site in a snug streetfront lot. Repeating gables step back as they rise from the original gabled facade. The rising brick stories

mimic the material and shape of the original facade's Dutch gable. In a modern vein, the gable sides are opened with rectangular windows and fronted with pipe rails.

The simple solution creates visual interest in a discreet composition of size, shape, and materials.

15. James Monroe Building
2001 Pennsylvania Avenue, N.W.
Skidmore, Owings and Merrill *1989*

Despite the vague historical references of the facade—a defined base, corners marked in a contrasting material, a gabled roof, and even chimneys—this is clearly a contemporary building. Its windows are flush with the curtain wall, which cannot re-create the depth of a load-bearing wall. Even the three gables that poke above a balustrade are perched lightly on the roof edge.

The building appears to occupy a single site, but its development involved a complicated combination of history and urban planning. The building's size reflects a transfer of development potential from the nearby Arts Club of Washington, originally the home of James Monroe. By selling its right to develop a larger building in the

future, the club has preserved its building and gained income to maintain it.

The building's height was increased from the allowable base of 90 feet to 125 feet because it faces a federal reservation, the small triangle of park created by the intersection of Pennsylvania Avenue and H Street. Since building height is related to street width, the open area here allowed a taller building. Finally, the developer agreed to participate in maintenance of the park.

This building illustrates the complicated tradeoffs between commercial advantage and public benefit that create the city.

16. 20th and K Streets, N.W.
Skidmore, Owings and Merrill (David Childs) *1986*

Although the text of the 1910 height limit allows spires, minarets, and other decorative roofs to rise above the permitted height, modern architects who had abandoned such frippery rarely took advantage of this aesthetic loophole. At the same time modernist designers ignored the importance of an emphasized corner as a point of convergence in the urban fabric. Building corners were the meeting of two walls, rather than an entrance or focal point.

A corner articulated with a tower highlights the building on the street, makes it clear where the entrance is, and directs the hierarchy of the facade. On this site, the corner is marked with a rounded turret topped with a perpetually flying bronze flag. The building's other street-fronting corners are

anchored by square-topped towers. The masonry wall is clearly divided along classical lines into a base, shaft, and top, and at ground level the street is enlivened with shopfronts. The building is an early postmodern breach of the height limit, and today it seems cartoonish; its details are simply drawn and overscaled.

Although corner towers have become formulaic, and architects have since moved to a more sophisticated expression of facades and rooflines, towers did herald a return to an

ATRIA AND TOWERS

ALL ZONING REGULATIONS are rules in a game, and the better you know the rules, the better you play the game. Occasionally someone reinterprets the rules and changes the way the game is played. So it is with two rules Washington architects must play by: floor area ratio (FAR) and the height limit. Working within these strictures, architects and developers in the mid-1970s began to apply two innovations that have changed the way Washington office buildings are designed and the way the city looks: atria and towers.

Washington's downtown office buildings are often built around spacious and airy atria. These vast buildings seem to dominate their sites, with repetitive curtain walls that stretch the horizontal city. These buildings are created by a peculiarity in the way FAR is measured.

FAR is meant to control the bulk of buildings by measuring the ratio of the building's floor area to that of the site. What it does not measure is empty space. So a large, 10-story office building may have an atrium that itself has the volume of a slender, 10-story building, but only the floor

area of the atrium is counted toward FAR. The bulk of the building however, increases dramatically.

The developer wants to build on as large a portion of a block as he can. A larger project creates a total environment that is easier to lease, has a geometry that usually yields more window offices, and a large building size that provides certain economies. The FAR does not allow that much bulk, and the real estate market cannot lease floor space in the vast windowless center of the building.

The atrium solves these problems. The unleasable center is turned into a dramatic amenity that becomes the building's signature, without a density penalty. The building now has two facades, an outer one facing the street and an inner one surrounding the atrium.

Atria are innovations of private office buildings, but they are an evolution of the courtyards that provide light and air to interior offices in older, large government office buildings. Atria are simply covered courtyards providing the year-round comfort we are familiar with in suburban shopping malls. They are controlled

important element of the baroque city. An articulated roof finishes the outdoor space, making a transition between earth and sky, man and nature.

17. Lafayette Center
20th and L Streets, N.W.
Welton Beckett *1987*

The flat facade of this complex of four buildings opens at the ground floor with round-cornered rectangular openings. The three arches of the main

environments, some starkly contemplative with sculpture and fountains, others boisterously mercantile, with shops and restaurants.

The draw of the atrium is that it is more attractive than the street. We are indoors, yet we are not really inside. Placed between the completely public street and completely private offices, the atrium exists in the semipublic realm of lobbies and foyers, yet it presumes to be more—a new communal space.

Unfortunately, with atrial excess, the street is forsaken; attention and investment are focused indoors. Ironically, where this city, as others, has promoted a mix of uses to instill vitality beyond office hours, those uses also find a welcome home inside the atrium.

A similar loophole allows the more recent proliferation of towers. The 1910 height limit only counts space that can be occupied, exempting "spires, towers, domes, minarets, pinnacles." Decorative penthouses and finials are also exempt.

The vertical projections take many forms. Some architects append turrets onto the traditional Washington box. Many of the city's traditional buildings use this form. Modern architecture's rationalism banished turrets as picturesque and unnecessary. Other approaches contort the building's roofline, engaging a tower or varying penthouse heights, or stepping the facade to simulate verticality.

A few have gone so far as to design a "tall building" within the constraints of the height limit and a reasonable additional height. From the base upward, all elements of the building's detailing and massing work together to create a vertical emphasis. The building does not have a tower, but is a tower.

This last permutation could have a profound effect on the cityscape. Washington is a horizontal city. Idealized, it would be like Paris, interesting facades and emphatic rooftops deferring to the streets. This new building type introduces towers into the horizontal city. The first skyscrapers of the 19th-century American city were short by today's standards. Almost all could fit within Washington's height limit. Yet there is no mistaking that they represent exclamation points in a different kind of city.

entrance rise four stories, shopfronts rise two stories. Flush windows are grouped in bays of two marked by incised lines in the brick facade.

The four buildings are arranged around a midblock courtyard that creates a shortcut to 21st Street. The courtyard serves the same purpose as atria in other downtown Washington buildings. It pushes the buildings on this large site out to the lot line, maximizing rental space by creating two facades, an interior and an exterior, within the height limit.

This building introduces some interesting variations into the streetscape, yet much of its effort is dated. The very flatness of the facade seems to be a pointless relic of modernism to a contemporary eye that favors dynamic and idiosyncratic massing. The courtyard and shortcut, though pleasant amenities, are not fully used in this location. The courtyard lacks the people and uses that would make it lively, and there is no traffic or destination that warrants a shortcut.

18. 1150 18th Street, N.W.
Don Hisaka and Associates *1990*

In this history-obsessed city and decided capital of architectural contextualism, Don Hisaka consistently goes his own way. While he is sensitive to the street and site he avoids both modernist and historicist formulas.

Here he has used modern materials—glass and steel—to form his facade. But rather than creating the ascetic rhythm of Mies or his mimics, here steel divides the glass into infinite planes. They jump across the facade in syncopation, dividing it into a recessed central bay flanked by two towers. A round cartouche of sorts marks the center bay.

The building's white facade is a reference to the work of Le Corbusier and his disciples, who emphasized aesthetic purity with white, exposed structural elements. The color also sets the building apart from its beige masonry neighbors.

19. Demonet Building

Connecticut Avenue and M Street, N.W.
Skidmore, Owings and Merrill *1984*

The personable Victorian building on the corner seems to linger as a friendly anomaly, unrelated to the newer, blank facades behind it. At the time it was finished, this mix of old and new buildings was considered a successful and desirable outcome. Today, the detailing of the new building, particularly the glass wall with the round window, seems faddish and trite.

The original building is a rich brown and is virtually iced with details. Variously shaped and sized windows topped with lintels and divided by corbeled stringcourses pile up on the facade. The whole is crowned by a faceted, gilded dome elaborated with bull's-eye dormers and concluding in a spire. Its scale and detail create a friendly and visually interesting streetfront.

The much taller office addition is stepped well back from the original, and from some angles seems unconnected to it. In a kind of aesthetic concession, the new facade has an arched window and corbeled cornice that echo the dome and cornice of the original. The rest of the new building, which takes off at various angles, is a mundane facade of flush windows in smooth brick and concrete.

21. Sumner Square
M Street between 16th and 17th Streets, N.W.
Hartman-Cox Architects *1985*

20. B'nai B'rith International Headquarters
1640 Rhode Island Avenue, N.W.
Fisher and Elmore *1956*

In an era of renovation and refacing, this building retains its modernist stance. Its freestanding, sculptural character is emphasized by a different treatment on each facade.

The L-shaped building is arranged around a single-story pavilion on a corner site. The inner facade is a steel frame supporting bands of glass and blue metal panels. The elements of this facade take full advantage of the open site and are sculpted as separate and distinct planes. The facades facing L Street and Rhode Island Avenue are solid, white-glazed brick detailed with a linear pattern of projecting courses.

The mosaic at the entry success-fully incorporates art into the facade, usually a feature of older Washington buildings.

In this complex the architects have created a small cityscape with buildings woven together by materials, shape, and style. It is one of the few places downtown that has the idiosyncracy of jumbled buildings reflecting layers of time. The complex leaves clues to the earlier character of this neighborhood. The Sumner and Magruder schools had been abandoned by the Board of Education as the residential population shifted away from downtown. After years of neglect a design competition for the site was held. The winning proposal called for renovating the two schools. A two-bay ell was added to the Sumner School, and the Magruder School was disassembled and moved to be the centerpiece of the new streetscape. The new building, a dark glass box with gray masonry quoins, sits behind the schools, wrapping around them in an L shape. Where the new building meets the street its facade is more postmodern, with quoined corner bays, individual rather than ribbon windows, and masonry walls.

Across the street, the National Geographic Society buildings are a similar complex of old and new. Together the two projects make an interesting urban block.

22. National Geographic Society Complex
M Street between 16th and 17th Streets, N.W.
Hornblower and Marshall *1902*
Arthur B. Heaton *1932*
Edward Durell Stone *1964*
Skidmore, Owings and Merrill *1985*

The two earlier buildings in this complex, which covers a block, are classical in their massing, materials, and details. After the completion of these buff brick and limestone buildings a revolution took place in architecture, and even if this client had

wanted a classical reprise that would have been unthinkable in 1964.

Stone's plain temples and boxes are classical in attitude, but he strips them of ornament and detail. This building, like his others in Washington, is a boxy mass articulated with vertical elements. Dark glass windows are framed with black granite and separated by vertical fins of white marble. The shaft is topped by the thinnest of perforated overhangs—a trademark of Stone's designs. In other Washington work, particularly the Kennedy Center, where the program allowed him to enclose the uses within sheaths of marble, Stone created more perfect boxes. By comparison, this is a very glassy building.

The latest addition to the complex plays off Stone's vertical elements. Long horizontal lines of pale pink concrete alternate with strips of dark glass. The floors step back to create landscaped terraces. This addition defers to Stone's self-contained temple by

receding and creating a plaza.

The newer buildings are a somewhat sterile pair, but they are enlivened by the play of vertical and horizontal. Taken together, they contribute to an interesting and varied streetscape on this block.

23. 1615 L Street, N.W.
Jung-Brannen Associates *1985*

This sleek building is tucked in the middle of a short block, but a bit of its crisp facade rises gently behind the three-story Benjamin Franklin School of Accountancy building on 16th Street.

The three-story brick base, which steps up as it turns the corner into an alley, transforms itself into a lush green glass-banded facade. Three notched balconies at the upper corner reflect the simple rectangular shapes of the brick arcade at street level. A glass and steel entry canopy projects through the brick, completing the image of interlocking parts.

The entrance and lobby are richly finished with colored and geometrically patterned marble, which presents an interesting contrast to the sleek exterior. Developers love to brag about the acres of marble in their building

lobbies, but the colors and craftsmanship here are so fine that there is no hint of ostentation. Through the lobby the building fills its lot around an interior atrium.

The building succeeds in creating a presence for itself while blending into the skyline and streetscape.

24. 1501 M Street, N.W.
Hartman-Cox Architects *1991*

These architects gently insert their work into the Washington streetscape. Even their most spectacular buildings, like Market Square on Pennsylvania Avenue, pick up on scale and detail for a good fit.

This building, while less ambitious and visible than the firm's work along Pennsylvania Avenue, fits into Washington's mercantile rather than monumental past. The building is on the edge of the K Street neighborhood, both physically and visually. The firm makes a slight nod to the glass boxes of K Street and returns to the more ornate Victorian period.

Two-story Tuscan columns support arches on the ground level and then stack up for four levels to a balustraded cornice line and recessed attic story. The corner is marked with an offset tower capped by a dome. These frilly precast concrete details are surface ornament. They lack the hierarchy of a true classical building and are a screen for the contemporary glass building behind. Ironically, the high ratio of glass to solid concrete gives the building the lightness of cast iron rather than the heavy mass of masonry.

The building may not have a classical rigor or a wild inventiveness; after all, it is a speculative office building, but it contributes to a pleasant streetscape.

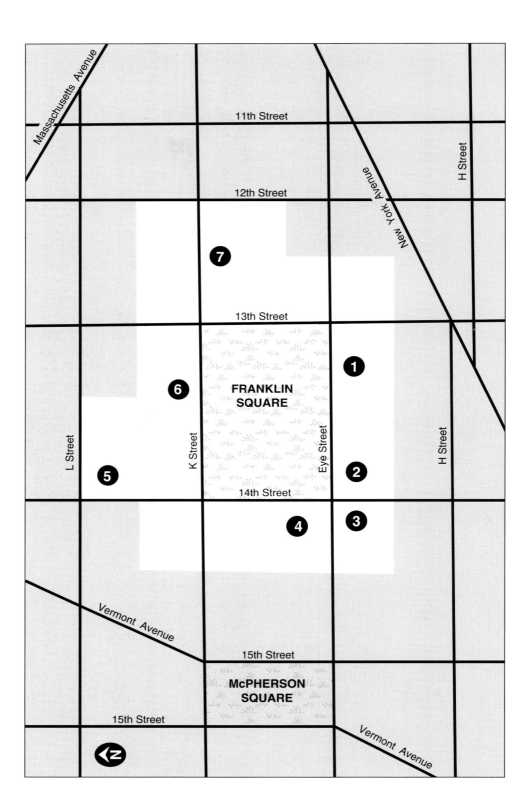

Franklin Square

The city itself is unlike any other that was ever seen, straggling hither and thither, with a small house or two a quarter of a mile from any other; so that in making calls 'in the city' we had to cross ditches and stiles, and walk alternatively on grass and pavements, and strike across a field to reach a street....

HARRIET MARTINEAU, 1835

Even though it is on K Street, Franklin Square is different from its western neighbors, McPherson and Farragut squares. Unlike them, its was not designated in L'Enfant's plan as a public reservation; instead it was divided into building lots. Franklin Square is also larger and more like a park than the urban McPherson and Farragut squares. These two squares are green complements to the buildings that edge them. Franklin Square is large enough to feel like a respite from the surrounding city.

Franklin Square's building lots were acquired in 1829 when natural springs were discovered on the site. Development was forestalled and the springs became one of the city's earliest water sources. For a time, wooden pipes from the springs served the White House.

Early downtown development focused on the White House, the Capitol, and the Navy Yard. When Secretary of State John Sherman moved with his wife to 1321 K Street in the mid-1800s, she felt they were out in "the country." One of the area farmsteads that had been part of the original colonial land grant, John Davidson's frame house and its dependencies, survived well into the 19th century. Despite the distance, Mrs. Sherman soon had fine neighbors; Secretary of War Edwin M. Stanton lived next door, and before he was president, James Garfield lived at 13th and I Streets. By 1851, the square was enclosed as a park. A decade later, during the Civil War, the square was requisitioned for military use as an encampment of the 12th New York Volunteers.

While Alexander "Boss" Shepherd was paving streets and planting trees in the rest of the city, he turned his attention to Franklin Square, planting it in the romantic, natural style of the time. The square was later redesigned, more formally in 1936, and again in 1964. In 1970, the National Capital Planning Commission noted in a survey of downtown Washington's historic landmarks that Franklin Square "is situated in an ever-changing neighborhood, formerly residential, then small commercial, and now large office buildings." The shifting fortunes and character of the square put the Franklin School in danger. Once the best public school in the city and designed by Adolf Cluss, architect of the Arts and Industries Building on the Mall, the building had been stripped of its exuberant Victorian detail by 1970, and needed a sympathetic buyer willing to rehabilitate.

Franklin Square has always had the potential to be one of Washington's most pleasant downtown parks. It fits neatly into the street pattern, yet is large enough to provide relief from the surrounding city. But, until the 1980s, the square was abandoned, making it feel unsafe and unpleasant. By that time, however, Franklin Square's fortunes began to shift again. Downtown development was moving east as Dupont Circle and K Street filled up, and as Pennsylvania Avenue was revitalized into an attractive office location.

Today new development and successful restorations, including a rehabilitated Franklin School, nearly surround the square. The height and bulk of the new buildings create a defining edge that contrasts with the park's large trees. Office workers are active users of the park. At a sunny lunchtime, Franklin Square is all that an urban park should be. ■

1. Franklin Square
1300 I Street, N.W.
John Burgee Architect (Philip Johnson)
1990

Often tempted to the outrageous, Philip Johnson uses a subtle classicism here to give a speculative office building weight and solidity. Rather than following the more decorative yet pared down classicism popular in the late 1980s, the architects looked to German neoclassicism and modernism of the early 20th century, particularly the work of Ludwig Mies van der Rohe and Peter Behrens. The building bears a compositional resemblance to an influential building by Behrens,

the Turbinenhalle in Berlin.

In the classical style, the building's length and height are articulated, but detailing and motifs are reduced to simplified elements. Slender, 11-story columns across the facade establish a rhythm that culminates in massive planes of limestone at the corners. Behind the columns, a glass curtain wall runs uninterrupted to the top story, a modern feature belying the building's classical organization. The limestone sheathing refers to the standard set by the Federal Triangle for the way a serious Washington building should look. The building's grand lobby is evocative of earlier German classicism, the work of Karl Friedrich Schinkel. Overall, the building is free of the sentimentalism and nostalgia of 1990s postmodernism.

The facade provides a grand, well-scaled edge to Franklin Square, its glass wall offering an open reflective face to the park and its limestone tops and sides providing definition. The heavy, rusticated northeast corner engages in a dialogue of solids and voids with the similar corner of 1300 New York Avenue one block south.

This is a restrained, well-detailed building by the architect who initiated high-end corporate postmodernism with New York's AT&T Building 10 years earlier.

2. 1350 I Street, N.W.
The Weihe Partnership *1989*

This is one of the earlier buildings that began the transformation of Franklin Square into a prestigious office address. Its reflective glass and polished stone, combined with the building's twin towers and clock face, mediate between old and new. The glass and stone place the building firmly in the here and now, but the towers hark back to a time when light wells were used to bring natural light into a building's interior. The clock is a retro touch that is quickly becoming a cliché.

A park the size of Franklin Square gains definition from a clear edge, but this building's surface reflects the square and does little to frame it. Instead, the polished glass acts as a mirror, and the building dissolves into the park.

3. United Press International Building
1400 I Street, N.W.
Arthur Cotton Moore *1985*

This is the usual downtown Washington office building, sheathed in brick, striped with ribbon windows, and lifted off the ground with concrete pilotis, but it reflects this architect's particular affinity for swooping curves and grand gestures.

The thin membrane of the Metro tunnel beneath the site could not support the office building and made it necessary to carve out the corner of the building. The space beneath the carved-out corner was intended for lively shopfronts. The sidewalk entrance is marked by a circular white metal gate elaborated with curlicues, and its ceiling is painted with a trompe-l'oeil sky. But the facade's overwhelming character comes from its ribbon windows, which have a faceless quality and make the storefronts seem hidden and dark.

4. Franklin Tower
1401 I Street, N.W.
Vlastimil Koubek *1990*

Most of the buildings that surround Franklin Square were built within a few years of each other and use classical imagery to define the street and park edge. The buildings vary though in their treatment of the details. Some are deep and molded, others applied to the surface.

This facade is an enthusiastic pileup of shapes—square and circular medallions and windows centered on slender columns. The first-floor retail space and human-scaled details create a pleasant streetscape. The elements are clearly a veneer and in interesting contrast to Johnson's Franklin Square building, which also applies nonstructural classical elements but with a depth and simplicity that are almost serene.

another layer of disembodied historical detail. The building does not front directly on Franklin Square, but its tower gives it a presence there. The tower dominates the front facade and thrusts past the roofline, which sets back at the tenth floor. On each side of the tower's top, a single three-story Tuscan column set within a dark opening emphasizes the building's height. This composition creates a classical temple atop a 20th-century skyscraper. Franklin Court's massing and tower ensure that the building is seen amid nearby emerging towers in the new Franklin Square.

5. Franklin Court
1099 14th Street, N.W.
Kohn Pederson Fox
1991

In Franklin Square, as elsewhere in Washington, architects refer to existing context. Rather than using the monumental historical context so prevalent in the city, postmodern architects pick and choose from a library of historic details. In Franklin Square some architects have chosen to refer to the ornate Art Deco and Victorian mercantilism of 7th Street. Franklin Court's bronze storefronts and precast concrete, steel, and bronze detailing create an appealing retail streetfront.

The architects of this building have added

FLOOR AREA RATIO

ZONING ORDINANCES ORIGINALLY used height, lot coverage, and setback to define a building's envelope and its relationship to the street. Although these standards are still used, another was developed to control the bulk of a building: floor area ratio, or FAR. By basing allowed development on a general degree of density, development potential can be distributed more fairly. Regardless of the site's size, it will have the same density as neighboring sites.

FAR is expressed as a ratio of the allowable building area over the lot area. For example, an FAR of 1 would allow a one-story building that covers the entire lot, or a two-story building that covers half the lot, or a three-story building that covers a third of the lot. In an urban environment, FAR's tend to be high, around 6 or 7 in a dense mid-rise area like downtown Washington, and around 19 or 20 in midtown Manhattan. To planners and developers alike, FAR is the most fundamental dimensional standard of the zoning code. It determines the development potential and value of a lot. An FAR of 4 is worth twice as much as an FAR of 2.

FAR is a rational tool, but it is coarse in its application its and effect on the street. Within one FAR level, three very different buildings could be created within the limits of the site and building technology. Theoretically, the final shape of the building is unknown, but the exigencies of real estate development make it unlikely that a developer will build a one-story building in a downtown where land is expensive and office space is at a premium. Other standards such as height and setback fine tune a building's shape; human-scaled details at the street level are usually left to the architect and developer.

FAR controls bulk as if bulk were the major determinant of urban quality, yet it ignores the more important nature of buildings and the details that combine to create a city and its urban experiences. FAR is most effective in urban environments on relatively small lots whose value will force a certain type of high density development. The street profile can then be influenced by other zoning ordinance standards like setback or build-to lines, and by planning guidelines, which may recommend plazas or arcades.

FAR is a less effective tool in a suburban or developing rural area where the character of the community is changing and undefined, and where lots are significantly larger, carved out of former farms and estates. The suburban landscape is too diffused by sky, road, and open land to be seriously affected by the overly bulky building. In an unbuilt landscape the effect of a four-story building is not significantly different from that of a six- or even an eight-story building. Other details will have more impact: the building's proximity to the street, the character and width of the street, the landscaping, the siting of the building, and its surrounding parking will all affect our perception of the landscape. A major aesthetic shortcoming of many suburban buildings—that they are set behind an expanse of cars—is neither addressed nor controlled by FAR.

On very large rural tracts, using the applicable FAR can yield huge amounts of office space. Each large farm could potentially be built to the size of downtown Miami. The real estate market, more than FAR, limits the ability to build up these tracts.

6. One Franklin Square
1301 K Street, N.W.
Hartman-Cox Architects *1990*

Referring to this building in
Architecture magazine, George
Hartman said the firm "needed to
transform its [Franklin Square's] area
rather than draw from a strong historic
context." More than neighboring buildings, One Franklin Square has changed
the area into a gracious urban space.
If you squint at them, the twin towers
look as if they belong at the edge of
Central Park.

The pyramid-topped towers of the
granite-clad office building introduce a
vertical character not seen in earlier
Washington office buildings. The towers are visible on the skyline from

across the Potomac. Because the zoning code allows unleasable space to
exceed the height limits, these towers
rise 90 feet above the limit. This, and
the site's slight rise above the street
and square, emphasize the building's
vertical profile.

The small, Moorish-inspired Almas
Temple to the west was dismantled and
moved to its present location to make
way for the new building.

7. 1200 K Street, N.W.
Hartman-Cox Architects *1993*

This brick building with limestone
detailing—balusters, spandrels, windowframes, a penthouse, and a
columned entry—takes a general historic stance with vague references to
the Franklin School next door. Just as, a
generation earlier, modern architecture
was adopted by the urban real estate
market and replicated ad nauseam, one
can imagine today's architectural fash-
ions creating a new generation of
ersatz historical cities.

Developers must establish a building's leasing image to attract tenants.
They hang out banners, give their
buildings names, offer special services,
and hire architects to maximize
leasable space and create a physical
image, all within the budget. Here the
architect and developer have chosen to
create an old-fashioned-looking building at Washington's newest office
address.

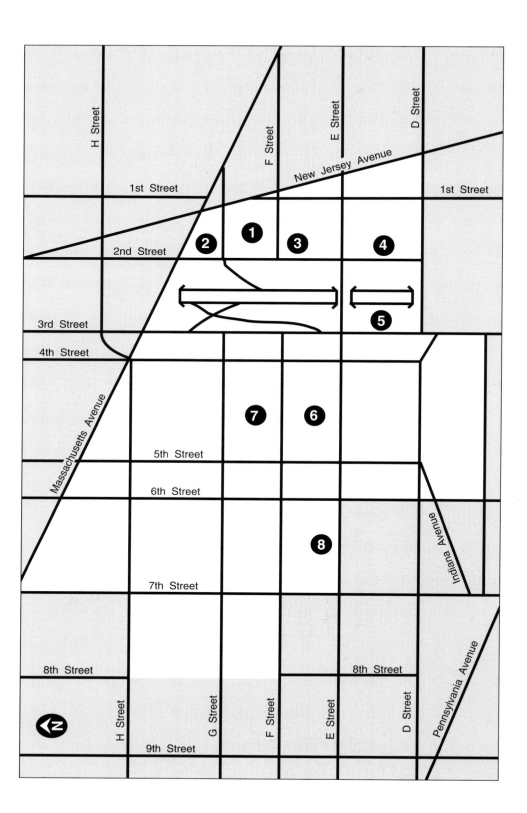

The East End

*Washington was spacious avenues that begin in nothing and lead nowhere;
streets a mile long that only want houses, roads, and inhabitants; public buildings that need but a public to be complete; and ornaments of great thoroughfares which only need great thoroughfares to ornament...*

CHARLES DICKENS, 1842

The East End is located between Metro Center and Capitol Hill, yet it is off the
beaten paths of Pennsylvania Avenue and K Street. It seems that the blocks of
office buildings marching eastward here flag in their energy. Between the new historicism of Franklin Square and the Beaux-Arts confections of Union Station, the
East End is a mixture of uses without a strong identity like that of K Street or
Georgetown. The East End is in the throes of becoming. Massive government
offices and warehouses bump up against freeway abutments. New office buildings
sit next to single, forlorn town houses in the middle of weedy lots. On this frontier
of development, few investors take risks in use or design. Rather than choosing to
mix housing and offices in exchange for higher density, developers build smaller
office buildings.

This area north of Pennsylvania Avenue around 6th Street was high enough to
be safe from Tiber Creek flooding and attracted early development. As a residential area on the fringes of the commercial downtown, it served as a starting point
for Jewish immigrants. Construction of the Old Adas Israel Synagogue was begun
in 1873 on its original site at Sixth and G Streets to serve this population. As the
neighborhood changed the synagogue was used by a Greek Orthodox congrega-
tion, and later as a barber shop and market. In 1969, it was moved to 3rd and G
Streets, and designated a historic landmark. This portion of the East End later
became home to Chinese newcomers. A small Chinatown still exists around H
Street, marked with a large, ornate Chinese-style arch near 7th Street. Its shops,
restaurants, and older housing serve an immigrant population who work hard to
move out and gain a toehold in the suburbs.

The East End, along with rest of downtown, began to decline in the late 1940s
in the face of increasing suburbanization and the westward shift of the downtown
office district. In 1968, riots stalled downtown investment, leaving low-rent offices
and some marginal stores. Although the area was included in the Downtown
Urban Renewal Area defined by the Redevelopment Land Agency in 1970, redevelopment efforts began at the western end of downtown. Later, the PADC's
efforts on Pennsylvania Avenue focused attention on the eastern end of downtown, but redevelopment is just beginning to reach the East End.

Public and private investment in revitalization of the Metro Center neighborhood just to the west includes metro stations, the Convention Center on H Street between 9th and 11th Streets, Tech World along 8th Street at Mount Vernon Square, and a pedestrian plaza along F Street in front of the National Portrait Gallery. Although the Metro station is a transportation hub, the other projects have been less than successful, disrupting important axes and access points, and creating characterless urban environments peopled by transients ranging from convention-goers to the homeless. The city's involvement in the redevelopment of Gallery Place—vacant sites north of the Portrait Gallery—has slowed the process and missed market opportunities. Now a sports arena proposed for this site has engendered debate about the project's fiscal wisdom, its contribution to an active downtown, and the efect of a megaproject in the grid of downtown streets. This development and lack of development has acted as a perceptual wall, making it hard to see potential redevelopment possibilities in the area of the East End.

Even a new proposal for a New York Avenue Development District, modeled along the lines of the PADC, begins at the eastern edge of Mount Vernon Square and travels north, again neglecting this area of the city. For urban pioneers, though, this area is convenient, offering buildable lots in a downtown location at less than downtown prices. The American Association of Retired Persons completed its new headquarters in 1991, and Georgetown University has established a law school campus convenient to city and federal court buildings. As a result, parts of the East End have developed as neighborhoods within a neighborhood, further fracturing the area's image.

As Metro Center and Pennsylvania Avenue build out, the East End will be the downtown of coming decades. It remains for future architects, developers, planners, and residents to determine the neighborhood's future. ■

1. Georgetown University Law Center
600 New Jersey Avenue, N.W.
Edward Durell Stone *1971*

Edward Bennett Williams Law Library
111 G Street, N.W.
Hartman-Cox Architects *1989*

Bernard S. and Sarah Gewirz Student Center
120 F Street, N.W.
Hartman-Cox Architects *1993*

Located near the city's court buildings, this complex is the beginning of a campus. The buildings are laid out to relate to each other and to create casual meeting spaces for students. In this

neglected part of the city they create a critical mass, and though, as do all campuses, they tend to separate themselves and to form a studious enclave, their edge at the sidewalk improves the street and the public environment.

All three buildings share a classical attitude that lends a weight appropriate to a law school. They use classical architectural language to send messages of collegiality and seriousness—grand staircases, repeated columns, and podium settings.

The oldest building of the three is typical of Edward Durell Stone's work, simple box forms articulated with vertical elements. Here he has designed a buff brick box, its flat roof topped with an attic. Brick piers define strong vertical lines. Their profile is stepped, with the most prominent face highlighted by a subtle change in brick pattern at every other course. The building front is set on the pedestal created by a grand staircase. At the rear, a terrace begins to define campus space.

The law library is a solid building in the tradition of Washington Greco-Deco. The formal, sometimes elaborate language of classical architecture is pared down to solid forms and shallow, carved ornament. It is streamlined, but retains the strength of a masonry mass. The building is organized around a center drum that is oddly off axis with the space defined by the long side of the Law Center and the front facade of the student center.

The student center follows the language of pared down classicism. It is also buff brick on a masonry base. It rises 10 stories around a central curved bay that echoes the curved drum of the library. The facade's windows are highlighted with solid rectangular lintels, columns, and window grates. The detail has a solidity that speaks quality.

2. John L. Young Homeless Shelter
425 2nd Street, N.W.
Studio Project—City College
Achitectural Center *1987*

Architecture is not only high style.
Here, a surplus building and student
labor combined to create a shelter for
some of Washington's homeless. The
World War II temporary government
office building was used for a time by
the University of the District of
Columbia, but by the mid-1980s was
completely dilapidated. Beginning in
1984 the Community for Creative
Nonviolence occupied the building as
squatters for two years. In 1986, after a
dramatic hunger strike, closely covered
by local and national media, the group
forced the Reagan administration to
lease them the building.

Its renovation was funded by grant
money. A limited budget and complicated mix of uses dictated simplicity
outside and inside. The facade is decorated with a checkerboard pattern that
articulates a base, middle, and top and
highlights the entrance and windows.

The building's interior was laid out
using a "village" concept that creates
small, private sleeping quarters and
communal eating spaces. The shelter
also provides office space, medical and
counseling facilities, and large food
preparation areas.

The building is one spare but efficient answer to one of the cities most
persistent problems.

3. United States Tax Court
400 2nd Street, N.W.
Victor Lundy *1976*

If architecture sends messages, then the
dark cantilevered blocks of this building must certainly project the animosity
Americans feel about paying taxes. The
building is assembled from four
masonry blocks set on a pedestal. A
200-foot-long courtroom block that
seems to be supported only by glass
around and beneath it is cantilevered
over a broad staircase leading to a
recessed entrance. The building's structure, provided by steel tension cables,
is hidden.

The dramatic building achieves
authority while eschewing the classical

motifs used in other federal government buildings, but it is not city-friendly. The main entrance is closed for security, and, as just another empty urban space, the broad stairs lose their impact. The stairs overlook a tree-filled park, but the park and building are divided by a depressed access road that seems like a moat between the two. Instead of being a green foreground for the building, this dismal stretch of concrete over a freeway is unclaimed space.

There is a bit of unintentional urban irony in the court's location across the park from the homeless shelter. How many plaintiffs who enter the building think, "there but for the grace of a tax court judge, go I"?

4. National Law Enforcement Officers Memorial
400 E Street, N.W.
Davis Buckley *1993*

Intended by L'Enfant for the federal judiciary, this reservation instead became an area of local government, with a jail, the 1820 city hall, and later a school and hospital. The square was landscaped as a park after the Civil War, but the atmosphere was soon changed by an 1881 addition to city hall and a year later by the construction of the Pension Building. Four court buildings were constructed in the 20th century—Police Court, Municipal Court, Court of Appeals, and Juvenile Court—establishing the square's current character. A Metro station was added in the 1970s.

This memorial to law enforcement officers is appropriately sited amid the local halls of justice, and it reflects a return to the use of allegory to express shared community emotions. The entrances to the memorial are marked by bronze lion figures, male and female, guardians of the lion cub figures on nearby benches. The memorial itself consists of two curves of marble panels, creating low walls on which the names of fallen officers are inscribed. Space is provided to inscribes names for the next 100 years. Low benches complement the form of the name walls. Elevator shafts for the Metro station are incorporated into the design with a pergola and a gazebo, and the site is edged with planting beds and red oaks.

While some memorials are objects in the landscape, this memorial creates a landscape. It is at once part of the park and a separate, contemplative space. The memorial forms a dignified and balanced forefront to the Building Museum and, though some feel the incorporation of the Metro station is awkward, it was an unavoidable necessity.

5. National Building Museum
401 F Street, N.W.
General Montgomery Meigs *1887*
Keyes Condon Florance *1985*

After the Civil War, the federal bureaucracy began to grow into the behemoth

ZONING

IF YOU WANT to add a deck onto your house and have to hop through permitting hoops, blame zoning. If a high-rise office building is forcing out the little toy store you grew up with, blame zoning. If you do not have to wait for a promotion to have an office with a window, thank zoning. Zoning is the hidden force in shaping our cities. It produces the rules by which developers (and their bank balances) rise and fall.

A zoning ordinance's allowances for size and type of development are used by a municipality to protect its property values, generate a tax base, and create new environments. Zoning recognizes the thin line between the rights of a property owner and the needs of a community to protect its citizens.

As cities grew more complex they also grew more noxious. Factory noise and waste made living nearby dangerous and unpleasant. The need to protect safety and property values emerged. In 1916 New York City established a set of codified building regulations that separated the city into districts, keeping industry and tenements away from luxury homes and shopping. The ordinance also defined the shapes of buildings, requiring roof setbacks to allow sunlight into city streets.

The use of zoning as an application of municipal police power to protect public health, safety, and welfare was upheld in the 1926 Supreme Court case Euclid v. Ambler. A landowner who wanted to use residentially zoned land for commercial uses sued the town of Euclid, Ohio, claiming that zoning was unconstitutional and removed the land's value, for which he deserved compensation. The court ruled that zoning was constitutional and that a reasonable use— building houses—remained. Towns and cities all over America moved

forward with ordinances designed primarily to reinforce their existing development patterns.

Since then zoning has been an accepted part of land development and community building, but it has gotten more complex as our notion of public welfare has changed. No longer used just to isolate noxious uses, zoning influences the quality of the environment, allowing and even encouraging a mix of uses and building types. Zoning can regulate the bulk of a building, the height of a building, how far that building is set back from its neighbors and the street, and the proportion of a lot that can be covered. As Justice William Douglas wrote, "The concept of the public welfare is broad and inclusive....The values it represents are spiritual as well as physical, aesthetic as well as monetary." His judgment opened the door to zoning ordinances used to protect views, to encourage community redevelopment, and to require public art. Planned-unit development and cluster and floating zones all encourage flexibility of site design, use, and timing to create a desired mix of activities, supply infrastructure or amenities, or protect the natural environment.

Zoning is what sparks land development battles. When a property owner hears about master plans and map amendments, the lawyers are called in. What is just a line on a map to a planner is money in the pocket of a developer. A careful reading of the zoning ordinance regulations and their creative application may reveal a loophole that creates more leasable space for the downtown developer or more houses per acre for the suburban builder.

The average homeowner or business person assumes that everything will stay the way it looks today. But beneath the calm surface of a community rumbles the potential for redevelopment generated by revised zoning ordinances that may burst forth when the bureaucracy or market dictates.

we know today. An army engineer, Meigs designed this building to house the hundreds of clerks charged with dispensing pensions to those wounded and widowed by the Civil War. The building's design is loosely based on the Renaissance Palazzo Farnese, but its size is incredible—it employs 15.5 million bricks. The huge facade is modulated by repeated details. The gable and arch-topped windows set up a pleasing rhythm across the facade, which is tied together by a molded terra-cotta frieze beneath the cornice and a stringcourse between the second and third floors. The building's interior is a huge atrium divided into three sections by two rows of brick columns painted in faux marble.

After Congress authorized the Building Museum's location here, a two-phase renovation and update of structural systems returned the grand central hall to its former glory and made the changes required to accommodate a museum, including exhibition and research space, offices, a library, and conference rooms. The fantastic atrium has become a favorite for grand events—inaugural balls and a dinner for England's Prince Charles—but one can imagine disgruntled Civil War veterans gathering beneath its frosted glass roof to compare notes.

6. AARP Headquarters
601 E Street, N.W.
Kohn Pederson Fox *1991*

Architectural movements tend to drift into one another as the eye comes to accept what was once outlandish. Postmodernism returned us to classical detail leavened with witty reversals of meaning. But now, as architects have returned wholeheartedly to classical organization and ornament, meaning is less clear. The deep recesses and huge scale of this building's details may be ironic or may be architectural muscle-flexing. It is hard to tell.

The project's two buildings cover a city block and are classically organized, each section articulated by its materials and details. The base is composed of a rusticated first floor, second and third floors of long windows, and a fourth floor of round medallions alternating with square windows.

The building is sheathed in yellow Roman brick and highlighted by precast details: lintels, columns, and windowframes. The focus of the facade is a central pediment above an arch that links the site's two buildings. The pediment and arch are deeply recessed, as are the rectilinear pavilions on either side of the pediment and the rounded tower marking the 6th Street corner.

The building's large size and muscular details create a sense of power and solidity not usually seen in a speculative office building.

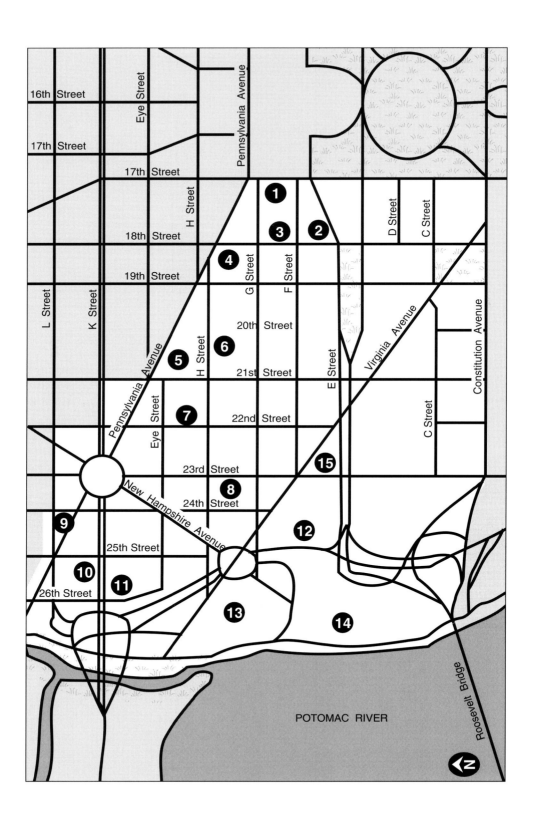

Foggy Bottom

A nation's capital should embody the finest in its contemporary architectural thought. Its architectural form should reflect the dignity, enterprise, vigor and stability of our national government.

JOHN F. KENNEDY, 1961

Foggy Bottom developed as an independent riverfront community, originally called Funkstown for its founder, German immigrant Jacob Funk. Its access to the river and a connecting canal to Georgetown encouraged industrial development: a brewery, a glassworks, and gas storage facility. Housing sprang up around these industries for laborers who did not have the money to move farther out. Thus, in the 1840s, this area was a motley combination of houses, industries, and farmyards.

Foggy Bottom was overlooked as downtown growth focused on Capitol Hill, Lafayette Square, Dupont Circle, and later around the Federal Triangle and the Mall. At the same time, streetcars opened up outer suburbs for those who could afford it. Foggy Bottom's town houses were left to those with limited choices, and the industries continued in the absence of economic pressure to redevelop.

The town houses of this intown neighborhood became attractive after the passage of the Alley Dwelling Act in 1934, a slum clearance effort that cleared the densest and most dilapidated housing. In 1947, the State Department relocated to Foggy Bottom and Washington Gas and Light dismantled its gas storage facility, which had loomed over the neighborhood for nearly 100 years. In the 1960s, new construction, including the Kennedy Center and the Watergate, encouraged town house renovations and new residential construction. The proximity to the State Department drew embassies and other offices, and Foggy Bottom became a small, sophisticated downtown enclave.

The institutional development that initially revitalized Foggy Bottom also threatens its small-scale residential character. Town houses convert easily to offices, and large institutions can afford to buy and raze entire blocks to meet their own development plans. George Washington University and its affiliated hospital have acquired blocks of neighborhood buildings for their needs. The World Bank and other quasi-public institutions, including the Federal Deposit Insurance Corporation, the Federal Home Loan Bank Board, and the Federal National Mortgage Association, have created a financial focus at the east end of Foggy Bottom near the White House and the Treasury.

Today Foggy Bottom is an eclectic architectural mix, including modest 19th-century town houses, visionary megaprojects of the modern era, and postmodern whimsies and facade preservation projects. ■

1. Federal Home Loan Bank Board
17th and G Streets, N.W.
Max O. Urbahn Associates *1977*

Almost unbelievably, this building was a conscious effort by the architect and client to create a lively, interesting corner of the city. It was completed in an era when architecture was lumbering away from sleek modernism but had not yet found postmodernism, and at a time when the most popular urban planning solution was to create a plaza, whether or not it was warranted. The result is a mundane redundancy.

The building is typical of 1970s explorations of refined brutalism that used poured-in-place concrete to express structure and function. Here a modulated concrete frame of incised joints, subtle variation in formative marks, and robust structural elements create one of the finest brutalist works in the city. But despite the attention to detail, the effect on the streetscape is forbidding. Entrances are obscure, and the building seems no different from many Washington office boxes.

The plaza, which connects through the block to adjacent streets, was initially enlivened with a skating rink and pool ringed by seating areas and a covered arcade. With the rink and pool removed, limited seating, and recessed shopfronts, the space is blank.

A few simple elements make a space appealing: a place to sit, a view to admire, even a convenient stop for a cup of coffee. Instead this project goes through complicated gyrations, only to fail.

2. American Institute of Architects
1735 New York Avenue, N.W.
The Architects Collaborative *1973*

The national headquarters for an association of architects must be an exemplary building, and in many ways this one is, despite the labored process of its design. For many years the American Institute of Architects (AIA) was headquartered in the historic Octagon House on the corner of the site. When that space became too small and its value as an architectural relic became evident, a design competition was held.

The first proposal of the winning firm, Mitchell/Giurgola, had to be redesigned after the AIA changed its program in a way that required enlarging the design. The Commission of Fine Arts objected to the redesign, believing it would overwhelm the Octagon. The Commission decided that the second submitted revision, which gave the Octagon more room on the site, was "too theatrical" and did not create a simple background for the historic building.

Mitchell/Giurgola resigned in 1968, and the project was continued by The Architects Collaborative (TAC). TAC adopted the basic form and solution set out by Mitchell/Giurgola and modified the facade to a simple curve, striped with glass and textured concrete.

Despite this inauspicious start, the building is successful. Its facade and siting work together to create a building that stands on its own yet at the same time defers to the Octagon. The building is set above the street by a graceful flight of stairs that offer enough of a view to draw pedestrians into the brick plaza. The plaza sets off the Octagon garden, and its paving pattern echoes the curves and stripes of the building facade. An ill-conceived plaza renovation replaced its concrete detailing with granite, which clashes with the buildings rather than drawing them together.

Although the glass ground floor was originally intended to be an active and open space featuring galleries, security and space demands have limited access to it. But the brick paving slides right under the glass walls, drawing eyes and feet to the dramatic stair rising through the lobby.

4. World Bank
1818 H Street, NW
Kohn Pederson Fox *1992*

It is almost as if postmodernism has opened up a time warp of history in which architects rehabilitate styles nearly as fast as examples can be dug out of the archives. Now modernism itself is being revisited. For the World Bank and its constituents, modern architecture still evokes progress and a hopeful future. Accordingly, the building—both renovation and new construction—invokes modern images with a contemporary twist.

Ornament on the white limestone and aluminum walls is derived from the visual character of structural elements, not their function. The

3. Federal Housing Finance Board (Michler Row)
1777 F Street, N.W.
Skidmore, Owings and Merrill *1981*

The original house on the corner was built for Brigadier General Nathaniel Michler of the Army Corps of Engineers in 1870. It later housed a dry cleaner, an Asian restaurant, and a liquor store.

The office addition behind the house makes no particular concessions to its historic forefront, except for a stepped massing that vaguely echoes the house's bays. The addition is a typical, ribbon-windowed Washington office building.

For the pedestrian, the Michler Row facade, the Dacor-Bacon House across the street, and the Octagon House down the steet all create a pleasant visual break from the institutional architecture of this part of Foggy Bottom.

building is topped with a mast and a cable-hung canopy, not structural necessities to roof the building, but structural elements used decoratively. Likewise, the vaulted glass roof over an interior courtyard is supported by five branching steel columns. The branches are not needed to support the roof, but are used to emphasize the tensile strength of steel.

At street level, and at its most visible corner at Pennsylvania Avenue and 17th Street, the building is somewhat blank, offering no sheltering or welcoming entrances, windows, or spaces. But overall, it has a refreshing crispness against the sky.

5. Red Lion Row
2000 Pennsylvania Avenue, N.W.
John Carl Warneke with Hellmuth, Obata and Kassabaum *1983*

Red Lion Row is an early lesson in facadism and a hard lesson in the deception of architectural renderings, which no doubt showed this building as a gentle pink cipher behind the lively historic facades.

In fact, the precast concrete and ribbon-windowed building looms over the town houses. The view from across the large traffic triangle created by I Street's intersection with the diagonal of Pennsylvania Avenue emphasizes the sheer size of the new building. The block-long, horizontal sweep of the facades offered the architects no convenient twists and turns to hide bulk.

Nevertheless, the building does more than many later projects of this type. The older buildings are preserved here in their entirety, including side and rear walls, which were dismantled and rebuilt after construction. The town houses have been reused as retail and office space. The building also creates an interior mall between the new and old buildings, made lively by shops and the rear facades of the town houses.

The project does connect with George Washington University, its landlord, through a nearly hidden courtyard path. Despite this link the building is a wall creating a campus enclave for the university and hiding campus activity from the street.

keystone in the arch over the walkway are also oversized. Although the facade lacks the flamboyance of some postmodern buildings, in typical postmodern style the historic details here are reordered and resized.

6. George Washington University
Jacob Burns Law Library
716 20th Street, N.W.
Mills, Petticord and Mills *1965*
Keyes Condon Florance *1984*

This building addition around an original expands the law library but also serves to define a quadrangle space on this urban campus. Two red brick wings on either side of a brown brick neocolonial original provide an edge for a central campus green space. The rear of the addition meets the quad with doors onto a stepped plaza containing bike racks, benches, and low walls that encourage informal gathering. An arched walkway on the building's south end connects the sidewalk and the quad.

The building's street facade picks up the gables and varied window patterns of neighboring town houses. But its postmodern architecture arranges oversized historical details on asymmetrical bays cut in and out of the facade. The large brownstone window lintels have a flat profile that projects scale rather than weight. The voussoirs and

7. George Washington University
Academic Center
801 22nd Street, N.W.
VVKR *1982*

It is a well-known urban fact that artists like the lofty and light-filled space of old factory buildings. Since Washington is a singularly nonindustrial city, loft space is hard to find. For this university building, though, the architects designed a structure with paned glass windows and hard edges reminiscent of a utilitarian factory building.

Stepped layers of dark glass and buff brick arranged around a corner plaza rise up to a more regular facade that wraps the outer edge of the site. A multipaned glass stairwell at the street edge is the most striking feature.

8. B'nai B'rith Hillel Foundation
Gewirz Center
2300 H Street, N.W.
Imas Gruner and Associates *1987*

This spirited building on a corner site continues the scale, materials, and details of its town house neighbors, but reorders the facade into a series of blocks and shapes.

The brick building is composed of stacked boxes highlighted with rounded windowframes, sills, and flat spandrel panels in precast concrete. Either side of the building's corner is pulled back, leaving a column-like section of building marked by a vertical window at the corner. Narrow arched entrances on either side are lit with three hanging globe lights that become decorative elements.

The building meets the street awkwardly. Its basement level is recessed, lifting the building off the sidewalk and, although the double flight of stairs cascades to the corner, the stairs are narrow and steep.

9. 2401 Pennsylvania Avenue, N.W.
Keyes Condon Florance *1991*

The light-hearted approach of this building is unusual in a serious city like Washington. Within its classical organization of base, shaft, and top, the facade is decorated with political imagery—donkeys, elephants, and flags—applied in an almost cartoonlike way.

Every bit of the eye-filling building is embellished. The brick facade rises out of a banded masonry base. Intricately mullioned windows and balcony balustrades add layers of pattern to the facade. Cables running from donkey and elephant heads support metal canopies at the first floor. The

building widens to follow its site along the diagonal of Pennsylvania Avenue, and the facade sweeps into a curved entrance, peeling away at the corner to reveal curved a glass and metal window, topped with a spiky pergola.

This is one of the city's few truly postmodern buildings. Its ornament is applied tongue in cheek. The architects have neither chosen neither allegorical figures of truth or beauty nor inscribed serious quotations on the building's facade. Instead, editorial-page images of donkeys and elephants ring the building.

10. Barclay House
2501 K Street, N.W.
Martin and Jones *1980*

In its height, setback, and massing this apartment building is compatible with its neighbors, fitting into the larger

11. The Griffin
955 26th Street, N.W.
David M. Schwarz *1984*

framework of the neighborhood. But within its own frame the building deconstructs before our eyes. At each floor and bay it peels off bits of its facade to reveal more frame and facade beneath.

The building begins with a modernist posture—a flat roof, rectilinear organization, and pilotis—but quickly shifts into a postmodernist stance as the building's structural logic is abandoned. Bays appear to hang from pilotis rather than be supported by them. Other bays dematerialize into a brick frame overlaid on the face. Even the entrance is topped by a wildly uneven archway.

The building is one of a number by the same architects that quietly tweaks our notions about architecture and construction.

In this apartment building, the architect uses details he has used in other Washington buildings to create a solid facade that reflects a comfortable domesticity. Gathered windows divided by white stringcourses beneath a gabled roof combine to create a nostalgic facade.

The use of historic details here is successful because they are not the superficial veneer of a cheap copy, but are integral to the massing and scale of the building. Despite its historicism, the building is not strictly postmodern. A postmodern building takes historic details and literally turns them upside down, to challenge our notion of structure and architectural propriety. On this building all the details appear where they should; gables are up and stringcourses bind the facade. The result is a gracious building in an ungracious setting of grade-separated streets and ramps.

12. Columbia Plaza
2400 Virginia Avenue, N.W.
Keyes, Lethbridge, and Condon *1967*

Hanging over the expressway, Columbia Plaza seems to be a brave new world of urban residential life, particularly in proximity to its older row house neighbors. In fact, this urban renewal project attempted to create its own environment by replacing old row houses with a self-contained complex of apartment buildings and duplexes arranged around a central shopping area.

This concept of a contained environment is similar to the urban vision of Le Corbusier and other modern masters, but the architecture is not strictly International Style. The buildings have variations in color, a facade hierarchy is established by giving the cornice line greater weight, and the grand sweep of apartments over the expressway is articulated like a honeycomb.

Despite its mixed uses and varied architecture, the complex is not an active place. Cities are made active by people who do not want to work, shop, and live in the same place, but who

travel through the city, experiencing its variety. It seems that the logical approach of the modernists is lost on human beings, whose behavior often defies logic.

13. The Watergate
2500–2700 Virginia Avenue, N.W.
Luigi Moretti *1965*

The Watergate project took its name from an expanse of steps just up river at the base of the Lincoln Memorial, where concerts used to be held until noise from airplanes approaching National Airport became too loud. In turn, the project has given its name to a generation of political scandals.

The project name and its design both changed the image of Washington. Sections of 26th, 27th, and G streets were closed to accommodate its large size. In its review of the project, the Commission of Fine Arts balked at the height and riverfront treatment, believing that the Lincoln Memorial and unbuilt Kennedy Center should retain their prominence.

Accordingly, the height of the Watergate was limited to 140 feet and riverfront villas proposed by the developer were removed.

Also in response to commission review, colored panels were removed from the design, the balconies were simplified, and the bright white color proposed by the designer was changed to a warmer tone. The five curvilinear buildings combine offices, apartments, and retail uses with views to the river, set above landscaped gardens. From the sidewalk, however, the project is overpowering. It blocks views and access to the river, instead offering vistas of concrete abutments and parking garage entrances.

Nonetheless, the Watergate has become a symbol of established Washington power, home to senators, Supreme Court judges, and French restaurants and clothing stores.

14. John F. Kennedy Center for the Performing Arts
New Hampshire and Virginia Avenues, N.W.
Edward Durell Stone *1971*

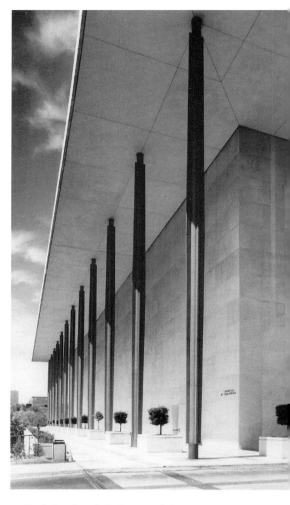

The Kennedy Center is a kind of culture mall, combining music, film, theater, and opera beneath a single roof. It was conceived in the era of urban renewal, to draw a moneyed clientele to a safe, isolated environment. Unfortunately, condensing an area's arts activity creates a neighborhood that offers no low-rent, start-up space and none of the spin-off effects generated by arts uses—cafes, studios, or shops. An opportunity for urban vitality is lost.

Much has been said about the building's appearance, and its proximity to Watergate and Washington Harbor has earned it a place as what the editors of *Architectural Record* called the "weird sisters of the Potomac." Literally a temple to the arts, the building reflects Stone's fascination with white marble, metal detailing, and a building with no back end. Although he originally proposed a curvilinear structure, which in turn influenced the design of the Watergate complex, Stone returned to a rectilinear form. This temple in a modern vocabulary rises above the river and expressway on a platform. Its marble wall panels alternate with grouped full-length window panels. A deep overhang is supported by golden cruciform columns.

Although, like Watergate, the building blocks views to the river, it becomes undeniably appealing once you are "on" it: on the promenade that cantilevers over the highway and seemingly over the Potomac facing the wilds of Roosevelt Island, or on the roof enjoying a picnic lunch or watching Fourth of July fireworks, or even onstage at the Christmas-time Messiah sing-along.

15. Pan-American Health Organization
525 23rd Street, N.W. (at Virginia Avenue)
Roman Fresnedo Siri *1965*

Latin American architecture has combined sculptural fluidity with the refined rationalism of the European modernists. Shapes and forms are arranged to challenge our sense of structural logic and pattern takes on an eye-filling richness.

Although observers have noted that the Uruguayan architect has here "suppressed his sculptural bent," the result is still striking in the rectilinear city of Washington. The facade of a slightly curved office block is articulated with vertical fins and serves as a backdrop for a cylindrical building housing a conference room. The round building is sheathed in a metal screen of a curvilinear pattern. Height restrictions as well as siting along a freeway ramp limited the building's impact, but the bold shapes and relationships among the forms create a dynamic symbiosis of space and form.

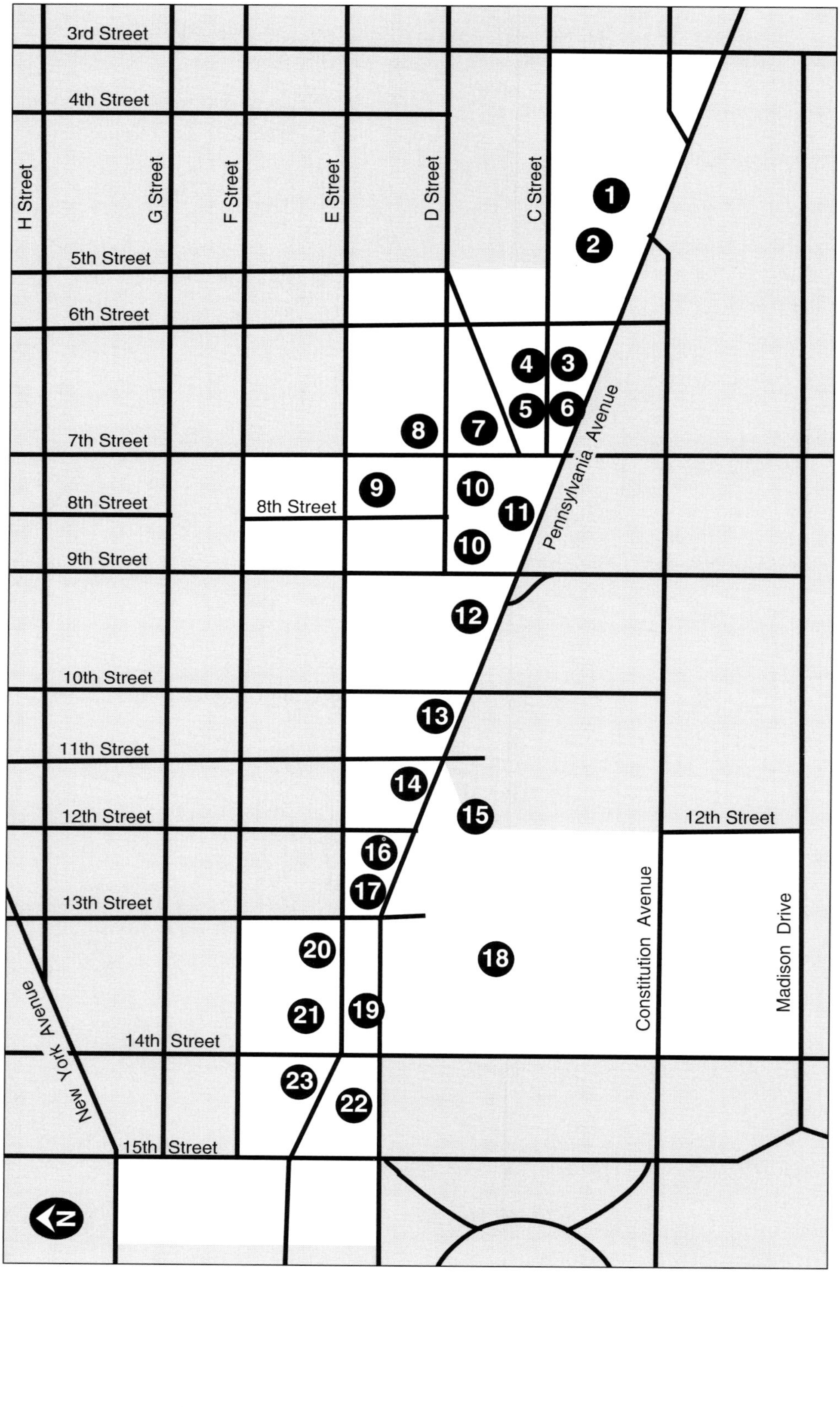

3rd Street
4th Street
5th Street
6th Street
7th Street
8th Street
8th Street
9th Street
10th Street
11th Street
12th Street
12th Street
13th Street
14th Street
15th Street
H Street
G Street
F Street
E Street
D Street
C Street
Pennsylvania Avenue
Constitution Avenue
Madison Drive
New York Avenue
N
1
2
3
4
5
6
7
8
9
10
11
10
12
13
14
15
16
17
18
19
20
21
22
23

Pennsylvania Avenue

Yet, with all its faults, Pennsylvania Avenue is a glorious street. It has length, breadth, perfect profile, and a fine terminal feature. . . .One weeps because it is not better, but one gives thanks for what it is.

ELBERT PEETS, 1928

Pennsylvania Avenue has been called America's Main Street; it is the street that links the branches of our government and serves as the presidential inaugural route. Its name immediately brings images of parades and pageantry to mind. It was intended by L'Enfant to be "grand and majestic" as well as "agreeable" and "convenient." It has taken almost two centuries, but today Pennsylvania Avenue is all those things.

L'Enfant laid out the avenue in 1791 as the centerpiece of the ceremonial and symbolic city, linking the Capitol with the President's House. He envisioned it lined with "rooms of assembly" and "academies" to attract both sociable and serious residents.

Creating a capital out of nothing is an expensive undertaking, and the new nation faced financial limits. Congress did not finally settle on Capitol Hill until 1800, and even then it was in session only part of the year. The members were hardly concerned with building a city in which they spent so little time. After fighting off the British for the second time and moving the nation's boundaries westward, they turned their attention again to Washington. Major civic buildings constructed after the White House and Capitol were the Treasury Building (1836–1865), the Patent Office (1836–1867), and the Pension Building (1883). The last two were built off of Pennsylvania Avenue, defining other points in the L'Enfant Plan.

Meanwhile, Pennsylvania Avenue became a busy commercial street. The turning basin of the Washington Canal at 8th Street became a natural gathering point for merchants, and over time the Center Market was established there, on the south side of Pennsylvania Avenue. In 1816, the dozen or so blocks between the White House and the Capitol were lined with sixteen dry goods stores, seven groceries, two stationers, three tailors, two hardware stores, two china and glass shops, one leather store, three jewelers, two drug stores, three milliners, three cabinetmakers, three confectioners, two hat and shoe shops, one chair factory, two hotels, and a reading room.

By the mid-1800s, the north side of the avenue had a reputation as a genteel shopping street, while the south side was seedy, descending into dangerous. In the

1890s the federal government began investing in the south side with construction of the Post Office Buidling at the corner of 12th Street.

In 1901, the McMillan Plan envisioned the Federal Triangle as a district of civic buildings along Pennsylvania Avenue's south side. This massive complex of neoclassical buildings between 6th and 15th streets would consolidate an expanding federal government and evict the seedier uses on that side of the street. The plan's powerful vision of white buildings and symmetrical courtyards inspired an image of the federal city as a place separate and distinct from the local city. On the street, the triangle creates a colossal wall of classical orders. Columns begin well above street level and support massive cornices and attics. Initially it all looks the same, but close examination reveals a subtle transition from highly detailed classicism at the west end to a stripped down Greco-Deco at the east end.

In 1926, President Coolidge signed a land acquisition bill for the Federal Triangle, and construction began soon after. The members of the McMillan Commission were City Beautiful advocates, and the triangle's design was based on the plazas and closed courts of the Louvre. Elbert Peets wrote that "while its red-tile roofs were still being laid, the Triangle became a landmark, a thing of the past." Its solid classicism made the buildings timeless, even if they lacked the romance of their Parisian model.

But while commissions and architects lavished attention on grand plans, the north side of Pennsylvania Avenue slowly began to lose its best commercial tenants to a growing shopping area just north along F Street. After World War II, downtown shopping was seriously challenged by suburban shopping malls, and local legend has it that when Kennedy rode down the avenue for his inauguration in 1961 he commented on the street's sorry state.

That comment started a series of political actions that focused attention on Pennsylvania Avenue and led to its ongoing renewal. In 1967, the avenue was declared a National Historic Site and commissions and task forces began to define a plan for its renovation. In 1972, the Pennsylvania Avenue Development Corporation (PADC) was formed with the power to acquire land, request congressional appropriations, and borrow from the Treasury. In 1974, the PADC issued a plan that recommended housing on the east end of the avenue, a retail focus on F Street between 8th and 9th Streets, office development at the western end of the avenue, a revitalized Willard Hotel, and high-quality public spaces, including sidewalks, parks, and plazas.

The PADC began its work at a time when architects were rediscovering classicism—an apt architectural symbol for all that Pennsylvania Avenue aspired to. At the same time, in the early seventies, bolstered by the nation's bicentennial, historic preservation began to take hold of the popular imagination. The Willard, which had closed after the 1968 riots, and the Old Post Office, which had been judged obsolete just after it opened, became, through renovation, two of the avenue's earliest success stories. Although in early PADC plans there was talk of raised sidewalks and housing based on Italian hill towns, these planning clichés were laid aside for effective and simple solutions.

Today Pennsylvania Avenue is a planning success story. Careful attention to market realities, a few well-timed leaps of faith, and a long view have created a street that is recovering a pedestrian liveliness with shops and restaurants, is a grand ceremonial space that links the local and federal cities, and may even become a downtown residential neighborhood. America's Main Street is a place of variety, levity, and solidity that reflects L'Enfant's initial goals. It is both agreeable and majestic. ∎

1. John Marshall Park
Pennsylvania Avenue, N.W. (between 3rd and 6th Streets)
Carol R. Johnson *1983*

One of the PADC's revitalization strategies was to install improvements in the public domain to encourage private investment. It worked on the avenue's western end, and John Marshall Park was the first PADC public improvement on the avenue's eastern end. The formal, tiered park is divided into three areas that mediate between the monumental setting and the park, creating a human-scaled space of color and comfort. L'Enfant's plan shows these few blocks as a smaller park perpendicular to the avenue. In later years it became a formal front lawn for the old City Hall. In the 1960s, it was envisioned as a driveway for the U.S. Circuit Court and Canadian Chancery on either side. Now, the gentle rise in elevation from south to north brings the park up into view from Pennsylvania Avenue, effectively displaying the fine planting and paving materials.

2. Canadian Chancery
501 Pennsylvania Avenue, N.W.
Arthur Erickson Associates *1989*

As is appropriate for embassies, this one is marked with symbolism. The site is a special one, between the White House and the Capitol, a metaphor for the friendly relations between the United States and Canada.

Furthermore, the public is allowed within the perimeter of the building. A raised plaza over which the building extends allows visitors to enter what is technically foreign soil. The building is clearly modern: a sculptural mass in which interior functions are expressed on the exterior rather than screened behind a facade of classical details. The architect did work within the monumental context of Pennsylvania Avenue. The building's marble is powdery gray, the preferred material and color for monumentality.

The building defines its edge of Pennsylvania Avenue by maintaining the same cornice height as its neighbors. Rather carrying a decorative cap that finishes off a screen of columns, here the building itself is the cornice, soaring over the plaza below. The very corner of the property and the intersection of Pennsylvania Avenue and John Marshall Park is defined with an anchoring corner column. The corner is further emphasized by a tempietto that provides sweeping views of the avenue. Under its dome, voices echo and bounce, sounding almost electronically amplified.

third element: bright white with its own proportions and rhythm. Here the architects introduced more detail, recessed window surrounds and railings set back on the top floors. This added detail exaggerates the minimalism of the bare addition.

Critics of the building admit that it follows all the rules of contextualism, matching cornice lines, picking up the facade's hierarchy, and stepping back upper floors. *Historic Preservation* commented, "The recipe had been followed, and still the chef had produced frozen turkey."

3. 601 Pennsylvania Avenue, N.W.
Eisenman/Robertson *1983*

Facadism in Washington varies in its degree of assimilation and differentiation. At 601 Pennsylvania Avenue it is clear what is old and what is new, but the relationship between additions and original is subtly marked. On either side of the original building, the addition extends cornice lines and window placement through crisp joints in the precast concrete. These facades are a warm gray monotone of concrete and featureless black rectangular windows. The only relief is the joints between precast panels. This reductive composition avoids mimicry but highlights important geometries in the original. Above this careful composition is a

4. Pennsylvania Plaza, The Pennsylvania
601 Pennsylvania Avenue, N.W.
Hartman-Cox Architects *1993*

One of the PADC's goals is to enliven Pennsylvania Avenue with a variety of uses, creating a place where residents, workers, visitors, and shoppers mingle. The price of downtown land and the incompatibility of residential and office floors in a single building sometimes works against this goal, but Pennsylvania Plaza overcomes this by creating two separate buildings.

The residential building to the north

faces Indiana Avenue and is marked by a clock tower sheathed in brick and varied with projecting bay windows, concrete details, and balconies. This treatment creates a domestic appearance. The office building, oriented to Pennsylvania Avenue, is covered entirely in precast concrete compatible with the white walls along Pennsylvania Avenue. A park between the two buildings extends the line of C Street to Indiana Plaza in front of the Argentine Naval Building and Sears House. The park is small but lushly planted and balances intimacy and openness.

5. Argentine Naval Building (Riggs National Bank)
301 7th Street, N.W.
James G. Hill *1889*
P. T. Astore/Vlastimil Koubek *1982*

6. Sears House
633 Pennsylvania Ave N.W.
Alfrerd B. Mullett *1887*
Hartman-Cox Architects *1984*

These renovated historic buildings make an interesting composition of buildings that vary in scale, material, and attitude from their newer neighbors. The buildings bring an older 19th-century Washington down from F and G Streets onto Pennsylvania Avenue, which is otherwise dominated by neoclassical and newer buildings. They are reminders of the avenue's commercial heyday. Sears House was once the studio of Civil War photographer, Matthew Brady. In a later incarnation it was the Apex Liquor store, with the ironically sited Temperance Fountain outside its front door.

The buildings are complementary in their solid massing, rough-hewn ashlar walls, and deep stone-edged window reveals. Their towers and turrets add rooftop drama. A connecting stair tower has been added to Sears House. Together they create a pleasant urban space further enlivened by a trompe-l'oeil mural expanding the Argentine Naval Building's exuberant facade.

7. Liberty Place
325 7th Street, N.W.
Glenn Brown 1882
Keyes Condon Florance *1991*

For most of its ceremonial length
Pennsylvania Avenue is the city's most
monumental street, but near 7th Street
it seems as if a local, mercantile
Washington is intruding. This is where
the Downtown Historic District meets
Pennsylvania Avenue.

This addition to the historic
Fireman's Insurance Building accom-
modates the developer's desire to create a prestigious Pennsylvania Avenue
address by stepping the building up to
the southwest corner and placing the
entrance there. The graduated steps
also echo the original building's
tower—crowned with a gilded dome—
which was rebuilt for this project. The
prismatic folding of the facade, the
light detail, and the spandrel panels
between windows give the addition a
1930s feel that is different from the
neoclassicism chosen by many architects for downtown projects.

8. Gallery Row
401–413 7th Street, N.W.
Hartman-Cox Architects/Oehrlein and
Associates *1987*

This addition is tucked in a recycled
streetfront of commercial buildings and
combines them into a single building
through a connecting stairway. In order
to create leasable space for the contemporary real estate market, the developer needed to create larger floor areas
and so combined the buildings. The
addition is clearly modern in its expression of the stairway but, sheathed in
slender columns and incised panels
reminiscent of the late 19th century, it
makes an easy link between the two
ornate Italianate buildings constructed
circa 1877. City zoning has established
an arts district along 7th Street, and
zoning provisions encourage arts uses
and street and sidewalk improvements.
The goal is to encourage a local arts
community anchored by the National
Gallery of Art and the National
Museum of American Art/ National
Portrait Gallery.

9. The Lansburgh
420 E Street, N.W.
Graham Gund Architects *1992*

This large, nearly one-block project avoids a monolithic streetfront by convincingly breaking up the facade with fanciful gables, receding niches, and projecting bays. At the same time, it is a single unified project with an identity that can be sold to lenders and real estate agents.

The work of a Boston architect noted for oversized, playful detailing, the building takes a stance appropriate to this part of town. Its exuberant details complement its neighboring Victorian and Italianate commercial buildings. Any closer to Pennsylvania Avenue and this levity might have been interesting, but not acceptable.
The white terra-cotta former Lansburgh Department Store was built, rebuilt, and expanded in seven phases between 1860 and 1950. The new, brick-fronted Lansburgh meets it as a separate building, although the arched gables of the new building recall the curved lintels of the old. The architect did not try to weave a new building seamlessly into the old, instead allowing both to stand, separate but sympathetic. Rather than

appearing as a megablock, the project appears as a composition of individual buildings, the way cities used to be built.

The uses include a commercial first floor, apartments, an outpost of the Folger Shakespeare Theater, and offices—a mix designed to generate activity in the slowly growing 7th Street Arts District.

10. Market Square
701–801 Pennsylvania Avenue, N.W.
Hartman-Cox Architects *1990*

Market Square defines the meeting point of two important axes defined by L'Enfant's plan: 8th Street and Pennsylvania Avenue. Eighth Street links the Carnegie Library, the Patent Office, and the National Archives to the Mall and, across it, to the Hirshhorn Museum. It is a site that warrants monumentality.

This building departs from the McMillan Plan, which kept classicism to the south and used Pennsylvania Avenue as a boundary to divide the local and national cities. The PADC treats the avenue as a corridor, a space to be shaped, and these buildings, form a hemicycle faced with columns, creating a scale and profile usually associated with public projects.

The architects really ran with classicism; these are some of Washington's most impressive columns. Their five-story height atop a three-story base topped by a several-story attic nearly dwarfs the scale of the Federal Triangle across the street. The two buildings are a dramatic backdrop for the Navy Memorial.

The project mixes a variety of uses—commercial, office, retail, monumental, and residential—in an effort to return life to the downtown by creating places for activities that draw different people at different times of the day.

street; a departure from the awe-inspiring white marble and from the lone marker placed in a contemplative landscape. Sometimes, however, the sailor looks a bit lost amidst cafe-goers and tourists.

The monument is arrayed around the lone figure standing on a world map in the paving around him. Two low hemicycles echoing the Market Square buildings are faced with bas-relief scenes of naval battles and service. Of course, a navy memorial must include water, and these fountains were dedicated with waters from world's seven seas.

11. Market Square Park—Navy Memorial
701–801 Pennsylvania Avenue, N.W.
Conklin Rossant Architects *1990*

The combination of this memorial with the Market Square buildings behind it is a happy meeting. A building of such monumentality requires a monument, and a monument of such simplicity requires a backdrop.

The monument's architects wanted to create a "living memorial" that contributed to the environment of the

12. J. Edgar Hoover FBI Building
10th Street at Pennsylvania Avenue, N.W.
C. F. Murphy *1975*

The book *Pennsylvania Avenue: America's Main Street* states that the FBI Building was intended to represent the "finest in American contemporary architectural thought." Perhaps it best reflects the paranoia and power of the man it is named for. Security concerns

led to surrounding the building with a skirting of concrete walls that create a moat on three sides, and to this day the Pennsylvania Avenue facade is a blank wall. Shops were intended there, then lighted vitrines were considered, vetoed, and replaced with static, poorly designed display panels about presidential history. The building's looming mass is designed simply to compete with the Justice Department across the street.

It is a product of its time, when the subtlety of modern architecture began to descend into repetitive banality. But the building is poor even by these standards, ponderous and cold in its materials, massing, and detailing. If not for bureaucratic inertia, the whole north side of the avenue might have been variations of this.

13. 1001 Pennsylvania Avenue
11th Street and Pennsylvania Avenue, N.W.
Hartman–Cox Architects *1986*

This chameleon–like building, completely driven by context, is different on every side. The limestone base, shaft, and capital of the Pennsylvania Avenue facade are classically correct and make no big gestures to draw unseemly attention. The 10th Street facade embeds and steps back from older buildings, introducing brick among the limestone. On E Street the facade is mostly brick and stepped in layers that run across the depth and face of the building. As it steps back, each layer of facade becomes simpler.

This approach achieves a comfortable contextualism and brings the building, which covers an entire block, down to a human scale at the street. The architects have created visual interest by carefully detailing the materials and applying them following a classical hierarchy appropriate to each facade.

While this contextualism may sometimes have stultifying results, one cannot help comparing this building favorably to its brutal neighbor, the FBI Building, across 10th Street.

14. *Evening Star* Building
1101 Pennsylvania Avenue, N.W.
Marsh and Peter *1908*
Skidmore, Owings and Merrill *1990*

The original *Evening Star* Building, named for the defunct Washington newspaper, is an exuberant Beaux-Arts confection. White marble, sumptuous details alternating with crisp simplicity, and a slender profile on the acute corner formed by Pennsylvania Avenue and 11th Street make this building one

of Washington's commercial landmarks. Its original profile, long on 11th Street and very narrow on Pennsylvania Avenue, made the *Evening Star* seem slender and lofty by Washington standards.

In the late 1980s the *Evening Star* was renovated and expanded. The addition was built directly to the west on Pennsylvania Avenue. By this time, Washington had seen so many variations on facadism that there were a number of precedents to choose from. The designers here chose to put an equivalently sized, proportioned, and detailed structure next to the existing one. The addition, like the original, is classically organized with a base, shaft, and capital. It continues the banding and cornice lines of the original, and it treats details like window surrounds and corners in a similar way. The addition is not an exact duplicate, yet it is close enough so that it is neither a background building to the original, nor a large modern building with an antique front, but an extrapolation of the original.

Unfortunately, the addition is designed along literal classical lines without the strength or sureness of the original. The proportions and locations of window openings are awkward, and the overly large entrance feature surrounds an opening that is much too small. Most significantly, the addition changes the prospect of the original. The horizontal bands have strapped the two buildings together, so that the original's slender profile no longer exists. The sharply curved, acute corner of the older building, which played off the knife edge on the west side, is softened and camouflaged by the curve on the oblique west corner of the new building. The *Evening Star* used to point to the corner; now it flatly faces Pennsylvania Avenue.

15. Old Post Office
Pennsylvania Avenue and 12th Street, N.W.
W. J. Edbrooke *1899*
Arthur Cotton Moore/Benjamin Thompson Associates, et al. *1983*

This Romanesque Revival pile was repeatedly threatened with demolition as various generations of planners and visionaries took a shot at monumental Pennsylvania Avenue. The building's style and placement just made it stick out. Even at its completion in 1899 it looked dated to a taste returning to classical architecture. The 1901 McMillan Plan could hardly recommend destruction of a building only three years after its completion, and when the Federal Triangle got underway, the building was saved by the lack of funds brought on by the Depression. In the 1960s, PADC plans showed a complete Pennsylvania Avenue with only the clock tower of the post office preserved. As historic preservation took hold, the building was seen as valuable, but this new appreciation raised the question of what to do with it. New technology and the changing role of downtown made the building and its location obsolete for post office uses. After renovation, with offices on the upper floors and a shopping and restaurant court below, the building now serves the two groups Washington has plenty of—bureaucrats and tourists. Like Union

Station, it draws tourists in search of a cool drink, postcards, and a place to sit out of the sun.

Inside, a visitor who can tear his eyes away from the neon signs and banners will look up and see what a huge space this is and imagine postal workers scurrying along criss-crossed catwalks. On the exterior, the heavy entrance arches are repeated up the facade, growing smaller at each level. The building is topped off with round towers clustered around a central

clock tower. Anything that is not classical in Washington stands out, and this building has taken on its own landmark status.

16. 1201 Pennsylvania Avenue, N.W.
Skidmore, Owings and Merrill (David Childs) *1984*

The PADC started its renovation efforts at the western end of Pennsylvania Avenue. This was the first modern

COMMISSION OF FINE ARTS

IN 1910, WHEN THE Commission of Fine Arts was established by an act of Congress, both the L'Enfant and McMillan Plans had been filed away in the basement of the Library of Congress, nearly forgotten. The Capitol and the White House anchored their ends of L'Enfant's grand axis, but between them lay the Central Market, surrounded by sheds and barrows, and the Baltimore and Potomac Railroad station on the Mall at the base of the Capitol. The Washington Monument was complete, but the Lincoln and Jefferson Memorials were years away from completion. The commercial city envisioned by L'Enfant was thriving, but the monumental city was still a hazy dream.

Inspired by the 1893 World's Columbian Exposition in Chicago and the City Beautiful movement that grew out of it, a group of artists and architects lobbied President Roosevelt to create a Bureau of Fine Arts to advise on all elements of design in the capital. The first members of the commission included Daniel Burnham, Daniel Chester French, and Frederick Law Olmsted, Jr., who took as their assignment the resurrection of the L'Enfant and McMillan Plans. They began their

work at a time when designers, under the influence of the Ecole des Beaux-Arts, were returning to classicism and when America's political and economic powers were expanding throughout the world.

The City Beautiful as expressed in Burnham's plans for Chicago and Manila was one of civic centers and opera houses linked by broad avenues. Like any aesthetic movement it was a reaction to what had come before, in this case, to the dark intricacies of Victorian brick architecture and the economic imperatives of industrialization that put train stations in parks.

The vision of the City Beautiful fit perfectly with L'Enfant's diagonal boulevards linking national civic buildings. With the political will and the purse to back it up, the Washington we know began to be built. Initially, the duties of the Commission of Fine Arts were limited to review of public monuments. The commission's review was expanded under presidents Wilson and Harding to include public buildings, private buildings adjacent to public areas, and coins, insignia, and medals.

The Commission used as its

office building to be built this far east along the avenue. When a prominent Washington law firm rented out most of its floors, success moved down the avenue.

The building's angled facade mediates between the older buildings, which are closer to the street, and the newer buildings built behind deeper PADC-required setbacks. The deeper setbacks pulled buildings away from the street to emphasize the broad avenue and to accommodate the

blueprint the L'Enfant and McMillan Plans. Two of its first projects, the Lincoln Memorial and the Reflecting Pool, were both recommended by the 1901 McMillan Plan, but alternative sites had been proposed, including Meridian Hill, the site of the Soldiers' Home, and even a memorial highway to Gettysburg. The commission recommended the Potomac Park site, which, while extending the axis created by the Capitol, the Mall, and the Washington Monument, also consolidated a monumental core.

The columned, marble pavilion in which Lincoln sits is a perfect expression of the Beaux-Arts aesthetic; its classical details and large scale so adaptable to monumentality. The Lincoln Memorial was not the first white building in Washington but it contributed to a critical mass that made white seem the only appropriate color for the federal city and contributed to its timeless feeling. As history is set before the viewer it is also denied. Washington's monumental buildings offer few clues to their age.

In seeking to create grandeur, the commission has pulled applicants back from the brink of grandiosity. In the 1960s, when plans for the western end of Pennsylvania Avenue called for

the Willard and the Hotel Washington and the street in front of them to be replaced by a paved National Square, the commission encouraged and eventually approved a smaller, more landscaped plaza framed by the two hotels.

Most recently the commission has addressed the proliferation of monuments. Meanwhile, the number of sites within the L'Enfant plan has dwindled. In the 1980s, Congress, with the support of the commission, passed legislation limiting Mall sites to memorials of "preeminent historical and lasting significance to the Nation." Military memorials are now limited to a specific war or to service branches of the Armed Forces.

While critics may comment that its watchdog role stifles creativity and initiative, the commission has succeeded in enriching the allegory of nationhood that defines Washington as a city and which further defines our American character. From Lincoln's weary gaze to the black gash of the Vietnam Veterans Memorial, America's history and values are laid before us so that we may learn, gather, and speak out as history is created.

crowds that turn out for processionals and parades.

The example of simple, clean modern architecture marks Pennsylvania Avenue's renaissance as a prestige office location.

18. International Cultural and Trade Center
Pennsylvania Avenue between 13th and 14th Streets, N.W.
Pei Cobb Freed and Partners *1996* (projected)

This massive building is the completion of a federal office enclave begun in the late 1920s as an element of the McMillan Plan. Since that time this particular site has been used as an 11-acre parking lot.

The building was originally planned as an international trade center, but the Bush administration proposed using it for government office space. The Clinton administration has returned to the notion of a trade center. The building will house federal agencies involved in trade, trade offices of foreign governments, and conference facilities, exhibition space, a performing arts theater, retail space, and restaurants.

The building is, of course, in the neoclassical style of the surrounding Federal Triangle buildings. In this era of contextualism and postmodernism, it could hardly be anything else. But it will not be exactly like its neighbors, for even they are not alike. Although they share scale and setback, their detail varies from the rich intricacy of the Commerce Building to the boldly sculpted Art Deco of the Justice

17. 1275 Pennsylvania Avenue, N.W.
Original architect and date unknown
Smith, Segretti, Tepper, McMahon, Harned *1987*

This twist on facadism stripped the building of its 1950s ribbon-windowed facade and refaced it with a classically styled one. Architecture is clearly a fashion. To appeal to buyers or renters, a building must look up-to-date, even if that means looking old-fashioned.

This renovation is a kind of redecoration. The old building's green glass ribbon windows added little to its unique site—an intersection of diagonal Pennsylvania Avenue with the orthogonal street grid. The curtain wall, hung on the building's steel frame, was changed like a slipcover to keep up with the latest fashion.

Building. Despite the building's huge size—three million square feet—it must function as a background building, part of the larger composition of the Federal Triangle that allows the Old Post Office, City Hall, and National Archives to stand out as exclamation points along the avenue.

The building's most pronounced aspect, a strong diagonal axis from Pennsylvania Avenue into the site, is a departure from the formal rectilinearity of other Federal Triangle buildings, but this building is not intended to be an imposing wall along the avenue. Its inviting design and variety of uses are part of the PADC strategy to introduce new uses that will revitalize America's Main Street.

19. Freedom Plaza
Pennsylvania Avenue and 14th Street, N.W.
Venturi, Rauch and Scott Brown *1981*

This once meager traffic triangle formed by the diagonal of Pennsylvania Avenue meeting E Street has been transformed into a long, rectangular plaza abutting the north side of the avenue. It was once intended, in the late 1960s, to be part of a vast, austere plaza—National Square.

A little over a decade later it was designed in a way that broke away from the abstract minimalism of modern monumentalism, but also avoided the robed allegorical women of traditional designs. The designer took a literary approach, literally. The plaza's main feature is a superscaled reproduction of the L'Enfant Plan for Washington, and its surface is inscribed with the words of the city's famous observers.

Two controversial features—models of the White House and the Capitol, and two tall pylons straddling original visual axis of Pennsylvania Avenue—were deleted by the Commission of Fine Arts. The pylons would have provided a focused view to this end of the avenue and, with the models, relieved the overwhelming flatness of the plaza.

For all its national pretensions and symbols, this plaza serves as a local space. It is directly across from the District Building, Washington's city hall, and is a place for local music performances, cultural festivals, and honoring the Redskins after a Super Bowl victory.

20. National League of Cities Building
1301 Pennsylvania Avenue, N.W.

The Shops at National Place
14th and F Streets, N.W.
Frank Schlesinger *1982*

Although it has been called a dignified backdrop, the National League of Cities building has about as much character as an unpainted theatrical flat. The beige concrete facade is broken only by a grid of rectangular windows. The 13th Street facade sets up a more interesting pattern as the facade steps up the hill. The demand for dignity at this important location coupled with

The gray glazed brick of this facade is marked by a bright blue vertical line of glazed brick. The color is very un-Washington, and the utilitarian facade does not read as that of a luxury hotel. The plain exterior belies the lobby's sparkling glass and deep pile carpets. The hotel building is set back to defer to the National Theater but juts out at the corner of 14th Street, blocking a view of the Willard's corner tower from Pennsylvania Avenue. One of the trickiest aspects of architectural design is deciding which buildings should have precedence on the street.

the minimalism of modern architecture results in visual boredom.

The Shops at National Place is an interior shopping mall, a winding space that eventually links the Marriott Hotel lobby with F Street and the renovated National Press Building. The shops are arranged mostly along F Street, visible but not accessible from the sidewalk. The link between Pennsylvania Avenue and F Street echoes the Willard's Peacock Alley and outdoor gallery. While the Willard presents a grand facade to the street, The Shops at National Place duplicate an existing streetside path and draw activity off the street. Unlike the Willard and European arcades that create charming and useful paths through the city, this space does not contribute to the area around it.

21. National Place, National Theater, J. W. Marriott Hotel
Pennsylvania Avenue and 14th Street, N.W.
Mitchell/Giurgola *1984*

22. Pershing Park
Pennsylvania Avenue and 14th Street, N.W.
M. Paul Friedberg and Partners/Jerome Lindsey *1981*

Twenty-five years ago the area of Pershing Park might have been swallowed up by the vast hardscape of the proposed National Square envisioned as the grand terminus for Pennsylvania Avenue. Fortunately, things do not always happen easily or swiftly in Washington.

Stone walls commemorating General Pershing and his military campaigns, heavily landscaped berms, and cascading greenery isolate the pool and patio of this park from the surrounding traffic on 15th and 14th streets and

Pennsylvania Avenue. The park's north-ern edge opens easily to the renovated and new facades of the Willard. The success of the park is that it provides an intimate oasis in the midst of monu-mentalism. This contemplative space is in the middle of a grand processional avenue, but it in no way stops the pro-cession or deflates the scale of its sur-roundings.

The problem with this western end of the avenue—that it dribbles away, without the strong terminus and focal point of the Capitol at the eastern end—has existed since construction of the Treasury Building obscured the White House in the 1830s. Pershing Park lightly punctuates Pennsylvania Avenue while making a transition from the avenue to the White House.

22. Willard Inter-Continental Hotel and Willard Office Building
Pennsylvania Avenue and 14th Street, N.W.
Henry Hardenbergh *1901*
Hardy Holzman Pfeiffer/Vlastimil Koubek *1986*

A hotel has stood on this site virtually since the founding of the city, but the 1968 riots changed the profile of

downtown, and the Willard closed in the same year.

In developing plans for Pennsylvania Avenue, PADC consid-ered options included razing the Willard and the neighboring Hotel Washington to create a massive National Square. There was enough opposition to this proposal to convince the PADC to save and restore the hotels, even though it would be an expensive venture.

The addition to the Willard mimics the original building's elaborate roofline with curved, cascading mansards shot with bull's-eye dormers. The two buildings create a stepped plaza enlivened by shops and restau-rants. The walkway between the two buildings mimics the famous Peacock Alley inside the original Willard, and both are worth a stroll.

Some feel the proportions and detailing of the addition are simple mimicry, but its placement and setback from the original create a good urban space. The new Willard is like a grand lady spreading her skirts: the focus remains on her imposing front, while the authority comes from her purpose-ful expansion.

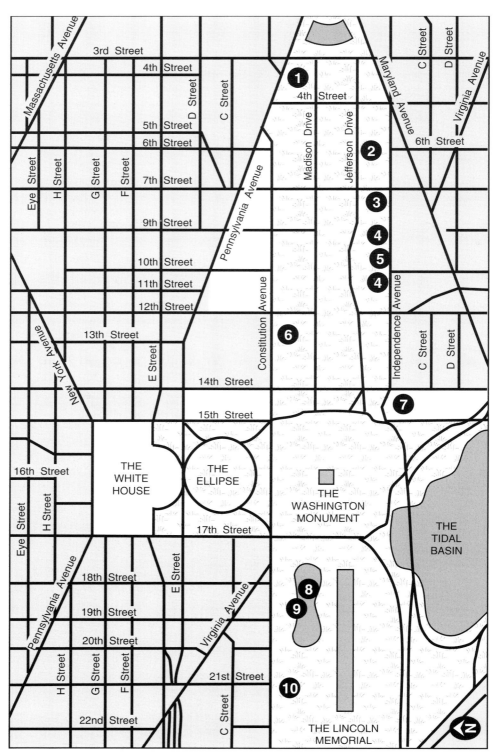

Strictly speaking the Mall is the area lined by museums between the Capitol and the Washington Monument. But most residents and visitors to Washington think of the green spaces that continue to the Lincoln and Jefferson Memorials as a monumental core.

The Mall

That men who have participated as leaders in the rise of American industry, who have shared its magnificent upward progress, its ceaseless and inexhaustible ferment, should turn for expression to the pale temples of an imaginary Greece, is, I think, one of the strangest phenomena in the psychology of idealism.

JOSEPH HUDNUT, 1949

The Mall is Washington's seminal space. It is the monumental city's culmination, it is the postcard views and tourist memories. The Mall is a record of our history and the marker of our national image.

Our visceral experience of the Mall is one of aching feet, tired children, and information overload. The point of the Mall is not human scale, but the vastness of the United States and the extent of American achievement. Human scale is found in the infinitesimal detail of American history and life held in the Smithsonian collections: Judy Garland's ruby slippers, the cramped seating of a Gemini capsule, the Hope Diamond's necklace setting.

The Mall, as a physical, urban place, is full of contradictions. It is a formal, ceremonial space filled with joggers, Frisbee players, a carousel, and a skating rink. The Mall provides the distance from which to view the buildings that line it, many of which are obscured by meticulously nurtured elm trees. It is a central place in Washington, around which streets and neighborhoods are organized, but in its activities, size, and buildings, is clearly distinct from the rest of the city. More than any other place in any other city, the Mall is a place of unified design and purpose, but it has been held and overseen by a variety of government, quasi-governmental, and private interests. The Mall has some of Washington's most carefully designed modern buildings, yet it seems timeless.

Just as the purpose and character of the Mall vary, so has its appearance through history. It was first laid out in 1791 by L'Enfant who envisioned a grand promenade lined with embassies. A boulevard in plan, in reality it was an undulating ground of fields and swamps used for grazing until British scientist James Smithson's bequest of more than $.5 million in 1840 refocused the Mall on cultural and scientific uses. Robert Mills, the architect of the Washington Monument, created a plan for the Mall as a zoological, botanical, and horticultural center that would be lined with the houses of Smithsonian officers. The Mall only stretched as far west as the Washington Monument, where it ended at the banks of the Potomac, which reached into the city as the Tiber Canal along the Mall's north side.

In 1848, Andrew Jackson Downing was consulted by the Washington National Monument Society and the Building Committee of the Smithsonian on a design for the Mall grounds. Downing's work was a departure from the symmetrical formality of classicism. His landscapes instead contrasted the orderliness of man-made construction and the beauty in nature's irregularity. He sought designs, as he explained in his *Treatise on Landscape Gardening,* with lines that united "agreeably and gradually with those of the surrounding country," while removing or concealing "everything uncouth and discordant." Downing's design for the Mall was based on a maze of sinuous paths linking meadows and groves. His goal was to create a national park that would be a living museum of trees in the natural style and that would influence the nation's taste in landscape gardening.

Like many projects in every generation of Washington's development, Downing's plan met political and financial obstacles. But while his vision was only partially achieved, his ideas influenced the next generation of improvements. Fifty years later the McMillan Commission was faced with a lush, natural landscape.

When the McMillan Plan was issued in 1901, the Mall's green meadows were facing encroachment from an expanding commercial city. At the base of the Capitol were the burgeoning Central Market, with its hurly-burly of sheds and stalls, and the train sheds and station of the Baltimore and Potomac Railroad, whose tracks crossed the Mall at 14th and at 6th streets. The Tiber Canal had been filled and a scenic Potomac Park was proposed on yet more filled land beyond the Washington Monument.

The McMillan Plan, issued at the height of the classically inspired City Beautiful movement and created by designers educated at the Ecole des Beaux-Arts, proposed a return to L'Enfant's formality, though in the form of a greensward rather than a promenade. The plan regularized the Mall's plantings, lined it with public buildings, and extended it as a grand axis on filled land beyond the Washington Monument to the future site of the Lincoln Memorial. The formality proposed in the plan reinforced the Mall as a separate and inviolable place. The details of individual buildings were subsumed into regularized setbacks and height limits. The commission traveled, studied, and surveyed to develop a properly scaled allée that would create a unified, symbolic environment.

The McMillan Plan both resurrected L'Enfant's plan and significantly changed it. The formal Mall we see today, which is the foundation of L'Enfant's plan, exists because of the McMillan Commission's monumental vision. L'Enfant's Mall, however, was not a mecca of monumentality, but a busy promenade, an integral part of the city's daily life.

The expediency of governance struck, and World War I saw the construction of temporary office buildings on the Mall and on East and West Potomac Parks, southwest of the White House. The "tempos" were placed so that the roads, paths, and open spaces of the McMillan Plan would be preserved. During World War II another round of wartime emergency building filled many of the Mall's open spaces with barracks-like office buildings connected by boardwalks and catwalks. Bureaucracy's inevitable expansion and self-perpetuation delayed the removal of the last "tempo" until the 1970s.

Despite the Mall's timeless appearance, most of its buildings and gardens have been constructed since World War II, some as recently as the 1970s. The strong image created by the McMillan Plan, and the oversight and stewardship of the Commission of Fine Arts have solidified a shared image and expectation of what the Mall should be. Even when buildings appear to depart drastically from that image, as does the concrete pillbox of the Hirshhorn Museum, a close examination will reveal that the architectural designs fit closely into context and history. Over time, the Mall evolved, functionally and physically, into the expression of our history. But also over time our notion of what is historic and how to express it has evolved and continues to change. We have moved from what J. Carter Brown calls white "carved soap" architecture to a black gash, from unified memorialization to the recognition of subgroups. As the prime sites on the Mall are occupied, we must face questions of what in our history must be remembered, how it must be expressed, and where it fits in the city of Washington. ■

1. National Gallery of Art—East Building

4th Street between Madison and Constitution, N.W.
I. M. Pei and Partners *1978*

The East Building is the preeminent modern masterpiece in Washington. Its thoughtful conception and fine execution set a new standard for the city's landmarks. Conceived at a time when modern architecture had seemingly lost its vitality and finished when modernism was increasingly blamed for the shortcomings of our cities, Pei's East Building is nevertheless a high point in the modern movement.

The museum is a freestanding addition to the National Gallery of Art. The original National Gallery (now the West Building) by John Russell Pope is directly across 4th Street. A cobbled plaza connects both buildings at grade, and a large tunnel connects the two below street level. In all, the new construction added a million square feet of floor space to the gallery complex, freeing the West Building's lower level for offices, and providing new gallery space and offices in the East Building.

This oddly shaped trapezoidal site is

created by the intersection of Pennsylvania Avenue, 4th Street, and Constitution Avenue. The resulting 19.5 degree angle is the basis for themes and motifs repeated at varying scales, from the building's overall massing of interlocking trapezoids and diamonds to the triangular coffers in the ceiling of the entrance porch.

Pei worked closely with the museum's director at the time, J. Carter Brown, who felt that art showed best in domestically sized spaces. Together they visited house museums all over the world in search of ideas and inspiration. In response, Pei developed a hierarchy of spaces. From the soaring atrium, space is sequentially broken down to intimately scaled galleries in the building's towers.

Pei was successful in relating the building to its prominent site and neighbors. The cornice lines of the towers and central connecting porch match the cornice lines of both Mall and Pennsylvania Avenue neighbors. From a distance the building seems to be covered by the white stone suitable for all buildings in Washington's core. Looking closer, one sees that the East building is sheathed in the same soft pink marble as Pope's West Building.

The relationship with the West Building is a special one. Brown points out how carefully Pei located the East Building by describing a visual link that the architect created: When you stand on the small balcony on the second floor of the West Building, look down; a line in the foyer's marble floor runs outside, across the "carpet of stone," between a niche in two of the plaza's glass pyramids centered on a granite bollard. The line continues to the center of the flanking marble towers of the East Building. Though nothing alike, the buildings are subtly linked.

The East Building combines the dynamism of movement and asymmetry of modernism with the repose of classicism. The exterior of the East Building is a composition of planes, solid forms, recesses, voids, and that impossibly sharp angle on the southwest corner. The elevations are different: the west massive and monumental, the east mostly repetitive windows and probably the best office curtain wall in the city. The north and south elevations use elements of each of the other two.

The East Building is entered through a deep, low-ceilinged porch which, like the exonarthex of a cathedral, brings the space close around the visitor to magnify the impact of entering the large, open space of the atrium. The atrium's skylights are screened by a grid of smooth aluminum tubes that soften the glare and minimize hard-edged shadows, permitting daylight but not taking away from the space.

Well over a decade past its completion, the East Building seems neither tired nor dated, but even better than when it opened. Unfortunately, it is doubtful that such a self-assured modern statement could be built today.

2. National Air and Space Museum
Independence Avenue and 6th Street, S.W.
Hellmuth, Obata and Kassabaum
1976, 1988

Some of Washington's modern museums are less temples to beauty than facilities for cultural mass consumption. To keep endless busloads of students and tourists moving requires that the architect have the sensibility of a traffic engineer as well as of an artist. This building has the largest capacity for exhibits and crowds of any museum on the Mall.

The architect relied on classical

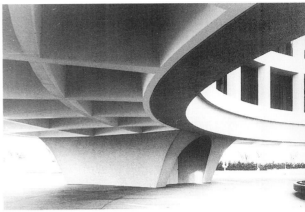

3. Hirshhorn Museum and Sculpture Garden
Independence Avenue and 7th Street, S.W.
Skidmore, Owings and Merrill (Gordon Bunshaft) *1974*

organization, which reflects the Beaux-Arts organization of John Russell Pope's National Gallery directly across the Mall. The building is made up of alternating marble-covered cubes containing galleries, and glass-covered cubes containing the largest exhibits. This composition is set on a podium base and rises to a cornice line marked by black window cutouts. Exposed trusses in the glass exhibit halls bring technology and engineering into the interior. The large interior space is simply organized allowing visitors to move easily around aircraft and spacecraft, and giving curators the flexibility to mount changing exhibits.

The glassy restaurant addition on the building's east side repeats the exposed trusses of the original but in a more sculpted, cruciform shape. Unfortunately, the United States Capitol is no longer a dramatic backdrop to exhibits; instead it is a view from a cafeteria.

Washington is a city for those with a long view. A museum for modern art was authorized by Congress in 1938. A design competition was won by Eliel and Eero Saarinen, father and son. Their modern design was viewed as inappropriate for classical Washington, too expensive for a nation coming out of a Depression and entering a world war, and by some as un-American. Their design was assigned to the purgatory that is unbuilt Washington, along with the arcade around the base of the Washington Monument and Robert Venturi's Capitol and White House models for Freedom Plaza.

Nearly 30 years later, Joseph Hirshhorn, a Latvian immigrant, who had indeed found the gold that supposedly paved America's streets, gave his art collection to the nation and endowed a museum to house it. The architect of the Hirshhorn, Gordon Bunshaft, has been described as a form-giver, a designer who gives shape to expansive ideas. In this building he departed from the rectilinearity of the

PUBLIC ART

IN HIS BOOK Edge City, Joel Garreau recounts the lingo of savvy developers who have reduced public art and architectural flourishes to bottom line price points. "Plop art," "blue water," and "hardscape" add to the "quality of life" by "animating" a "streetscape." The ends that planners and designers see as their mission are nothing more than the developer's price of doing business. Despite the effort, the results are remarkably unrelated to history or local character.

Public art was not always irrelevant. Incised gravestones and carved and painted ships' figureheads were expressions of grief and superstition, part of the ritual of community. The symbols of headstones—urns, willows, angels, broken staffs—were a shared language of allegory and metaphor.

As a city, one of Washington's roles is to pass along a shared culture. Both the plan of the city and many of its public buildings create ample opportunity to incorporate art that defines and memorializes history, from the squares, circles, and triangles of the L'Enfant Plan to the yards of carved masonry in the Federal Triangle. Early public sculpture used a language of references from classical antiquity, the Bible, and history to commemorate the great actions of great men.

This act of communication that is public art was easier when Trajan could erect a column recounting his martial exploits. Likewise, in a community that shared a common perception of who was great and what victory was, the language was readily spoken. In 19th-century Washington this may have led to public art that James Goode in The Outdoor Sculpture of Washington, D.C. calls "repetitive and unprovocative"; but simply through accretion, this work

has built a rich visual environment. And perhaps, one day stopping to read the inscription, we may discover the image of some schoolbook hero.

Modern buildings swept away entablatures and architraves, opting for sheer glass and metal. Even the thought of bas-relief and friezes became jarringly inappropriate. They seemed to represent a kind of dowdiness of thought and form that was just not modern. At the same time we began to reexamine history, studying the lives of common people rather than of generals and kings. The letters and diaries of women and members of minorities were reread and reinterpreted for clues to our past. History became not a seamless image of glory and right, but a sometimes clashing patchwork.

In the meantime planners and designers who see public art as a "placemaking" device have, through legislation and review, fostered an industry of artists and consultants who create happy floral images and lifelike sculptures of yuppies reading the Wall Street Journal. Will this revitalize our cities?

It seems that as our understanding of history has changed, our language to express it has not caught up. Occasionally, a Maya Lin breaks through and creates new metaphors so sharp that they hurt, but for the most part our public art is mute. Evanescent video pictures and ephemeral headlines make the latest scandal or disaster riveting. Before we have time to reflect on its import we are absorbed into the next event. What will a future monument be—a video monitor on continuous loop playing CNN footage of an interview with our general and equal time to our enemy, summed up with commentary from a soothing talking head?

Mall to create a round building that arranges galleries to receive natural light, but protects works of art from direct sun. The building is a hollow, three-story cylinder raised on four massive pilotis. The outside surface of the cylinder is unbroken except for the seams between concrete panels and a single projecting balcony on the north face. The inside surface is a glass wall admitting light to the circulation spaces. The centers of the inner and outer circles are eccentric, producing a slight asymmetry in the cylindrical volume.

Marble was the intended material for this building, but to meet the budget, precast concrete was substituted. Marble would have been a curious choice for such a building. The massive, monolithic forms of the Hirshhorn and similar sculptural buildings, such as the Department of Housing and Urban Development, by Marcel Bruer and Herbert Beckhard, seem better expresed by poured-in-place concrete. Unfortunately, the Hirshhorn's precast concrete panels look applied, not solid.

The plaza around the building (altered by landscape architect James Urban in 1993), was designed as a square concrete plaza enclosed by high walls from which the cylindrical building rose. Although it was unrelieved by greenery, it was liberally planted with modern sculpture. The building, the outdoor art, and the plaza seemed to form a single composition. Grassy areas were added to the corners and sides of the plaza, their edges reflecting the circle of the building. All the art was relegated to these green patches. The building now sits awkwardly, and the artwork is remote. Across the street from the museum building is the Hirshhorn Sculpture Garden. Sunken about one story into the Mall, the sculptures in the garden are cloistered behind high walls that are barely visible from outside. The vistas up and down the Mall are uninterrupted, and the sculpture is given a contemplative, isolated setting.

Many people feel that the Hirshhorn is too severe, but it came out of an era of bold statements in architecture. When viewed against fussier, more recent buildings, the Hirshhorn seems an appropriate setting for its collection.

4. Arthur M. Sackler Gallery/National Museum of African Art/S. Dillon Ripley Center
Independence Avenue between 9th and 11th Streets, S.W.
Shepley Bulfinch Richardson and Abbott (Jean-Paul Carlhian) *1987*

This project is a combination of sensitive architectural design and engineering tour de force. On this most central of Mall sites, surrounded by wildly eclectic neighbors—the solemn

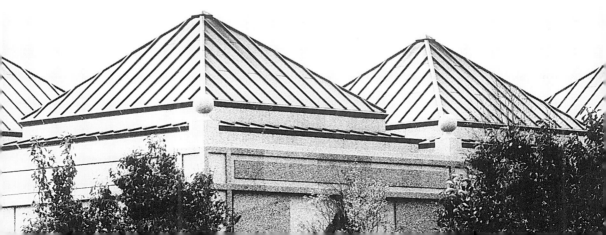

Freer, the cacophonous Arts and
Industries Building, and the nursery-
Gothic Castle, the architect has gently
inserted two full-sized museums and an
office and program center. This is
where the engineering comes in.
Except for the entry pavilions, most of
the space is underground.

    Above ground the pavilions are well
placed and designed to fit their unbe-
lievable context. The two larger
museum pavilions are placed on either
side of a central axis to create defined
garden spaces. The smaller entry to the
Ripley Center is placed closer to the
sidewalk to draw in visitors. One pavilion has a domed roof and the other a
peaked one, inspired by similar forms
in the Freer Gallery and the Arts and
Industries Building, but also reminiscent of festival architecture. The
friendly shapes gain dignity from both
their scale, carefully set to meet with
neighboring cornice lines, and their
materials, granite and glass.

    While Mall sites are becoming
scarcer, history and culture show no
sign of slowing down. As the consciousness and collections of the nation
grow, this underground solution may
be the museum of the future.

5. Enid A. Haupt Garden
Independence Avenue at 10th Street,
S.W.
Shepley Bulfinch Richardson and
Abbott (Jean Paul Carlhian) *1987*

While this garden may appear as a
sweet setting for the surrounding museums, a visitor will quickly realize that
the garden is also a roof over two
museums and a warren of Smithsonian
offices.

    The garden is in three parts. The
largest central garden is a foreground to
the Smithsonian's red sandstone Castle

by James Renwick. It resolves circula-
tion and links the entry pavilions for
the underground facilities: the Sackler
Gallery, the National Museum of
African Art, and the S. Dillon Ripley
Center. The garden also makes connec-
tions to the adjacent Arts and Industries
Building and the Freer Gallery of Art.

 On either side of this central north-
south axis are the museum entry pavilions and their complementary gardens
organized around vistas and outdoor
rooms. The garden of the Sackler
Gallery is focused on a circular pool
reached through a moon gate. A second moon gate is placed on its side to
create a seat. The African gallery's garden draws on the tradition of Islamic
gardens composed of free-flowing and
channeled water. Visitors walk around
an unenclosed water jet that is on axis
with the moon gate. These are inviting
and interesting spaces and small, pleasant respites from the scale and crowds
of the Mall.

6. National Museum of American History
Constitution Avenue between 12th and 14th Streets, N.W.
McKim, Mead and White/Steinman Cain and White *1964*

This building is the last gasp of the firm that was instrumental in returning classicism to America after the 1893 World's Columbian Exposition. Beginning at the turn of the century, McKim, Mead and White skillfully interpreted historical styles for the wealthiest clients. In cities and on college campuses across the country, their buildings have stood as luxurious examples of a bygone grandeur. The Museum of American History, though, is a stodgy attempt to fuse the principles of classical and modern architecture. In a characteristic Beaux-Arts composition, between a podium base and recessed attic the building's uniform facades are detailed with engraved panels—literal messages on this figurative temple. In the modern manner, the facade is created of mass rather than detail and it lacks a strong vertical or horizontal hierarchy. Perhaps this building's most modern detail is its setback from the sidewalk to accommodate a large, curved driveway.

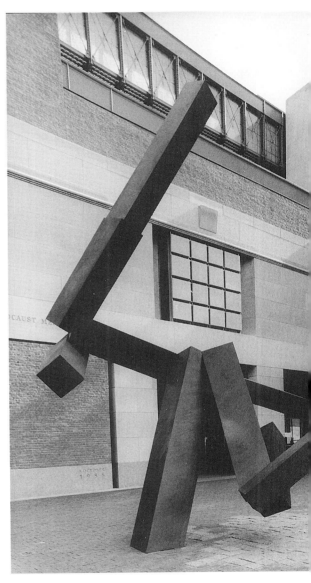

7. United States Holocaust Memorial Museum
Raoul Wallenberg Place (Independence Avenue and 15th Street, S.W.)
Pei Cobb Freed and Partners—James Ingo Freed *1993*

With what trepidation an architect must approach a commission like the Holocaust Museum. The emotions and politics surrounding it are daunting.

The events it commmemorates are almost too much to face. What manner of building can hold the artifacts of such history?

From the beginning, Freed viewed this building as a vehicle for thought and a construction in which the context of the Holocaust and the context of Washington must somehow meet. The building is sheathed in brick and limestone, compatible with its two neighbors, the Auditors Building to the north and the Bureau of Printing and Engraving to the south. From there the architect moves on to symbols of the Holocaust. As Benjamin Forgey noted in *The Washington Post,* the building turns certainties into uncertainties, just as the Holocaust did for its victims. Above the entrance is a window, but where the panes of glass should be are concrete panels, and where the supporting muntins should be are thin lines of glass. A window is no longer a window and view is restricted. Moving through the building, the glass skylight above shifts and fractures as its panes are set at diagonals. Walls meet each other at odd angles.

This museum is unlike any other on the Mall. There is no room here for glory. It is perhaps closest to the Vietnam Memorial in the way it addresses shame and death. It is also similar to that monument in being an experience. To enter into the museum is to enter a part of the Holocaust. Washington is a city of monuments, and metaphor is everywhere, from flags to buildings. Here Freed has developed new metaphors and a new way of facing our history. Even though the building is beautifully constructed, it is an ugly beauty, taking its details of steel reinforced brick walls and leaping catwalks from the concentration camps. The meanings are clear, and the message is powerful.

8. Constitution Gardens
Constitution Avenue and 17th Street, N.W.
Skidmore, Owings and Merrill (David Childs) *1976*

President Nixon was instrumental in convincing the reluctant Navy Department to leave its convenient location in the last "tempos" remaining on the Mall from World War II. Nixon had in mind a pleasure garden for this corner of West Potomac Park, described by project architect David Childs as a sort of combination of Walt Disney World and Tivoli Gardens. The activity-intensive plan that would have included two levels of underground parking was denied by the Commission of Fine Arts, and a second round of plans created a more gently landscaped area. Its curvilinear paths, tree clusters, and free-form pond are a departure from the strict axiality of the Mall.

The only jarring note to the gardens is their odd scale. The width of the paths and their broad curves lack the intimate scale of the romantic garden style. Trees and plantings will never grow in to reach the pond, thus creating tableaux of wood and water. The pond itself could hold Boston's entire Public Garden. Nonetheless, the gardens are a pleasant respite.

9. Memorial to the 56 Signers of the Constitution
Constitution Gardens
EDAW, Inc. (Joseph E. Brown) *1983*

This memorial is composed of sloped, slightly offset granite blocks set in a semiellipse. The blocks are organized by state, and each is engraved with the signer's signature, printed name, profession, and provenance. The addition of information about homes and profes-

sions adds a human touch; one can begin to imagine the risks these men took for the idea of nationhood. The memorial's small scale is appropriate to the intimate place that Constitution Gardens was intended to be. The opening of the ellipse to overlook the smooth pond would have had more impact if the garden had not been set amid an even greater openness. One might suppose that the memorial is so modest because, at its conception, the signers were not present to lobby Congress.

10. Vietnam Veteran's Memorial
Constitution Avenue and 21st Street, N.W.
Maya Lin *1983*

Lin's memorial not only ignited buried emotions and political activism, but gave a new form and language to contemporary monuments. Her solution is a departure from the classical white marble, sculpted forms that are traditional but that do not necessarily speak to contemporary society. Critics and observers have found moving metaphors in this work. As your hand reaches out to touch the names etched in the black polished walls, a reflected hand reaches back. As visitors move through the memorial, the land slopes

down and the walls rise up, engulfing them with the soldiers, listed in the order of their deaths—a reminder of America's reluctant but ever deeper involvement in Vietnam. The memorial is one of America's most moving places.

For those uncomfortable with this stark statement, the first of two representational sculptures was created. The first scuplpture depicts three infantrymen. The second representational work commemorates the contribution of the women who served in Vietnam. Both seem trite and sentimental next to Lin's powerful work; it is like setting up two greeting cards next to the Pietà. Fortunately, they are placed at a distance that limits their interference.

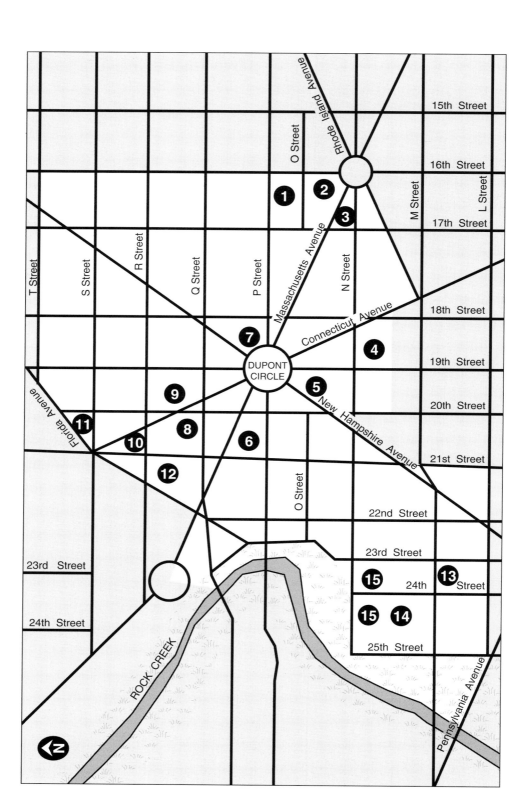

Dupont Circle and the West End

Having first determined some principal to which I wished making the rest subor-dinate, I next made the distribution regular with streets at right angle, north-south and east-west. But afterwards I opened others in various direction as avenues to and from every principal place, wishing by this not merely to contrast with the general regularity nor to afford greater variety of pleasant seats and prospects...but principally to connect each part of the city with more efficacy by, if I may so express, making the real distance less from place to place.

PIERRE CHARLES L'ENFANT

Although limned by the L'Enfant Plan, the area of Dupont Circle and the West End first developed as an area of farmers' gardens and slaughterhouses to serve downtown. After the Civil War, Washington became a boom town, provid-ing services for war veterans and turning civic attention to long-needed city improvements. Public investment in roads and bridges efficiently linked Dupont Circle with the rest of the city and encouraged more private investment. When "Boss" Shepherd's improvements included paving Connecticut Avenue through the circle, the area drew investors' attention.

In the 1880s, Dupont Circle was still at the city's westernmost edge. In 1874, when Senator Stewart of Nevada constructed his mansion on what is now the site of a Riggs Bank branch, it was called Stewart's Folly for its distant location. But other elegant houses soon followed. Designed by noted architects of the day—Stanford White, John Russell Pope, Carrère and Hastings—they housed ambas-sadors, senators, generals, and cabinet secretaries in an elaborate style that reflected the untaxed wealth and expansionist attitudes of the time.

Originally called Pacific Circle, it was renamed for Admiral Samuel F. du Pont in 1884 and marked with his likeness in bronze. The fountain there now was a gift of the du Pont family in 1921, and is the work of Daniel Chester French, the sculptor of Abraham Lincoln at his memorial.

The lavish development of Dupont Circle continued through the 1920s. President Wilson lived north of the Circle at 2340 S Street after leaving the White House until his death in 1924. During the Depression, large mansions and wealthy lifestyles became harder to maintain. With the outbreak of World War II, owners anxious to shed their gilded shells found a willing customer in the federal government, which needed office space. Other mansions were subdivided into apartments for an increasing population of wartime employees. Some of the large homes were turned into embassies. The Indonesian Embassy is housed in the mansion that belonged to Evalyn Walsh McLean, the last private owner of the Hope Diamond.

Meanwhile, the West End, divided from Georgetown by Rock Creek Park, developed as an area of small town houses and light industry. It was more like the riverfront industrial area of Foggy Bottom than fashionable Dupont Circle.

During the 1960s and 1970s the row houses of both Dupont Circle and the West End found new tenants. Young gentrifiers discovered an excitement in city living that their parents had rejected for the suburbs. They matured and invested in the area, renovating its town houses and attracting a lively mix of shops and restaurants.

By the 1980s, Dupont Circle was a thriving urban neighborhood, suffering the perils of popularity: high prices and no place to park. Looking for more of the same, developers turned their attention to the West End, an undiscovered corner of the city. Although planners saw this area's potential as a downtown residential neighborhood, the zoning ordinance allowed hotels to be defined as housing. Three luxury hotels were built on three opposite corners anchoring new office uses on 24th Street. This architecture has significantly changed the area's character. Supported by the grid street pattern and the strong edge of Rock Creek Park, the West End is now a distinct neighborhood.

Even though the gentrifying generation may have moved on—renovating a town house is one thing, but a school, police department, and entire municipal system is another—they left behind one of the few places in Washington that attracts people for its urban experience and not for its museums or monuments. Dupont Circle is one of Washington's most pleasant urban neighborhoods and continues to draw shoppers, strollers who enjoy the architectural variety of tree-lined streets, and visitors who come to browse in shops and sip coffee in cafes. The lesson here is not in history, but in humanity. ■

1. National Wildlife Federation
16th and O Streets, N.W.
Keyes Condon Florance *1990*

This project combines offices and apartments using elements of the Washington aesthetic to convey a sense of solidity and purpose. The result fits in well on 16th Street, lined with churches and institutions.

Three rectangular brick bays project from the front facade, the fourth masonry bay marks the entrance, and a recessed attic caps the building. A masonry first story composed of alternating bands of finished and rusticated stones marks the building's base.

This solid base, combined with the bas-relief panels of animals alternating with the windows and the building's setback from the sidewalk behind a small lawn, give the building the quasi-public appearance of an institution rather than a speculative office building.

2. Benjamin T. Rome Building
Johns Hopkins University
1619 Massachusetts Avenue, N.W.
Keyes Lethbridge and Condon *1961*

Architects have a variety of ways to articulate the facade of a building. They can manipulate bulk and mass, they can apply decoration, or they can highlight planes with void and solid. The architects here chose to emphasize planes with a series of overlaid frames that create a warmth and depth often unseen in similar office buildings.

A concrete frame over inset red–framed windows defines the building and gives the facade dimension. The red window frames are a pleasing contrast with the concrete and subtly emphasize the planes of the facade.

The building pulls back from the street to create a projecting block on one side of a small plaza. The scale here is just right. The small plaza emphasizes the entry and sets off the building, giving it a quiet presence on the street.

3. Embassy of the Philippines
Massachusetts Avenue and 17th Street, N.W.
Tower Group Architects *1993*

Embassies use architecture in varying degrees to represent their nations and aspirations in a foreign country. From the bold sculptural shape of the Brazilian Embassy, the special location of the Canadian Chancery, and the blocks of former mansions in Northwest, each country re-creates itself as budget and space allow.

Rather than move into a mansion or build a Philippine-style building in Washington, the government of the Philippines built a new embassy that looks like an old building. In the Beaux-Arts manner, the building has a base, middle and, top articulated by modern, stripped-down moldings and columns. At the site's sharp angle, the building is marked by a curved facade and two stepped, convex bays of windows, a common solution to the odd-shaped sites created by Washington's diagonal avenues. Within the Beaux-Arts frame, the building is filled with finely mullioned windows. The type of glass and austere details mark it as a

new building, its attitude and massing make reference to history.

The embassy is a formal and pleasant addition to the streetscape, though some have complained about the narrow sidewalks along the site, noting that new construction should offer an opportunity to improve the streetscape for the pedestrian.

4. 1818 N Street, N.W.
David M. Schwarz/Architectural Services *1984*

Facadism is a compromise between comfort and change, the comfort of the familiar that we know and understand, pitted against change that is the inevitable result of growth and investment. The compromise that saves an older building's facade while gutting the interior, and sometimes the rest of the block, to create a new building, is often an uneasy truce between developers and preservationists.

This building is more successful than most because the transition between old and new is a comfortable fit within the building and with its neighbors. On a corner site, the building retains the facades of five, four-story town houses dating from the 19th century, with the larger building rising to eight stories behind them. Despite the fact that only the facades are preserved, the joining of the new building with the old gives the impression of more substantial buildings.

The materials and elements of the new building echo those of the town houses. The stepped-back brick facades are detailed with lighter-colored concrete and varied with bays and balconies below a gabled roofline. This massing and detail create a complementary backdrop for the painted facades of the town houses, which remain prominent on the streetfront.

From the sidewalk, these substantial and well-maintained facades fit into the streetscape, with elegant detail that is a pleasant change from blank office fronts, but also with the weight to stand up to the larger surrounding buildings.

5. Euram Building
21 Dupont Circle, N.W.
Hartman-Cox Architects *1971*

Washington's traffic circles present architects with special problems. Awkward, wedge-shaped sites preclude the standard office building floor plan that arranges work space around a service core. On the street the building must mediate between the characteristics and scales of converging streets and avenues and the circle. This building responds to its context, but establishes its own presence with a graceful use of modern massing and materials.

The Euram Building was designed and built when Hartman-Cox had not yet picked up the language of neoclassicism so loved by developers looking for instant legitimacy. The client here, an Italian firm, was seeking a modern idiom. The building has been compared to a modern Renaissance palazzo, no doubt because of the client

and its strong street walls and massive, anchoring corners, which form an interior courtyard. Its modernity lies in the glass walls, which counteract the heavy brick corner elevator shafts.

The brick towers flank a center stair at the circle facade. From there, the building widens to fill the site created by a diverging street and avenue. The brick continues to frame and anchor the building along the side facades, which are filled in with bands of glass. The architects have used common materials—glass and brick—in a subtle yet interesting way to create a unique building.

6. Indonesian Embassy
2020 Massachusetts Avenue, N.W.
The Architect's Collaborative *1982*

This former mansion was built in 1902 for Thomas Walsh, a Colorado gold miner who was reputed to have embedded a lump of gold in its front stairs. His daughter, Evalyn, eloped with Edward Beale McLean, son of the owner of *The Washington Post,* and became prominent in Washington's social and political life.

After the death of Walsh's wife, Carrie, in 1932, the mansion stood empty for three years and then was rented to the Reesttlement

Administration of the New Deal. In 1937 the Rural Electrification Administration moved in and in 1940 the house was turned over rent-free to the Washington chapter of the Red Cross. It was purchased by the

Indonesian government in 1951.

The 1982 addition houses chancery functions, leaving the grandest parts of the mansion for entertaining. When the addition was designed, at the dawn of postmodernism, another firm might

THE PLANNED CITY: GEOMETRY

THE PLAN OF Washington—the layout of its streets, public spaces, and focal points—is unique among American cities. Along with the height limit, this web of green avenues connecting distinct public spaces is what makes Washington memorable.

The scheme consists of diagonal avenues overlaid on an irregular grid of orthogonal streets. The diagonals, at various angles, connect points across the city, recalling the baroque plans of Europe. The orthogonal grid is like that of most American cities and is a reminder that this city was planned on open land. The intersections of the diagonals with each other are punctuated with squares and circles—small urban parks. The intersections of diagonals and orthogonals create acute and oblique angles that stress the superimposition of the two plans.

Besides this intersection of two street plans, the diagonal avenues ultimately focus on the two most important sites of the plan, the White House and the Capitol. A segment of one avenue—Pennsylvania—becomes the link between these two buildings. In this sense, the plan is unbalanced, with this relationship taking place to one side of the main axis of the Mall.

The inspiration for L'Enfant's Washington can be seen in several European cities. Pope Sixtus V cut long, straight streets through Rome's tight, medieval fabric to connect religious sites. Essentially finished by 1590, this was the first baroque city

plan. Italian and French garden planning, culminating in Louis XIV's Versailles, forms another tradition, that of the extension of axes and vistas through forested countryside, expanding the king's view and power infinitely in all directions.

Baroque plans are about spaces and movement. Streets, squares, and parks defined by their abutting buildings and become outdoor rooms. Baroque architecture, with its elaborate bases and cornices, becomes the walls of these rooms. Movement through the baroque city is punctuated by squares and circles anchored with monuments expressing the power of church or state. But not all boulevards are anchored. The baroque plan also allows for the power of infinite view, leaving the impression that the reach of the king or community expands indefinitely.

Baroque design was encouraged by new technologies. Telescopes were expanding man's view beyond his own planet, and the increase in vehicular travel changed the perception of distance. The long avenues of baroque plans opened views, and their distances could be covered quickly in a swift carriage. These traditions of design were well developed, though not extensively implemented, by the time L'Enfant was planning Washington.

Another approach to design, the gridiron, was popular at the time, used in town after town in the middle and

have picked up directly on the elaborate detailing of the original. Yet this firm, founded by Walter Gropius, did not stray from his modernist ethic. TAC designed a glass box, but framed it in buff brick and placed it behind a sweeping, curved entrance that mimics the exuberant curves of the original. Pulled back from the street, the addition creates a formal entry space and allows the grand original mansion to remain dominant.

southern colonies. Nearby Alexandria and Georgetown—established seaports by the time L'Enfant was drawing Washington—typify the American gridiron plan. Washington's grid is analogous to the medieval city that European baroque cities were built on: It is the tight background against which we appreciate the baroque sense of vista and movement.

Washington has always presented designers with several challenges. Unlike plans carried out in Europe, L'Enfant's plan is only a diagram. Rather than being cut through a dense forest or medieval city, Washington was built on open land.

Generally, in all eras, the baroque plan is strongest when the distinction between the overlay and the background grid is heightened. One should have a sense of space opening up or closing down, of changes in direction, and of entry back into the general tightness of the city.

This frequently does not happen in Washington for several reasons. The streets, not just the avenues, are very wide. Often, these wide streets lack definition and are out of proportion to buildings that would make a comfortable urban space. Also, with some notable exceptions, most of the focal points of the plan are small parks with statuary. Unlike the Champs Élysées, with the Arc de Triomphe at one end and the Place de la Concorde at the other, Washington's axes are anchored by no strong architectural features and only occasionally by a prominent public building. In this regard, the parks are more like the squares in gridiron plans of other American cities like Savannah or Philadelphia.

Modern architects frequently treated L'Enfant's plan with disdain. They designed building curtain walls that shot upward repetitively and drifted off without firm conclusion. Often, when enough land was available, buildings were designed with a geometry that reflected nothing in the streets and public spaces around them. This happened most egregiously around the circles of L'Enfant's plan. In larger projects, architects and planners went so far as to bury portions of streets and avenues beneath a new vision of planning.

There are inspiring vistas and sophisticated convergences in Washington. The view down Pennsylvania Avenue to the Capitol or the gathering of avenues at Dupont Circle exhibits the plan's power. But just as often views are broken by topography or a departure from the plan, like the placement of the Treasury Building to block the view of the White House. Many circles are not tightly defined by building walls to emphasize breaks where avenues enter.

Washington's legacy is that, more than any other American city, its plan requires architecture to defer to the greater idea of the city. The deference goes beyond contextualism, which merely echoes its surroundings. Instead, architecture must both create and respond to the plan's potential.

Photo courtesy Eric Colbert and Associates

marked with steel and glass canopies designed to suit each location.

One of the most significant contributions of this project is the restoration and operation of the abandoned public restroom at its entrance in the small park on federal property. This rare species is virtually extinct and deserves to make a comeback.

7. Dupont Down Under
20th and P Streets, N.W.
Eric Colbert and Associates (K. C. Dutton) *1995*

On a 30-year lease from the city, this former trolley station has been transformed into an underground marketplace. The station was opened in 1949, was a terminus for trolleys to Mount Pleasant, and closed twelve years later when Metro planning was underway. As with many outmoded industrial and transit systems, despite the cost, the tunnel was abandoned until a new use could be found.

Festival marketplaces—fun places to eat and shop—have been a successful urban phenomenon for more than a generation. Baltimore's Harborplace and Boston's Faneuil Hall have focused new interest and investment in their downtowns by attracting tourists to spectacular buildings and sites. On a smaller scale and for a different market the developer here hopes to serve the neighborhood with a mix of restaurants and a health club.

The design for retail concourses in the tunnel preserves some of the simple, original tile work and introduces new cove lighting and lightposts that mimic streetlamps. Tenant spaces are reminiscent of trolley cars. Above ground, the existing entrance stairs will be renovated for service and customer access. Public entrances will be

8. 1600 20th Street, N.W.
Mariani and Associates *1989*

The buildings of the Dupont Circle neighborhood are an eclectic mix of lavish late Victorian that gently segues into a more restrained Arts and Crafts style. This addition to a brick corner building has used the details of these styles, replicating them in a sympathetic way.

The building follows the height and setbacks of its neighbors, but also picks up their eccentric ornament. The facade is finished in buff brick and detailed with sculpted terra-cotta panels, a detail seen often in the area. The facade is further embellished with buff and terra-cotta colored tiles. The rectangular windows are held in red frames. The facade is a harmonious blend of the brick and limestone tones so prevalent in Washington. Two bays project on the facade, the larger one culminating in a belvedere. The building is connected to an older freestanding corner building by a glass and paneled bay framed in the same red as the windows and overhanging a recessed entrance.

The real clue to this building's age is the two-car garage at street level, taking the place of a dooryard or stair.

9. 1629–1631 Connecticut Avenue, N.W.
John Wiebenson *1992*

While a building's height and setback are regulated by zoning, architects choose materials and details to fit into the context of a neighborhood. Here the designer has created a sort of shadow facade out of a metal frame that outlines features of neighboring historic buildings.

The two gables of the metal frame are like two tents over a deep sidewalk that also provides visibility and access to a basement level. The recessed glass facade is capped by a rooftop deck behind a cornice of curved precast concrete bays and railings. Behind the patio is more of the steel and glass facade.

The architect was interested in exploring the idea of a building as an entrance rather than a wall, and with its opened depth and layers of materials and spaces, this building seems to turn inside out. The facade projects the idea of a building, almost like a sketched note to put something here in

the future. A more subtle rendition could have powerfully conveyed this notion, but the decoration of this building makes it seems a festival marketplace jammed onto a small site.

10. 1718 Connecticut Avenue, N.W.
David M. Schwarz/Architectural Services *1982*

The architect here applies tools of composition that he has used successfully in other parts of the city. The closely laid brick and precast concrete echo the Roman brick and masonry of the neighborhood. The building's complementary scale and massing create a streetfront height the same as that of neighboring buildings and move the bulk of the building to the rear of the site. The varied details—window shapes and grouping, turrets, gables, and bays—echo the eclectic styles of Dupont Circle's town houses.

But with this building the architect has allowed himself latitude to make a statement. The broad-arched entry and clock tower are reminiscent of area treatments, but clearly unique to this building. Perhaps the most startling aspect is the building's rear facade, which is finished as a white modernist building. While playing architectural games, the architect was mindful of the client's bottom line. The towers house mechanical equipment, and the simple rear facade allowed for more elaborate articulation on the front.

11. American Geophysical Union
2000 Florida Avenue, N.W.
Shalom Baranes *1994*

This building is an interesting juxtaposition of old and new. Its rusticated stone base supporting a patterned brick facade of punched, paired windows picks up on the restrained elegance of its Dupont Circle neighbors. A frieze above the full-length first-floor windows creates a pattern of planets, waves, and rain, symbolizing the client's mission.

Like a glacier forced through a

fissure, an inverted pyramid of glass and steel juts out from the building's acute corner, dramatically marking the intersection of grid and diagonal streets. Glass and steel also frame a recessed attic story and an entrance marked with a shallow bow. The swooping shapes of the steel panels and pipe rails lie somewhere between the nautical forms that inspired early modernists and the fins of a 1950s Cadillac.

The building uses this variety of architectural techniques to relate to its site, client, and time.

12. The Phillips Collection
Goh Annex
21st and P streets, N.W.
Arthur Cotton Moore *1989*

The Phillips Collection is a small Washington jewel. This personal collection, established in 1921, was the first in the country devoted to modern art. Washingtonians find the pictures, in their intimate display in the rooms of the former Phillips family home, to be a welcome change from the vast collections, spaces, and crowds of the Mall.

Over time the mansion has been expanded to house the growing

collection, most notably in 1920, with a skylit gallery atop the library by McKim, Mead and White.

The most recent addition, the Goh Annex, increased the gallery space by 50 percent but retained an intimate scale and is compatible with the neighborhood. The addition shares the massing and cornice height of the original buildings and interprets details from its own complementary position.

The brick and masonry of the addition share the rosy tones of the brick and brownstone original. Windows are domestically scaled but dramatically linteled with curved brackets that echo the curves of balusters and bays. The panels that form a frieze just below the mansard are also repeated in the new construction but elaborated with square windows that become decorative elements. On the street, the Goh addition lightly makes its presence felt in an elegant doorway topped with the gallery logo set into a base marked with even squares.

uses precast forms and a rusticated base to build up a facade hierarchy of windows alternating with bands of brick and precast details. The entry is marked by a fan-shaped covering reminiscent of old apartment buildings.

13. Grand Hotel and Office Building
2350 M Street, N.W.
Skidmore, Owings and Merrill *1985*

When this hotel and office project was begun at the same time as the two hotels on opposite corners, the West End was a mongrelly area of light industry and small row houses. New development in the neighborhood was to be at a larger scale and for new uses. The architects took advantage of this changing character to create their own context.

It was also a time when architects were rediscovering classicism, which provided a rich vein of ornament or ostentation, depending on how the details were used. The language was perfect for a luxury hotel. This building

14. 1250 24th Street, N.W.
Don Hisaka *1988*

As in his other Washington work, here Don Hisaka finds his own way through the thicket of contextualism. Rather than using the neoclassical context created by Skidmore, Owings and Merrill in their adjacent office and hotel buildings, he instead refers to the neighborhood's former light industrial character.

The base of this white building is the two-story masonry facade of the original industrial building. Rather than a solid plinth, this base seems like a screen in front of multipaned windows that rise into a curved facade. The building's glassy planes make the

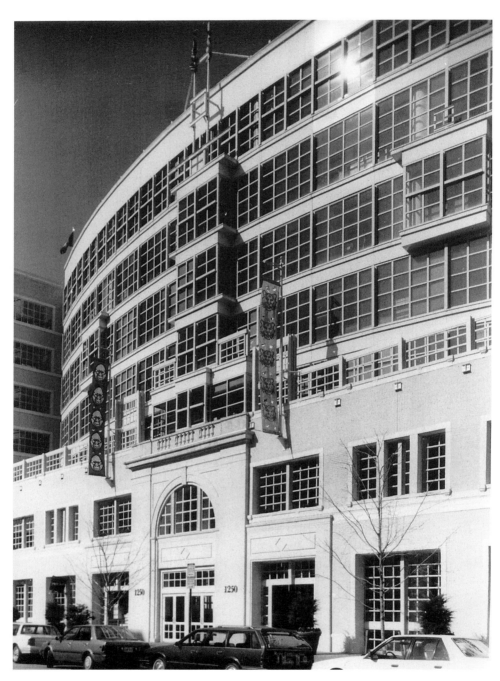

facade seem faceted. Despite this modern approach to the facade, the building is symmetrical in the classical style with a projecting center bay over the arched entrance flanked by project-ing rectangular bays. The cornice firmly tops the building, articulated with a heavy band that reaches down over the top row of windows to add another layer of muntins.

The windows of the upper floors refer to the light industry previously found in this area. They have a functional beauty, catching and reflecting the light. Hisaka has created a contemporary curtain wall that offers an appealing texture, detail, and scale to the street.

15. U.S. News and World Report
2300 N Street, N.W.

Carnegie International Center
2400 N Street, N.W.
Skidmore, Owings and Merrill *1985*

This matched pair of corner buildings with their concave curved facades created a gateway to the block, which has become a main street in the revitalized West End neighborhood. The buildings' neoclassical design also sets an aesthetic standard that suits the office buildings and luxury hotels lining the street.

The striped facades of the buildings, alternating between brick and precast concrete, were intended to be a transition between the white federal city and red-brick Georgetown. In a tentative step into postmodernism the designers used setbacks, projections, and striations to delineate the bases and cornices of the buildings.

Although the buildings have an appealing and eye-catching appearance, their scale and design elements have been used ad nauseam on this street, almost re-creating the sameness of K Street and proving that even red brick and friendly classicism can be too much.

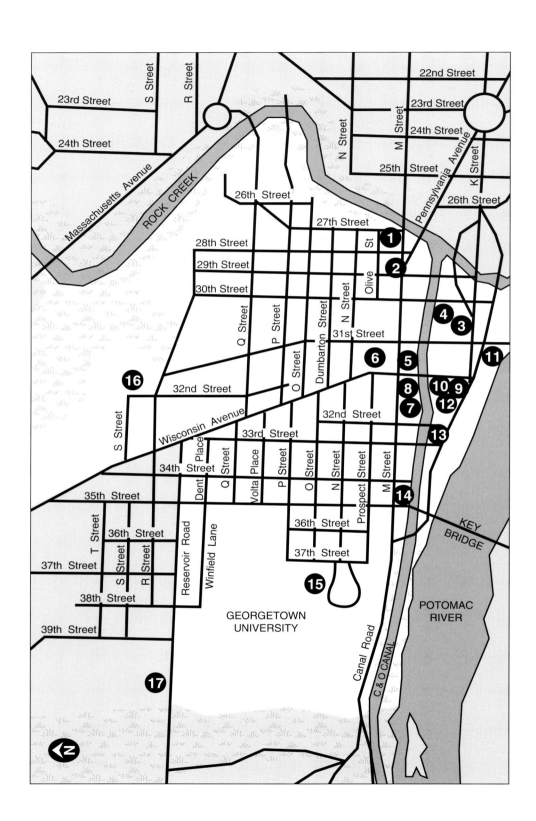

Georgetown

"Moving to that 'Indian Place,' where houses and kitchens have yet to be framed, the trees to be felled and the streets to be named."

Washington Past and Present, 1930

The 1938 WPA *Guide to Washington, D.C.* describes residential Georgetown as containing "fine small houses, occasional quaint cottages, and many pretentious mansions; here and there a shaded street is still laid in ancient cobblestones, and a sidewalk in smooth, worn brick." For the walker who ventures away from the stores and restaurants along Wisconsin Avenue and M Street, this scene is still intact. Change in Georgetown has come along the riverfront. Where the 1938 guide described crumbling old warehouses, the walker will now discover the neatly pointed brick walls of condominiums and offices. The only reminder of the industrial past is in their names—the Flour Mill, the Paper Mill, and the Foundry.

Georgetown was first established by the Anacostan Indians at the fall line of the Potomac, which enabled them to navigate upstream and down. River navigation later attracted colonial settlers, mostly of Scottish descent, and the settlement grew to be an active port and industrial center. By the end of the 18th century, the governor of Maryland declared Georgetown the largest tobacco port in the United States. During the Revolutionary War, Georgetown was an important base of supplies and munitions. In 1789 the town was incorporated, but by the 1840s, waterfront industry changed from tobacco shipping to milling. The Chesapeake and Ohio Canal expanded milling by supplying resources from inland farms and increased water power. With the advent of steamships and, later, railroads, the town's prosperity and importance waned. In 1871 it became part of the District of Columbia, which was booming after the Civil War.

As Georgetown was absorbed into Washington, its street names changed. Bridge Street became M Street and Water Street became K Street. At the same time its industry began to decline. In 1924 the canal stopped

operations and waterfront warehouses and factories drifted into obsolescence. At the same time, other Washington residential neighborhoods
were becoming more fashionable than Georgetown's old-fashioned row
houses. But as early as the 1920s, residents achieved enactment of a zoning ordinance that limited the size of new construction. Later, the
Depression brought the best and the brightest of New Dealers to town
and World War II flooded the city with war workers. Both groups found
Georgetown's row houses cheap, charming, and convenient. In 1950,
Congress passed the Old Georgetown Act, which protected the area's
physical character. By 1967, most of Georgetown had been declared a
historic district and listed in the National Register of Historic Places.

Today the residential and former industrial areas of Georgetown remain
distinct, divided by commercial M Street. New development in the residential areas north of M Street is careful infill, respectful of cornice lines,
height, and setbacks. Within that envelope contemporary architects have
experimented with materials, massing, and facade arrangement. South of
M Street architects and developers have had more leeway. The large sites
of former factories or their large building shells have left room for intricate
hidden courtyards, canalside plazas, interior shopping malls, and rooftop
gardens.

Georgetown above M Street

Carved out of colonial land grants, some of which still remain,
Georgetown above M Street is a mix of institutional uses, estate lots, town
houses, and single-family homes of varying scale and complexity. This is
truly urban fabric; a densely built grid of streets lined with buildings of
immense variety that have been constructed within a framework of development standards and historical imperative that created both consistency
and variety.

Lot sizes, a shared concept of appropriate building size, and the limita-
tions of materials and building techniques combined to create the consistency of Georgetown's streetscape above M Street. The neighborhood's
variety comes from individual buildings, each one different, each built at a
different point in time by people with more or less money than those
before. Small detached single-family homes sit next to large ones, all
linked by row houses. Some are just two stories high and two windows
wide, others are embellished with turrets, porches, and bay windows.

The wide availability of machine-made architectural detailing created
even more variety in these Victorian building facades. Pressed and glazed
brick, textured quoins, and lathed window lintels were combined in endless patterns. Today a tradition of painting brick has continued in
Georgetown, adding even more decorative options. Somber grays, exuberant pinks and lavenders, and genteelly flaking white create atmosphere

and attitude. One could stroll the streets of upper Georgetown and always find something to please the eye.

Georgetown along M Street

M Street, originally called Bridge Street for its span over Rock Creek Park, runs parallel to the canal and the Potomac. It links Georgetown with Maryland to the west and with downtown Washington to the east. Today the gold dome of the Riggs Bank at the corner of M Street and Wisconsin Avenue is a local landmark and the perceived center of Georgetown.

M Street has always been a primarily commercial street; the market established in 1795 at 33rd and M streets attests to the changes along this main street through history. The market was originally established to sell fish netted in the river. When Georgetown was absorbed into the city of Washington, the city took over the market and leased it to various vendors, including a car parts store as late as 1967. More recently the market building, built in 1865, has housed a dealer in posh provisions.

Although they have been reused and renovated many times, most of M Street's buildings retain their original scale, and many have their original details. The visual variety of the products in the storefronts is rivaled by the architectural variety of the second and third stories. Much of the new construction along M Street is in the shells or behind the facades of older buildings.

Today M Street in Georgetown is a center of entertainment. Its shops, bars, and restaurants draw both locals and tourists. It is the city's informal gathering place on Halloween or when the Washington Redskins win the Super Bowl. The excitement of Georgetown is created by the uses, not the building forms. The streets lined with Federal and Victorian-era buildings are similar to those in upper Georgetown, but for their commercial tenants. The grid street pattern leaves no room for sidewalk cafes, let alone plazas or squares, but the crowds eddy along M Street, reveling in an urban experience.

Georgetown below M Street

Georgetown's waterfront may have created the wealth that built the rest of Georgetown, but it has always been a poor cousin. The warehouses and factories that give their names to luxurious condominium and office developments were once the source of foul odors from flour and paper mills and an infamous glue factory. Now the only bits of urban blight that remain are a few ramshackle buildings along the riverfront at the far end of K Street and Whitehurst Freeway. While the elevated freeway is an eyesore to some, it is also a quick route downtown and a shady respite from Washington's steaming summer sidewalks.

This different character prompted discussion in the early 1970s when the area began to redevelop. Some factions felt the waterfront should be rebuilt in the image of upper Georgetown, focusing on small-scale town houses. Others felt it was more historically accurate to retain the large-scale and commercial uses that have always existed along the waterfront. Historical verisimilitude, buttressed by the large amount of money to be made, won out, and the area below M Street was redeveloped into residential condominiums and apartments, offices, and some shops in buildings that, if not the shells of the originals, retain the original scale and simplicity of the historic industrial buildings.

This area is one of the few places in Georgetown where such extensive new construction is possible, since the fabric of streets and previous development have left large lots offering a range of design options. It is also a part of Georgetown that, until recently, has not been valued for its appearance.

The area below M Street is just as interesting visually as the streets above it. Here the interest is generated less by architectural detail and more by idiosyncratic urban spaces: an art gallery overlooking the canal, a quiet courtyard, or a tiny cobbled alley. It is unique in Washington as a reclaimed industrial area on an intimate scale. ■

1. The Corcoran at Georgetown
28th and M Streets, N.W.
Arthur Cotton Moore/Associates *1986*

As with many Georgetown and Washington buildings, this project was completed after negotiations between the developer and the community and under the watchful eye of both the federal and local governments. After the District auctioned off the Corcoran School as surplus property it lay as an unsightly gateway to Georgetown. Rezoning that allowed both residential and commercial uses on the site gave impetus to redevelopment.

This infill project adds new construction (along M Street) to the renovated school (along 28th Street). Together the buildings form a midblock mews, landscaped as an urban garden in which the architect plays games with perspective, heightening the sense of distance with scaled gateways and decorative elements along an axis. Moore, who has played fast and loose with history in other projects, here has constructed a checkerboard brick-patterned wall topped with a glass mansard, and standing seam turrets and towers topped with small globes.

2. Madison Bank Building
2833 M Street, N.W.
Martin and Jones *1980*

This building exhibits the wit that made postmodernism such a fresh breeze in American cities. At a glance, the building looks like a creative rehabilitation of a historic building, with its somewhat awkward massing and deliberately mismatched bricks around the window openings. In fact, the four-story building, housing a bank and five apartments, replaced a gas station on this corner site.

The building is sensitively scaled to its Federal and Victorian neighbors and holds the street corner, becoming part of the urban fabric. Its facade however, takes liberties with our assumptions about architectural propriety. Columns sliced neatly in half support bluntly cut friezes at three places on the facade, gables of varying size intersect, and cornice lines drop and end midway. This postmodern play, combined with a strong sense of urbanism, make this building an asset to the street.

3. Jefferson Court
K Street between 30th and Thomas Jefferson, N.W.
Skidmore, Owings and Merrill *1985*

This building has been described as Richardsonian and has the bulk and corner-tower massing associated with his work, but there is no mistaking it for a historic building. A thin, exterior brick veneer broken by punched windows with smoked glass panes makes it clear that this building is not supported by its masonry, but by an interior steel frame. Even the traditional tile mansard roof is lightened by being made of glass. The paired chimneys are another historical reference that here creates a varied roofscape.

The building's most appealing feature is a hidden interior courtyard that creates solitude amidst the city bustle. It is one of the intimate spaces that architects were able to create on the large sites below M Street. For the curious walker it is a serendipitous discovery. The courtyard's quiet is emphasized by the sound of trickling water in a central pool.

4. The Foundry
1055 Thomas Jefferson Street, N.W.
Arthur Cotton Moore Associates/ELM
Design Group
1975

This brick building, tucked along the
canal on the site of a former sand and
gravel plant incorporates the former
Duvall Foundry along Jefferson Street.
When it was built it was a bold investment in revitalizing an obsolete urban
environment. Since then, the value of
sites below M Street has increased.
New projects using historical references more flexibly make this building's jutting corners and abrupt
switchbacks seem arbitrary rather than
visually interesting.

    The first floor of this five-story office
building is designed as an internal
street lined with shops, culminating in
a piazza and fountain. This interior
mall was initially successful, but now
Georgetown streets have become entertainment in themselves, and an isolated
mall with a few shops cannot compete.

    The project's greatest asset is its
location along the canal, which offers
a unique natural but urban environment. A park that meets the edge of
the canal creates an intimate public
space.

5. Canal Square
1054 31st Street, N.W.
Arthur Cotton Moore/Associates *1970*

This rehabilitation of a former industrial
building was one of the first in
Georgetown and is also one of the
largest, stretching from the canal to M
Street. The building along the canal is a
renovated brick industrial building constructed around 1890. The facade of
repeated arched windows sits on a
stone base, just above the canal's stone
walls. The project's impact comes from
its simplicity and its site. The repeated
arches have a strength that is emphasized by the soft greenery of the canal.

    Along M Street the original
Victorian buildings and facades have
been retained. The entrance to the new
project, in the middle of the block, is
marked by an arched opening into a
breezeway, scaled to be consistent with
the original buildings. The new office
building is located in the center of the
block. Narrow entrances through the
older buildings open into a central
courtyard shaped by the crisp lines of
the brick and glass.

    At the time this building was com-
pleted postmodernism was a gleam in a
theorist's eye, and the only historical
reference Washington architects were

comfortable with was the use of brick. Brick has sometimes been used overwhelmingly, inside, outside, on walls and floors. Today the architect of a project such as Canal Square might use a more varied historical palette and take more risks with color and materials, especially on a hidden site.

6. Hamilton Court
1228–1230 31st Street, N.W.
Smith Blackburn Stauffer *1985*

One of the great pleasures of urban life is the juxtaposition of buildings, space, and activity that creates a sense of serendipitous discovery. The original owners of Hamilton Park combined thirteen buildings to create a complex of apartments, a restaurant and shops. During its heyday in the 1950s and 1960s the complex presaged the reuse of older buildings for mixed-use projects that would be instrumental in renovating neglected downtowns.

Close review of the 1985 renovation by the neighborhood and the Commission of Fine Arts called for the renovation of streetfront buildings to preserve the street's historic character. New buildings inside the block are organized around a courtyard garden composed of smaller spaces that reveal themselves as the walker ventures farther.

The facades of the three-story brick buildings are articulated with arched windows and skylights in the mansard roof that echo the details of neighboring historic buildings. Their ground floors are built at a human scale, breaking down and creating spaces with recessed entries and courtyard patios. The buildings step in and out of the courtyard space, which becomes not a single space, but a series of intimate, human-scaled spaces. The hard brick

edges are softened with landscaping, a small grove of trees, flower beds, and a fountain. A brick and wooden pergola along the side of the original building links it to the courtyard and new buildings.

The project is a creative and elegant use of a tight urban block that creates interesting found spaces.

7. Canal House (Georgetown Park Apartments)
1080 Wisconsin Avenue, N.W.
Chloethiel Woodard Smith/Lockman Associates *1977*

This Victorian-era coal warehouse was transformed into a complex of shops and apartments as part of a development project that crosses the canal. On the south side of the canal, retail space and apartments in a former warehouse are connected by three pedestrian bridges that link the building with the Georgetown Park shopping center on the north side. One of the bridges is a canalside plaza at an entrance that connects the project to the shopping center and to Wisconsin Avenue.

The project opens up views to the canal but also maintains the strong edges of the canal walls and building facades that grow out of them. To maintain the warehouse's original flat facade, the apartment balconies are recessed. During construction, the canal wall had to be shored up and additional windows and doors were cut.

By creating intimately scaled spaces where people can linger and enjoy special views or use as shortcuts, the architects have added to the overall urban environment.

HISTORIC PRESERVATION

LONG INFAMOUS AS the eccentric hobby of little old ladies in sneakers and mink, historic preservation has become intrinsic to our view of communities. In most communities historic preservation started with a threat of demolition or alteration. The Mount Vernon Ladies rallied themselves in the 1850s when Washington's home on prime Potomac River real estate was proposed for a hotel. They raised enough money in five years to purchase the home, and it has been theirs ever since.

Preservation received a boost to professional status in the early 1970s. With a backlash developing against modern architecture and the nation's bicentennial focusing public attention on American history, preservation became a degree program in architecture schools and moved into the mainstream.

Professionals developed studies, surveys, and standards to identify what should be saved and how. The values of historic preservation were inserted into the political arena through zoning ordinances and historic district legislation that limited redevelopment and tried to prevent destruction. Battles were waged over the color of a windowframe, and some developers became infamous for their tactical use of the midnight bulldozer.

More often, though, preservation has brought a new appreciation of local history, the skill of self-taught builders, and the inherent appropriateness of the materials at hand. It has added depth and meaning to communities while preserving a fund of human knowledge. The clever reuse of institutional buildings for housing or the concerted effort to fund, restore, and book an old theater has often brought new life and investment to downtowns.

Preservationists are often the good guys, fighting for the underfunded but not unloved. In politics, though, every cause and strategy can be turned on its head. Historic preservation can also be used to forestall redevelopment. When a developer submits a proposal for a high-rise office on the edge of a neighborhood, the savvy community quickly redefines an old shopping center on the site as exemplary of commercial architecture responding to a burgeoning car-dependent society. Quiet farms surrounding a rural hamlet suddenly become "viewsheds" when town houses are proposed. The edges of the Manassas Civil War battlefield saw a contemporary battle when a developer proposed a shopping mall overlooking the gravesite.

What we define as valuable further defines us as a society. Early preservationists valued the shrines of national icons like George Washington. Hundreds of years later we are beginning to recognize the more humble but equally unique American values of roadside architecture. One hundred years from now what we take for granted today will have become the precious past.

8. Georgetown Park
3222 M Street, N.W.
Lockman Associates/Berkus
Group/Clark Trible Harris and Li *1981*

This project's careful integration into historic buildings, its mix of uses, and its exuberant design elements make it the best sort of urban development. It adds to the critical mass of people and activity rather than taking away from it. The project covers a full block between the canal and M Street, except for properties that could not be acquired, including the historic firehouse on Wisconsin Avenue and a restaurant on M Street.

The Commission of Fine Arts required retention of the street's Victorian scale and facades. The project fits in well, using height (40 feet on the street side, 60 feet along the canal), material (brick), and detailing (corbeled cornice, gabled roof, and linteled windows) to create complementary contemporary facades. The project also makes a connection between the street and canal, maximizing access and retail space in a desirable shopping location.

The building is constructed in three horizontal parts: three underground levels of parking, three partly below-ground shopping levels, and apartments on the top three floors. The apartments are reached through a gated entry from Wisconsin Avenue to an elevator that provides access to a plaza level forming a street in the sky, with front doors facing each other across common space. The middle level, the shopping mall follows the unfortunate pattern of taking retail off the street but maintains a sympathetic street scale that contributes to Georgetown's thriving streetfront retail.

9. Dodge Center (Waterfront Center)
1000–1006 Wisconsin Avenue, N.W.
Hartman-Cox Architects *1976*

This building, at the corner of
Wisconsin Avenue and K Street on the
site of a former concrete plant, preserves the historic warehouse of Francis
Dodge, a merchant who traded
between New England and the West
Indies.

   The new building's stepped profile
along the Potomac River is a local
landmark, visible from Whitehurst
Freeway, which squeaks by between
the river's edge and the building. The
brick slope is notched with rectangular
window openings that remain in dark
shadow, creating a hard, graphic
facade. The architects used this same
approach in their Mount Vernon
College dormitory (see Chapter 5), but
here, using different materials, they
achieved a crisp edge.

   The building is 90 feet high,
exceeding the 40- and 60-foot height
limits used elsewhere in Georgetown,
but because of the land's steep slope, it
rises only two stories above the apartments on Cherry Hill Lane.

10. 1024 Wisconsin Avenue, N.W.
Shalom Baranes *1990*

Squeezed onto a hilly site, with most of
its frontage on an alley, this building
nonetheless achieves a presence without overwhelming the site or its historic
neighbors. Like the adjacent Dodge
Center, the design uses the hill to
define the building shape and emphasize the slope. The Dodge Center's
slanted roofline follows the hill. Here,
the architect uses materials and massing to build with the hill.

   The building's rubble stone base
steps up to the brick and masonry
building, which seems to grow from
the hill. The brick facade is lightened
with large windows broken by slender
mullions and capped with masonry lintels. The facade builds up to a square
corner tower topped by a seamed
metal roof. The top two floors are
recessed to give the tower prominence.
The mix of levels, materials, and details
recalls small Georgetown houses and
shops and makes the building seem to
float rather than loom above Wisconsin
Avenue on its precipitous site.

11. Washington Harbour
3020 K Street, N.W.
Arthur Cotton Moore/Associates *1986*

The large waterfront site of Washington Harbour is separated from the rest of Georgetown by the hill between K and M streets and by the Whitehurst Freeway, freeing the architect from the strict historic context of Georgetown. In fact, the building seems to relate more to its waterfront neighbors, the Watergate and the Kennedy Center.

The Commission of Fine Arts supported the community in its initial desire for a federal or city park on this

site, but when neither government was willing to pay for the land, various owners proceeded with development proposals. The commission established development guidelines for the site, which included a public park at least 160 feet wide along the river, a use mix that was 60 percent residential and 40 percent commercial to avoid creating a monolithic design and use, and the continuation of the existing street pattern through the site. Through various Commission of Fine Arts reviews, the overall height and bulk of developer proposals were reduced.

The architecture of the resulting project has the look of the 1980s: detail and drama, bright colors, and a facade

C&O CANAL

WALKING ALONG THE C&O Canal, on a warm spring day when the only noise is a splashing labrador urged on by laughing children, it is hard to imagine the scene along this busy waterway 100 years ago. The canal would have been crowded with barges hauling flour and coal, their crews calling out for the latest news and gossip, the mules plodding alongside. Today's jogger or cyclist would have been an odd sight indeed.

The canal has helped shape Georgetown's character through history. Originally it connected the Chesapeake & Ohio Railroad to a busy riverport with three custom houses, industrial mills, and rendering plants.

Along its course into Washington, the canal passes the remains of old mills, crosses breached aqueducts, and descends through a series of stone and wooden locks. The canal's natural setting is marked by ghosts of an industrial past. Once it reaches Georgetown the canal takes a quick,

straight path. For a time the canal was carried across the Potomac to Alexandria by an aqueduct, but now it merely trickles out into Rock Creek. As it flows below M Street, becoming visible as buildings open and close around it, the canal presents a glimpse into Georgetown's history.

In 1754, when George Washington began surveying a route to bypass the Potomac's shallows and make the river navigable, he envisioned economic progress. By 1784, the more ambitious Potomac Company was chartered and its investors began raising funds to construct a link between the eastern seaboard states and the markets and raw materials west of the Alleghenies. In 1828, a grand procession led by President John Adams moved up the Potomac to break ground. When the first thrust of his shovel into the ground hit a root, the assembled crowd did not read it as an omen.

That same day the first spike was driven in Baltimore for the Baltimore

articulated to within an inch of its life. Some consider it vulgar, but this is Georgetown, where Washington comes to play. In the more sober 1990s the building may look like an evening gown at a barbecue, but it will always turn your head. The project's focal points are a fountain of choreographed water sprays, a tower, and plantings. The space was initially designed to be a boat basin.

But underneath the frills there is good urban design: the project's axes make focused links to existing street patterns, its internal streets are lined with shopfronts, and it opens the river to boat and pedestrian traffic in a departure from the formal granite

bulkheads in front of the Kennedy Center and the Watergate. The mix of activities, shops, offices, park, and housing combine to draw activity to the riverfront. Ironically, one of the most spectacular times to visit Washington Harbour are those when the Potomac is cresting and the flood gates rise to block the waters.

Washington Harbour begs for a public works project backed by some farseeing bureaucrat with influence over a wealthy philanthropist: a bridge over Rock Creek to connect it with the Watergate and the Kennedy Center and eventually, along the Potomac, to Hains Point.

& Ohio Railroad, whose speed and power would quickly surpass the canal. The canal took years to construct. Without reliable labor, materials, or engineering expertise progress was slow. Canal construction was also plagued by political fights. Charles Carroll, a B&O investor, owned land crucial to the canal route and delayed its acquisition in the courts. He was also able to woo away canal workers to the B&O when union disputes arose.

With each mile the canal became more obsolete. At its conception it could move goods faster and cheaper than the poor or nonexistent overland roads. But the railroad could outrun the canal and would not be shut down by floods. The canal was finally completed to Cumberland, Maryland, turning a profit only during the 1870s. It was eventually operated under receivership and closed after the damages of a final flood in 1924.

The canal took on a new role in 1938, when it was purchased by the federal government for $2 million, to be operated by the National Park

Service. The Park Service originally proposed an automobile parkway, but those who recognized the canal's scenic beauty and recreational potential found a friend in Supreme Court Justice William O. Douglas. His 1954 hike along the canal's length drew media attention and rallied public support for a park.

Today the C&O Canal is a unique and well-used urban park. In Georgetown, where the canal runs parallel to M Street, enterprising shopkeepers and developers have made it a lively path lined with shopfronts and plazas. The seasonal changes of the canal's waters—iced over in winter or dappled with summer sunlight—bring nature into the city. In Bethesda and Potomac the canal is a linear park for day-trippers and overnight hikers punctuated by waterfalls, lock houses, bridges, and trails.

Where technology has forced change, old environments may be abandoned, but only temporarily. The failure of one generation becomes a pleasure for the next.

12. 3222 Cherry Hill Lane, N.W.
Arthur Cotton Moore/Associates *1979*

This well-hidden building is thoroughly
modern in its conception, responding
to the demands of the site and creating
a facade that reads as domestic without
reliance on typical residential details.
On this steeply sloping site facing a
narrow alley lined with two-by-two
row houses, the architect seems to
have balanced a brick facade that
quickly dematerializes into a sloping
glass wall. Ground-level apartments
are marked by curved brick walls that
enclose patios and create private
recessed entries. The building's other
apartments are reached though a common entrance off a shady courtyard.
From the rear alley the building rises
up the slope in an arrangement of
receding and projecting shapes.
Duplexes are stacked over duplexes
and triplexes over flats on the steep
slope, and each apartment is different.

Rather than mimic the small row
houses across the street, the architect
has created a charming urban residential environment by using a restrained
sense of detail and scale. The building's
sophisticated attitude is enhanced by
the private location, which happens to
be only a block or so away from the
middle of Georgetown.

13. The Flour Mill
1000 Potomac Street, N.W.
Peter Vercelli *1981*

This renovation of a 1908 mill building
is tucked away at the end of K Street,
under the Whitehurst Freeway. The
building runs between the canal and
the street, with a large brick plaza overlooking the canal and connecting the
street to canal paths and bridges. From
the plaza, this building and its neighbors frame views across bridges and
catwalks to the canal's stone walls and
busy M Street beyond. The building's
brick facade is pierced by triangular
balconies forming a hard-edged,
graphic facade that contrasts with the
softer landscape of the canal.

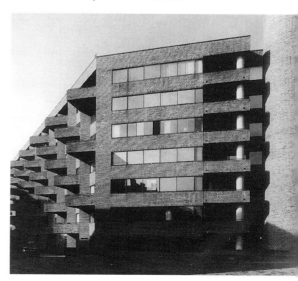

14. Francis Scott Key Park and Star-Spangled Banner Monument
34th and M Streets, N.W.
Oehme, van Sweden and Associates
1993

Key Park is the result of a private fund-raising effort to memorialize Francis Scott Key, whose house was near the park site. It turns a weedy, deserted lot into a contribution to the streetscape, as Benjamin Forgey described it in *The Washington Post,* "a place formed from a non-place."

The park is organized around a central pergola and is articulated with appropriately scaled and well-placed benches, walls, and curb edges amid plants of varying color and texture. Key is memorialized by a 15-star, 15-stripe flag, a bronze bust, and wayside plaques elaborating on the historical events of his time. The park mediates between the urban and natural environments, providing a gateway to Georgetown and connecting to the canal towpath.

The designers should be commended for avoiding specially designed wastebaskets or benches, novelty paving patterns, and flag images. All this elegance is created with simple, well-deployed design elements.

15a. Georgetown University Village A Student Housing
John Carl Warnecke *1978*

This building adds to the spiky profile of Georgetown University as its rises on a hill above the Potomac. Like many of the university's newer buildings, it defines an edge of the campus, here on a dramatic site.

The building is a series of stark, multistory apartment blocks linked by stair towers in open bays. The open bays puncture the building and offer glimpses of the river and Rosslyn, Virginia, to passersby as well as residents. The Erector Set structure of the towers seems to vault out into the view across the Potomac.

15b. Georgetown University Village B Student Housing
37th at N and O Streets, N.W.
Hugh Newell Jacobsen *1984*

Like much of Jacobsen's work these buildings are a distillation of contextual historic forms. The brick dormitories are three stories high with English basements. The rectangular windows echo the rhythm of windows in adjacent town houses, building up a facade capped by a simple cornice. At points the facade is punctuated by elaborately supported and topped multipaned bay windows. The dormitory, like its town house neighbors, is built to the street edge, but its bulk is arranged around a midblock courtyard that creates a hidden green space, allows service access, and permits rear entrances, thus creating a floor plan that maximizes the number of student apartments.

The interiors are simply and sturdily finished with studded rubber flooring in the halls. White surfaces in the apartments provide a neutral background for the clutter college students collect.

The sympathetic details and scale make these buildings as good a neighbor as a college dormitory can be in a tight urban environment.

15c. Georgetown University Village C Student Housing
35th and 36th Streets at N Street, N.W.
Mariani and Associates *1987*

This three-building complex marks the western edge of the Georgetown campus at the base of a hill. Unlike modern buildings, it is embellished with historical details, but unlike the historic buildings of the area, it is built at a huge scale. The red brick building sits on a masonry base. The facade is articulated with masonry trim, bay windows, and arched doorways and is topped off with stepped gables.

Campus buildings rarely have the luxury of a choice of sites. Ambitious building programs and limited budgets often force less than optimum solutions. This large complex could not be designed to step up the hill or be sited perpendicular to it to emphasize the slope and frame a view to older buildings on the quadrangle. Instead it is like a wall at the base of the hill with an unceremonious entry up a narrow service road.

15e. Georgetown University
Lauinger Memorial Library
37th Street between N and Prospect
Streets, N.W.
John Carl Warnecke *1970*

15d. Georgetown University
Intercultural Center
37th and O Streets, N.W.
Metcalf and Associates *1982*

As with many of the university's newer
buildings, this project is perched on a
hillside edge of campus and defines
both the outer edge and inner space of
the quadrangle. The two blocks of the
building meet at a tower that marks the
entrance and punctuates a small plaza.
One block slopes down the hill to
catch sunlight for its solar panels, while
the other block intersects to edge the
plaza.

    The building is modernist in the
manner of the 1970s, when architects
were inching away from the sleek glass
box to more sculptural shapes constructed out of contextually compatible
materials. The brick walls are decorated by rectangular windows broken
up asymmetrically by mullions lying
over the window panes. The sloping
roof is edged with reverse batten gray
metal fascias.

Unabashedly a modern building, this
library, named for the first Georgetown
University student killed in the Vietnam
War, nonetheless picks up on materials
and patterns of adjacent older buildings. Its rubbled concrete walls are similar in tone and texture to the masonry
buildings defining the quadrangle.
While the mass of the building is sculp-
turally shaped with jutting bays and
cutouts to meet the steep hill, its vertical lancet windows and towers echo
the older Healy Hall.

15f. Georgetown University
Leavey Center
Mariani and Associates *1988*

This multipurpose center, which houses
conference facilities as well as student
activities, runs horizontally between
the university's playing fields and its
hospital. It shares the brick and stone
palette of the Village C housing complex, both of which define a rear area
of the campus composed of fields
and parking lots. It also shares that

building's large scale.

The parking structure in the building's lower levels is detailed with arched windows. Upper levels are finished with turrets and towers, lending it an appropriately collegiate air.

16. Pre-Columbian Museum
Dumbarton Oaks
1703 32nd Street, N.W.
Philip Johnson *1963*

Dumbarton Oaks is a Washington treasure, a creatively conceived garden, luxuriously executed and carefully maintained. This building fits beautifully into that precious atmosphere.

The original Federal-style house was built in 1801 as part of a large estate. Under the ownership of the Bliss family, exquisite gardens were designed by Beatrix Farrand, beginning in the 1920s. In 1940, the Bliss' bequeathed the house, outbuildings, and sixteen acres to Harvard University. Since then, a neo-Georgian wing has been added to house Mrs. Bliss' landscape and gardening library.

This intimate museum, set to one side of the property, houses Mr. Bliss' collection of pre-Columbian art. The modern building passed Georgetown design restrictions since it is largely hidden from the street. Its plan is composed of eight interlocking circles arranged in a square around a central opening focused on a pool. Each circle is topped with a low dome. This plan is a modern interpretation of a Byzantine church plan, a link to the Byzantine collection of Dumbarton Oaks. The building is finished with luxurious materials, reminiscent of the fine finishes Philip Johnson used in the Kreeger House (see chapter 10): green and white marble and teak.

17. French Chancery
4101 Reservoir Road, N.W.
André Remondet *1984*

Embassies are perhaps the only buildings in Washington that are not influenced by the compunction of contextualism. In fact, a central tenet of their programs is to represent their countries, to stand out on the skyline as literal and figurative pieces of their nations. This embassy follows that notion and makes no attempt to fit into the brick context of Georgetown.

Situated on an eight-acre site in Georgetown adjacent to Glover Archbold Park, the horizontal mass of building is tucked into a sloped site. Bands of white marble and dark glass bend and twist around the complex of four buildings. The ground floors are set back and lifted by pilotis. A dark metal mechanical penthouse is recessed. Small offices are set into the slope around the site's perimeter.

Shortly after the building was completed, Philip Johnson commented in *Washingtonian* magazine, "No comment is the only possible remark." Given that in the same article Johnson criticized such classics as the cherry trees and the plantings around the base of the Lincoln Memorial and federal architecture in general, this is a truly scathing comment.

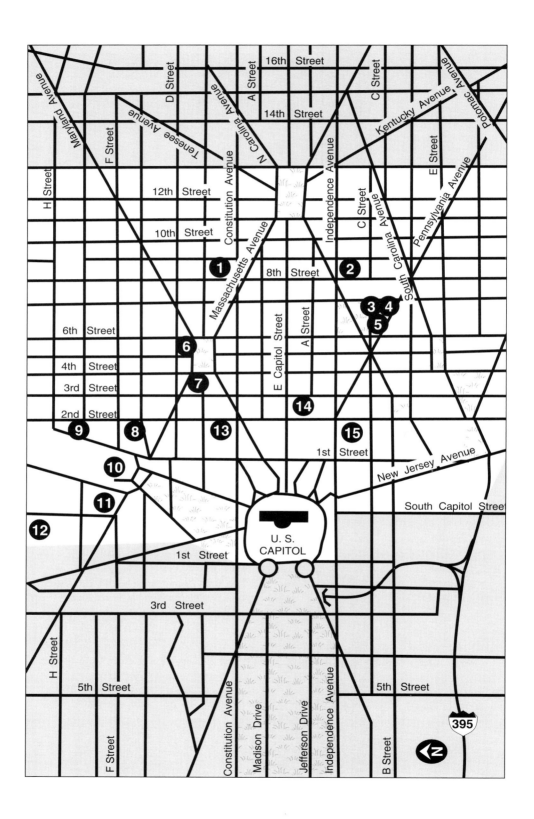

Capitol Hill

Everybody knows that Washington has a Capitol but the misfortune is that the Capitol wants a city. There it stands, reminding you of a general without an army, only surrounded and followed by a parcel of ragged little boys, for such is the appearance of the dirty, straggling, ill-built houses which lie at the foot of it.

CAPTAIN MARYAT, 1838

In surveying the city for his plan, L'Enfant described Capitol Hill, then called Jenkins Hill, as "a pedestal waiting for a monument." He proposed placing the Capitol building on this pedestal, giving the center of the young nation physical and symbolic prominence. In 1800, when Congress settled in Washington, it could not move into its new home, since only one wing of the Capitol was completed.

But L'Enfant did not stop at the Capitol. He drew East Capitol Street from the Capitol building to the Anacostia River as a 160-foot wide boulevard and envisioned it as a commercial street lined with shops. At the midpoint in its length he placed a park, later named Lincoln Park, giving this stretch of road balance and grace. The street did not develop with shops, however, and its houses are placed back from the sidewalk, behind lawns that contribute to Capitol Hill's atmosphere as a green neighborhood.

The workers who built the Capitol were among the first residents of the Hill. In 1790, the area had a mixed population that included whites and free blacks, at various levels of income. As Congress established itself in the city, boarding houses sprung up to house the peripatetic representatives. Other development focused around the Navy Yard. By the 1820s, Capitol Hill was the center of the city's social life. At the end of the Civil War, Washington's social center began to move to Dupont Circle, but the increasing number of federal workers and freed slaves found housing on the Hill. In 1873, Eastern Market was built and between 1875 and 1895 developers built block after block of formulaic town houses, varying and upgrading them with stained glass windows or slate roofs.

The McMillan Plan resurrected East Capitol Street as an important axis. It was envisioned as a mall lined with public and semipublic buildings, terminating in a riverside sports center. Except for reclamation of the riverbanks for parks in the 1920s and 1930s, this vision was never realized. Robert F. Kennedy Stadium, home of the Washington Redskins football team, was built in 1961, and plans to rebuild or remove it have pointed out how much a landmark it has become. Through the rest of the century, until after World War II, Capitol Hill remained a convenient intown neighborhood.

After World War II, Veterans' Administration loans, the Federal Highway Act, and a burgeoning Civil Rights movement gave whites and blacks more housing choices, and many chose the suburbs. Like other urban neighborhoods, Capitol Hill was left to lower-income residents. Capitol Hill was studied under various urban renewal proposals, but funding and construction priority was given to Southwest, and Capitol Hill was preserved by default. Renovation of the Hill's homes began slowly in the 1950s, and, although the 1968 riots slowed downtown investment, the Hill remained an attractive location because of its convenience. In the 1970s a new generation bought and renovated Hill town houses. Gentrification began at first in areas closest to the Capitol building.

Capitol Hill was declared a historic district in 1976. It is the city's largest historic district with buildings dating from 1791. Historic designation, however, does not guarantee a pristine preservation of the neighborhood and its buildings. Historians and neighbors face off over building renovations and additions to private homes and to public buildings like Eastern Market. Since 1976, further zoning restrictions have been overlaid to limit redevelopment to changes that are physically in scale with the existing town houses and that preserve the Hill as a residential neighborhood.

The character of Capitol Hill is created by a congenial layering of details that has developed over time. L'Enfant's grid pattern is broken by traffic circles and the larger squares, Lincoln and Stanton Parks, which form a walkable and varied street pattern. The buildings lining the streets behind dooryards make up a consistent streetscape of sidewalk, garden, and building wall. The scattered pattern of development over time finds single-family homes next to row houses and row houses that vary between stone and brick, some with arched windows, some with projecting bays, some with turrets and gables.

In the shadow of the Capitol a neighborhood thrives around the still-working Eastern Market. Butchers and produce vendors, crafts, antiques, and junk draw customers from the neighborhood and beyond to a now rare urban market experience. The popularity of the market has also served as an anchor for smaller surrounding commercial endeavors, prompting architectural renovations.

Today Capitol Hill remains a neighborhood that is home to senators and secretaries, blacks and whites. Its town houses have proven to be durable and flexible, serving as single family houses, apartments, and sometimes offices or stores. ■

1. Kaupp Residence
313 9th Street, S.E.
Weinstein Associates Architects *1989*

Amy Weinstein's work on Capitol Hill is a contribution to the cityscape and is an ongoing examination of urban and architectural themes. This row house addition is a simple conservatory-type space, largely hidden by a lush magnolia tree. Its scale is completely comfortable with the neighborhood and the original house, yet the detail is bold enough to stand out.

Weinstein describes herself as a modern architect, but finds, like many contemporary architects, that one of the faults of modernism was its rejection of small, scale-giving detail. Weinstein tries to incorporate that detail into her work while maintaining a modern stance. Her details are clearly informed by contemporary structural demands and capabilities; for example, her brick walls are screens rather than structural support. She does not literally copy historical details, but finds her own patterns and forms that refer to the past.

2. 816–820 East Capitol Street, N.E.
Smith, Blackburn, Stauffer *1992*

Much of the way a city looks is a product of time and economy. Because Capitol Hill's town house rows were constructed as simple homes for the middle class, their size and amenities reflected a modest market. They are small compared to today's homes, and their variations were made possible by machine-made details and decorations chosen from catalogues. The developer could make a profit with a simple building. Today new housing is built like a car: the profit is in the extras. Walk-in closets, whirlpool tubs, and

decks help the developer maximize the site and the profit, sometimes to the detriment of existing physical context. At first glance this row of town houses seems to have borrowed details from neighboring buildings, but a closer look will reveal that they alternately re-create details and add modern touches such as pipe rails. The buildings do not pick up on the rhythm of their neighbors, however. A typical Hill town house is divided into three bays, the doorway bay being the smallest. In these new town houses all the bays are equally sized, making a subtle change in the streetscape.

3. 303–305 7th Street, S.E.
Weinstein Associates Architects *1987*

This small commercial building, just down the street from Eastern Market, shares the height and setback of its modest neighbors, but its facade, highlighted with bold details, takes a different attitude from the neatly done renovations on the block. Its twin door-

ways beneath a single arch split by paired columns are historic in a vaguely Victorian way. But there is no strict historicism here; an exposed steel beam runs as a lintel above the doorways.

This is a delightful addition to the streetscape of comfortable commercial buildings anchored by Eastern Market. Its exuberance fits in with the bustle of a market street.

fronts help anchor this neighborhood commercial street.

As with this designer's other work, pattern is a defining feature of the facade. Rather than Victorian references, the motifs here are appropriately Art Deco. The pattern in the window lintels and frieze is based on a design drawn from a 1930s wallpaper pattern.

The pattern in the concrete sidewalk echoes the building's curves, and a change from concrete to brick between the Pennsylvania Avenue and 6th Street facades reflects a change in character from a main street to a neighborhood street. The facade was re-created by reusing original brick saved when glass storefronts were enlarged. The newer upper floors are distinguished by a glazed brick pattern.

4. 666 Pennsylvania Avenue, S.E.
Weinstein Associates Architects *1991*

An unstinting attention to detail makes this building a quiet tour de force. The former S.S. Kresge store was not eligible for landmark designation on Capitol Hill since the historic district includes only buildings built between 1790 and 1920. Nevertheless, the building's Art Moderne curve fits the Pennsylvania Avenue site, and its 6th Street store-

5. Penn Theater
650 Pennsylvania Avenue, S.E.
John Eberson, *1933*
David M. Schwarz/Architectural Services *1983*

This building, like its neighbor at 666 Pennsylvania Avenue, S.E, was ineligible for landmark designation because of its date of construction. Nevertheless, its redevelopment reflects the

designers' and the community's appreciation of the social and aesthetic value of older buildings.

Although the Penn Theater no longer offers entertainment to Capitol Hill residents, its vibrant facade remains a landmark. Renovation combined residential and office uses. A brick neo-Georgian addition with an entrance at 649 C Street provides a focus and image for the residential part of the project.

The commercial part of the project rises up behind the original Art Deco facade along Pennsylvania Avenue. Setbacks at varying heights echo the horizontal lines of the original, highlighting them in white brick against a blue glazed-brick background. The limestone storefronts are new construction. The two parts of the project are arranged around an interior courtyard.

6. 518 C Street, N.E.
Weinstein Associates Architects *1991*

In this office project, Amy Weinstein uses many of the motifs she has explored in her Capitol Hill work, but in a more complex way. Projecting, screenlike bays emphasize the use of brick as a veneer rather than a structure, brick patterns enliven the facade, and gables create an animated roofline.

The corner site on a traffic circle created by the L'Enfant Plan demands special treatment. A building must have a scale and weight that anchors such a highly visible site. This building's rounded corner tower, a slate-clad cylinder seen through a brick screen, is reminiscent of the churches on the intersection's other corners but, as with other work by Weinstein, this element is not a slavish copy of historical form or detail. Patterning is bolder and more varied than earlier work and the gable supports are more strongly sculptural, creating a plasticity and interest on the corner site.

7. 317 Massachusetts Avenue, N.E.
Weinstein Associates Architects *1985*

This four-bay building was the architect's first on Capitol Hill and introduces themes explored in her later work. Three gabled bays, punched out with half circles, rise as screens in front of sloped, greenhouse-type windows. Although the designer uses brick, a historical material, its application is clearly as a veneer and not structural. This modern approach within a historic context typifies this architect's work.

The building facade is further elaborated with patterned stringcourses at each floor level, highlighting the windows. In later work, such as 666

Pennsylvania Avenue (see number 4), Weinstein's use of pattern becomes bolder and more clearly defines the building facade. This building's large arched doorway in the fourth gable is reminiscent of other Victorian buildings on the Hill. This type of detail, along with attention to scale, height, and setback, makes Weinstein's work eminently comfortable in its setting.

8. Thurgood Marshall Federal Judiciary Office Building
2nd and E Streets, N.E.
Edward Larrabee Barnes (Michael Barratt) *1992*

The Judiciary Office Building finishes the composition of three buildings envisioned by McMillan Commission architect Daniel Burnham more than 80 years ago. In his plan, Union Station was to be symmetrically framed by equally ornate Beaux-Arts buildings. The Post Office was constructed in 1914, but this site to the east of the station remained vacant.

Here a contemporary building meets its classical neighbors. No doubt the architect was inspired by instruc-

tions from the Architect of the Capitol to design a building that would last 200 years.

The typical florid Beaux-Arts facade has been reduced here to a simple composition of repeated stacked rectangular windows topped with arched windows. A cornice line divides the upper portion of the facade, which is articulated with smaller rectangular and square windows. The building's two wings meet at a glass atrium entrance, which appears as a weightless cube framed by heavy masonry.

The building lacks the classical anchors that signal beginning, middle, and end and create a defining scale. The use of repetition to define a building and its space is most effective when it reaches a point of culmination, for example, a dome or central pavilion. In this meandering building there is no end in sight.

9. 900 2nd Street, N.E.
Daniel Burnham *1908*
Michael Oxman *1988*

This simple building, designed by the architect of Union Station, served as a railroad freight depot until the late 1960s. It is a utilitarian brick shed, but it has a graceful solidity that comes from the Beaux-Arts attention to detail. After sitting vacant for fifteen years, it was renovated for offices and lobby retail space after its purchase in 1984.

The three-story brick building runs between 2nd Street and the Union Station railyards. It rises above 2nd Street on a plaza level in order to stay at grade with the railyards. This change in topography was used to create below-grade offices that are naturally lit through skylights.

The impact of its facade comes from the repetition of arched doors and windows. The human scale and neatly finished details create a pleasing composition. A bonus is the serendipitous space created out of the former loading dock. Now a covered porch, it overlooks the railyards and runs the length of the building. For a train buff, this is a great place to eat lunch on a warm day and is the kind of found space that is scarce in such a meticulously planned city as Washington.

10. Union Station
Massachusetts Avenue between 1st and 2nd Streets, N.E.
Daniel Burnham 1908
Harry Weese and Associates/Benjamin Thompson Associates 1989

The location of Union Station behind the Capitol was a result of the McMillan Plan. The B&O Railroad had a station on the Mall until 1909. The noise, soot, and appearance did not fit in the McMillan Commission's vision of the Mall as a grand monumental space, and commission member and architect Daniel Burnham was instrumental in convincing the railroad to move. The dramatic site he offered provided a terminus for Massachusetts Avenue, an axis of the L'Enfant Plan.

The station's site and its architecture are archetypes of the Beaux-Arts school of design. Based on Roman models, the station's formal symmetrical massing sets up three central arches flanked by lower arcades and anchored by arched corner pavilions. The whole, inside and out, is decorated with a full complement of columns, garlands, and statuary. The flat planes of the facade are inscribed with maxims on travel as a necessity to commercial and cultural superiority. In the entrance plaza, Columbus in his fountain leads the way.

As train travel decreased, the station

lost its utility and began to look like a white elephant. For a time it was boarded up and turned over to pigeons. Travelers were routed to trains through a makeshift wooden tunnel, a sad contrast to the station's vaulted halls.

A 1976 renovation as a visitors' center was an ill-conceived failure. It was hard to draw tourists off their beaten paths to watch a slide show of Washington when the real thing was just down the street. Placing the exhibit in a hole excavated out of the main hall's floor made it even less appealing.

A 1989 renovation that combined boutiques, restaurants, and expanded train and Metro service capitalized on a renewed interest in older buildings and successes in other cities with festival marketplaces, which had recast shopping as entertainment. The station became a destination for visitors, whether they had arrived by train or not, and for residents of the Hill and the metropolitan area. A traveler who at one time could not have bought a newspaper before boarding a train now can buy a suitcase and everything to put in it—as well as a newspaper from any major American city.

The renovation also restored the main hall as a grand space while using smaller side halls and even spaces up under the arches. The concourse space behind the main hall is also filled with shops and restaurants, inserted on a mezzanine level that retains the openness of the hall. This approach preserves the vaulted halls while generating activity to animate them.

11. Postal Square
Massachusetts Avenue, North Capitol and 1st Streets, N.E.
Graham and Burnham *1914*
Shalom Baranes Associates *1992*
Florance Eichbaum Esocoff King *1993*

Sometimes the most significant impact on a city space entails no change at all. Because the Post Office was part of a building triad that terminated a grand axis of the L'Enfant Plan, it was important to find a new use for it that would

preserve its facade and scale.

In response to changing technology and shifting populations, the Postal Service moved in 1986 from this intown mail handling facility to one in northeast Washington. Once it was important to be near the train station; now airport and freeway access are vital.

Before moving out, the Postal Service explored on-site expansion and renovation, but the site could not accommodate the need for large, open horizontal spaces for sorting mail.

As a District landmark, the building was not threatened with demolition, and its renovation was reviewed by the Commission of Fine Arts. The facility was built to complement Union Station, and its renovation did not alter the facade. Moreover, it strove to restore public interiors to their 1914 appearance. The original 800,000 square feet of the building were renovated for offices and another 400,000 square feet were inserted into the interior courtyard. The completed building includes offices, a post office, and a

postal museum in the former courtyard, now a covered atrium.

The Postal Museum draws visitors into what would otherwise be just an office building. Its exhibits feature rare and valuable stamps and its design cleverly incorporates postal graphics, like the wavy lines of a franking mark, into a railing balustrade.

The building's architecture continues to frame Union Station, and its new uses complement the station's shops and restaurants. Its office workers are a ready market, and the Postal Museum draws tourists and visitors.

12. 800 North Capitol Street, N.W.
Hartman-Cox Architects *1991*

The work of Hartman-Cox has moved from a warm modernism that incorporated historic details to an almost imitative historicism that sometimes seems to begrudge modern details. This neo-Romanesque office building responds to the scale and materials of the adjacent Government Printing Office (GPO)

and Gonzaga High School.

The boxy mass of the building corresponds to the height and setback of the GPO and picks up its cornice line. Rectangular windows at the base run up the facade and define the corners that flank the facade's rounded arches. The arches are linked at the base and enclose a series of vertically stacked windows on the facade. The roofline is marked by smaller arched and rectangular windows beneath a heavy, bracketed cornice. Deep window reveals in the curtain wall create the illusion of massive, load-bearing walls.

This finely detailed, historically styled building is stealth architecture. It fits into its context so well that it gives few clues to its age and architect.

13. Hart Senate Office Building
2nd and C Streets, N.E.
John Carl Warneke *1973–1982*

The purpose and image of Washington require government buildings to be an embodiment of nationhood. In emulation of ancient democracies, early architects used classicism to express national goals. Modern architecture's break from the classical idiom has left designers searching for new symbols. The Hart Senate Office Building is a result of that search—a struggle highlighted by earlier Senate office buildings.

The formal hierarchy and rich ornament of the Russell Senate Office Building (Carrère and Hastings, 1908) make it an archetype of Beaux-Arts classicism. Fifty years later the Dirksen Senate Office Building (Eggers and Higgins, 1958) stripped the ornament and altered the hierarchy, placing a pediment without a door as an element to match the Russell Building's pedimented entrance. Further, its windows, rather than individual openings in a masonry wall, are ranged in vertical rows alternating with masonry panels.

A generation later the Hart Senate Office Building abandoned any pretense of Beaux-Arts hierarchy and orna-

ment. Only the marble sheathing remained. The facade is composed of an overall pattern of rectangular windows, and neither cornice nor entrance is marked. But modern buildings can convey monumentality: I. M. Pei's National Gallery is a rich and evocative work. By comparison, this seems a meanly conceived and finished work.

14. Folger Shakespeare Library
201 East Capitol Street, S.E.
Paul Philippe Cret *1932*
Hartman-Cox Architects *1983*

The scale, materials, and details of the original Folger Library mediate between the monumental and domestic scales of Capitol Hill. This sensitive insertion into an established fabric is continued by the Hartman-Cox addition.

The new reading room on the south facade is tucked into the space left by Cret's U-shaped building layout. The addition's impact on the street is minimal. The entrance remains on East Capitol Street, and the addition can be seen from an alley in the rear. The internal addition, however, is a light-filled barrel vault enclosing a serene space. The addition's exterior repeats the strong planes of the original with a

series of fluted marble panels hung on a steel frame.

15. Library of Congress, James Madison Memorial Building
Independence Avenue and 1st Street, S.E.
DeWitt, Poor, and Shelton *1980*

This stripped classical box was conceived in the 1960s but completed by 1980, when a taste for ornament and decoration in architecture had returned with postmodernism.

The plain facade of the building seems to go on forever. It is a mammoth box built using a simplified classical hierarchy in deference to its neighbors. Anchored corners flank a central bay of vertical marble panels. Slender columns support an overhang and the building is topped with a recessed attic story. The library is set above the sidewalk and behind a paved plaza.

The Madison building is silent. It speaks of none of the glories of knowledge or beauties of scholarship celebrated by the sculpture, mosaic, inscriptions, and design of the late 19th-century Jefferson Building across the street.

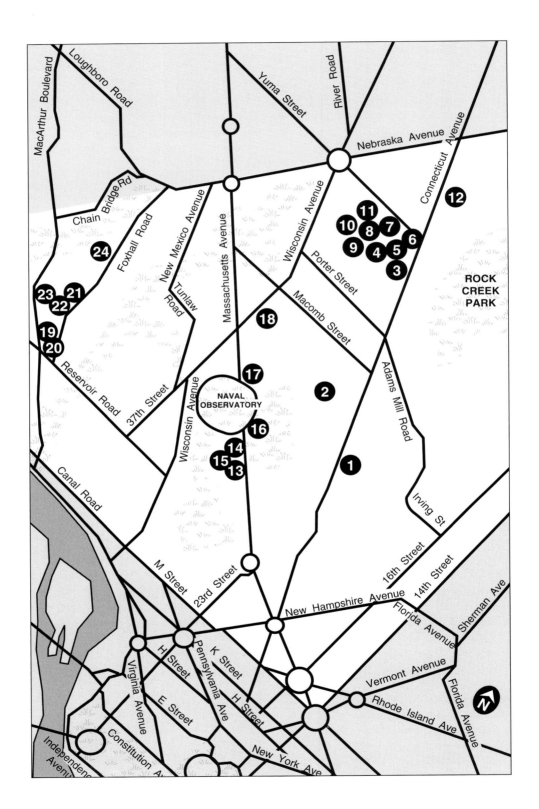

Northwest

It is a beautiful place, as American cities go, made beautiful by its trees, skies, fogs, rivers, low green hills, even by the rich chaos of its buildings, a chaos subdued by the city's magnificently ordered plan.

ELBERT PEETS, WPA GUIDE, 1942

The hills of Northwest Washington developed as country estates that were a cool escape from the city's infamous summer miasmas. Today these neighborhoods retain an air of repose and escape, of comfortable houses amid green parks. The Woodley Park neighborhood is named for the Georgian manor house, Woodley, and Cleveland Park is named for the president who found respite there from a White House without air conditioning.

Development of Northwest followed the pattern of many outlying areas and was influenced by social and political changes. The high ground of Northwest and its undeveloped parklike land tracts were attractive and healthful. The settlements and farms carved out of land grants later became attractive to wealthy residents, institutions, and embassies. As early as 1860, the Rock Creek stream valley was eyed for a public park. Congress was effectively convinced that the park had national value, and its boundaries were established in 1891.

With the opening of a streetcar line along Connecticut Avenue to the new community of Chevy Chase in 1892, the area became convenient for commuters. The large houses in Cleveland Park, architect designed and each one different, were expensive for their time at $5,000 to $8,000, and were intended for professional buyers earning salaries. In the 1920s, convenience shops were developed along Connecticut and Massachusetts Avenues to serve this new suburban population.

As in other Washington neighborhoods, the large houses of Northwest became less attractive during the Depression, and many were divided into flats and rooms-to-let under wartime housing pressures. Later generations found the old houses conveniently close to downtown business areas, restored them to single-family homes, and established neighborhoods of residents committed to protecting their community from threats of high-rise development and freeway construction.

The ancient Roman architect Vitruvius condensed the qualities of good architecture to three: firmness, commodity, and delight. It is a lasting notion that is expressed in the buildings of Northwest Washington and continued in new development. Commercial and apartment buildings along Connecticut Avenue respect the context created by their neighbors and project a distinct style in high quality materials. New institutional uses continue to add cachet to a community of rich and varied architecture. ■

1. 2631–2639 Connecticut Avenue, N.W.
Martin and Jones *1989*

Martin and Jones's work elsewhere in Washington exhibits a sensitivity to neighborhood context. They take subtle clues and give them a defining twist. Here, using simple materials in deference to the client's limited budget, the architects have created the kind of old-fashioned retail building that works well on an urban street.

Gray brick, stucco, and steel frame are composed to create a streetscape hierarchy. Horizontally the storefronts are flanked by two projecting bays that link the building to its row house neighbors. Vertically the second-story office space is fronted by a steel-frame pergola and the bays are topped by a heavy cornice. The simple composition is striking, and storefronts flush on the sidewalk, rather than hidden under an arcade or in an interior mall, are effective.

2. Embassy and Chancery of Switzerland
2900 Cathedral Avenue, N.W.
William Lescaze *1959*

Lescaze, a Swiss-born architect, was one of the earliest practitioners of European modernism in America. His Philadelphia Savings Fund Society building, completed in partnership with George Howe in 1932, became a modern icon. The PSFS was the first International Style skyscraper in the country. Its banking hall and office tower eschew ornament for a rectilinear expression of function and structure.

In the Swiss Embassy, Lescaze explores linear patterns in a composition of solids and space, defined by buff brick and glass. The building is composed of two pavilions linked by a glass hall. A long rectangular block of buff brick broken by regularly placed rectangular windows runs along the side of the site. This wing is connected by a glass hall to a smaller square pavilion of glass and metal frames anchored with a buff brick corner.

In contrast to the containment of a stately house such as the British

Embassy, here the asymmetry of modern architecture breaks itself apart to articulate uses. Offices are behind the repeated windows and ceremonial space lies behind the glass pavilion.

The building's scale and materials make it a comfortable fit in a dense neighborhood of homes and institutions of varying historic styles.

3. Intelsat
4100 Connecticut Avenue, N.W.
John Andrews International *1985*

Looking like one of its own satellites fallen to earth, this glassy assemblage of towers and cubes nestles on a hill over Connecticut Avenue. The

high-tech architecture reflects the space-age mission of this consortium of 110 countries.

Octagonal office pods are punctuated by stair towers and linked by atria in an arrangement that catches natural lighting. The atria, each one with a different interior design ranging from pastoral gardens to Russian Constructivism, are linked along a central corridor and intended as informal gathering places. The facade alternates brushed steel panels with windows covered by three-dimensional tubular steel framing hung with steel panels.

The building breaks the urban pattern of Connecticut Avenue which is lined with a variety of apartment buildings and shops, most of which edge the sidewalk. Intelsat is set back from the street amid lawns and trees. Along Connecticut Avenue the building is a distant object, while along Tilden the trees shelter a public park.

The building is designed to maximize passive solar energy and natural cooling. The mirrored glass block that sheathes the stair towers maximizes solar effects, and sodded roof gardens further insulate the building.

4. International Center
International Drive at Connecticut Avenue, N.W.
Edward D. Stone, Jr., and Associates
1970

Through its embassies, the world converges on the political, social, and physical landscape of a capital city. In Washington, embassies vary from estate sites, like the French, Danish, or British embassies, to town houses marked with national seals and flags that blend into the streetscape. At International Center, Washington has its first embassy subdivision.

In 1964, after a District zoning ordinance made it more difficult to locate embassy buildings in residential neighborhoods, Congress directed the State Department to establish an area for new embassies. A 1968 plan by landscape architect Edward D. Stone, Jr., was approved by the National Capital Planning Commission in 1970. The plan, for the former National Bureau of Standards site, allocated six acres for Intelsat and created 23 one-acre embassy sites. Plan standards mandated that embassies be domestic in scale, not more than four stories, and that they preserve the site's hilly topography. The center is only partially complete. Visitors will find curb cuts for future buildings and can imagine the dense complex this will someday be.

State Department standards also require that embassies at International Center reflect their national character, but the character of the subdivision—one-acre lots cheek by jowl—limits the architect's ability to make a statement. On an estate site, with a setting that creates presence for the building, an embassy can be daring or even outrageous. But line up the Brazilian, French, Danish, and Finnish embassies on one-acre lots along a residentially scaled street and dignity begins its slide into Disneyland. Most designers have opted for simple buildings lightly ornamented with regional references.

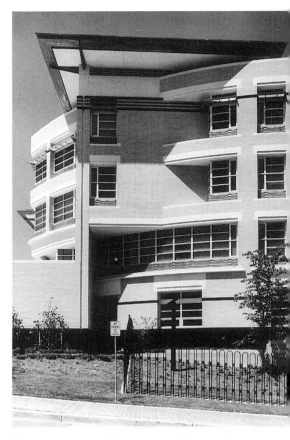

4a. Chancery of Singapore
3501 International Place, N.W.
RTKL Associates *1993*

The State Department's requirement that embassies in the International Center reflect national character can sometimes place both the architect and the nation in the difficult position of interpreting history and current events.

The country's indigenous architectural style may be a vernacular or residential style inappropriate to the scale and requirements of a modern embassy, or it may reflect a colonial past at odds with national goals.

The Singapore Embassy solves the problem by applying a few local motifs—the overhanging eaves of bungalows and wood windowframes, mullions, and louvers—to an artfully detailed, scaled, and sited building. The use of these motifs is simple, direct, and in proportion to the contemporary building they decorate. The broad-pitched roof is a firm finish to the building. The windows are grouped in pleasing patterns, and their wood framing adds warmth to the facade.

In an interesting transfer of influences, these motifs are reminiscent of the work of Frank Lloyd Wright who was, in turn, influenced by the subtleties and clean lines of oriental art and architecture.

4b. Israeli Chancery
3514 International Drive, N.W.
Cohen, Haft, Holtz, Kerxton *1981*

4c. Embassy of Ghana
3512 International Drive, N.W.
Brown and Wright *1989*

4d. Jordanian Embassy
3504 International Drive, N.W.
Leo A. Daly *1983*

4e. Bahrainian Chancery
3502 International Drive, N.W.
The Architect's Collaborative *1982*

The embassies of the Middle Eastern nations of Israel (4b), Jordan (4d), and Bahrain (4e) use a similar design approach. Their buildings are sheathed in various sand colors and are composed of massed rectangular shapes, and are punched with artfully placed and shaped openings. The buildings evoke images of desert strongholds with thick walls to hold in the cool air and small windows to ward off the sun. In these embassies and in the neighboring embassy of Ghana (4c), activity is focused on a private interior, not the

public exterior. The buildings seem to be small pieces of their countries transplanted to a green Washington hillside. Ghana and Israel both use decorative motifs based on cultural symbols to further distinguish themselves. The fence of the Israeli embassy repeats a menorah motif, and the tribal motifs on the wall of the Ghanian Embassy are taken from patterns originally stamped on cloth expressing ethical, aesthetic, and religious values.

4f. Chancery of Kuwait
3500 International Drive, N.W.
Skidmore Owings and Merrill, New York *1982*

This is International Center's most elegant building to date, a satiny aluminum steel cube atop a glass base. It takes its sharp elegance from a dramatic use of its materials.

The metal box of the building opens at a tilted corner cutout containing large square windows marked by diagonal struts. The downward and inward direction of the struts emphasizes the building's entry just below. The struts also emphasize the visual tension created by a seemingly weightless glass box supporting a dense metal mass.

The building's rectilinear design

motif is continued on the interior. Through the frosted glass of the base one can just make out an elaborately detailed screen in Islamic patterns of squares and interlocking diamonds.

stodgy phoniness that is shown up by its elegant and sometimes challenging neighbors. There is no wit in the use of historical details, and the facade's lightness is insubstantial rather than graceful.

4g. Federal Building
3507 International Place, N.W.
Leo A. Daly *1990*

Ironically, the State Department has ignored its own requirement that buildings in International Center reflect a national style. Its own administrative center has Georgian massing and Palladian windows and is decorated with an English rose motif. Perhaps its most American characteristic is the pastiche of historical styles haphazardly used to create an impression of authority and solidity.

Two blocklike wings flank a central, recessed entry whose primary feature is a grandiose window. The gables and cornice lines topped with a tile roof, along with the other details that give scale to the building, lack the solidity of their Beaux-Arts big brothers in the Federal Triangle.

Overall, the building has a sort of

4h. Egyptian Embassy
3521 International Court, N.W.
Daniel, Mann, Johnson and Mendenhall *1993*

So many ancient Egyptian images—pyramids, obelisks, sphinxes—have been absorbed by the architecture of American popular culture, from old movie houses to new casinos, that it is hard to design an Egyptian-style building without creating a comic book version of an ancient temple.

The architects here have shown restraint in topping a white, flat-roofed, modern office box with a flared cornice and articulating the facade with long, paired rectangular windows. The building is fronted by an Egyptian-style gate whose wide base narrows as it rises to a flared cornice. In its simple way, the building meets State Department requirements and maintains its dignity.

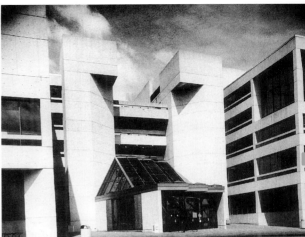

4i. Embassy of Austria
3524 International Court, N.W.
Boeckl/Gates *1992*

The embassy architect faced with a
requirement to reflect national character has two choices. The first is to create a standard office block with
adjustments for site and particular
needs, which announces its nationality
in applied decoration. The architect's
second option is to create a building
expressive of national concerns and
goals. *Architectural Review* noted that
the transparency of the new Finnish
Embassy opens views to "almost
untouched woodland," and appropriate
gesture from a "nation of tree lovers."

The Austrian Embassy uses the
graphic, rectilinear decorative motifs of
the Vienna Secessionist movement.
This group of artists, architects, and
craftsmen believed in an integration of
all the arts and expressed their work in
cubic, geometric forms. The flat planes
of the building are the blank canvas for
a linear design of windows and squares
arranged to create a simple frieze. The
rectilinearity is further emphasized by
pulling each facade slightly away from
the corner.

5. University of the District of Columbia
4200 Connecticut Avenue, N.W.
Bryant and Bryant/Ellerbe Becket *1972*

Campuses are special places, especially
in the city. By walking a fine line
between self-enclosure and connection,
they have a quality of respite that
comes from an arrangement of buildings and spaces that do not always
have to meet the imperatives of real
estate economics. Even a modern campus that lacks the patina of ivy-covered
walls can be a friendly place of human-
scaled buildings arranged to create
both formal and intimate spaces.

This complex of concrete-walled
buildings is in the tradition of 1970s
modernism that used blank facades and
meaningless protuberances to articulate
buildings. Entrances are not symboli-
cally marked, and dark glass windows
further distance the facade.

It is hard to imagine the brutalist
buildings of UDC ever taking on the
authority of age. Their urban location is
irrelevant. The austere buildings lack
scale-giving detail and are connected
by a maze of hard-edged plazas that
create an image of stultifying bureaucracy rather than active learning.

6. Van Ness Station
4250 Connecticut Avenue, N.W.
Hartman-Cox Architects *1983*

Van Ness Station suffers from the architectural malady of "complex-itis," too much building built at one time, no matter how delightfully detailed or thoughtfully sited. The primary symptom is an enervating sameness of streetscape.

Van Ness Station is nicely detailed. Curves and stripes of a darker color in the buff brick recall 1930s commercial architecture. The glass window bands of the upper-story offices are broken by mullions. A lively postmodern touch is a central column in the middle of the entrance that supports a broken cornice.

The building's ground-floor storefronts pull away from the street to create a large sidewalk plaza around a Metro station entrance, but the space is undefined, and the eddy of activity that should flow around a metro stop and office complex next to a university does not materialize.

7. The Saratoga
4601 Connecticut Avenue, N.W.
David M. Schwarz/Architectural
Services *1989*

Zoning along Connecticut Avenue created a street lined with apartment buildings broken every half mile or so by a two-block commercial area. Most are served by a Metro station or bus stop, and the more interesting ones have taken on an urbane character of active mixed uses. As the city expanded outward, the style of the apartment buildings changed from neoclassical to fantasy Moorish to streamlined Art Deco to sleek modern. The complete environment is a pleasant mix of apartment buildings alternating with single-family homes, parks, and commercial centers.

The Saratoga fits in well as the latest addition to the time line of architectural styles expressed in grand apartment buildings. The building uses details seen elsewhere on the avenue: gables, balconies, and limestone detailing against a brick background. Rather than merely applying these details to a modern box, the architect follows through, adjusting the building to its site to create spaces and setting up vertical and horizontal hierarchies in the facade that finish the building in a solid way and gracefully relate it to the street.

Photo courtesy Pireo Sartogo

8. Italian Chancery
Whitehaven Street and Massachusetts Avenue, N.W.
Piero Sartogo *1996 (projected)*

In a selective competition of nine Italian architects this embassy requested designers to create a building that "would somehow be Italian." The winning design takes its inspiration from the Italian palazzo, which served both as the center of community and a as stronghold against outsiders. Similarly, an embassy is both a representative of its country and a refuge.

This design, however, is intended to do more than imitate. It is a contemporary interpretation that relates to its client and its site. The battered masonry walls rise out of the sloping site, to be punctuated by a rhythmic arrangement of windows. A thin copper roof rests lightly atop a recessed reveal.

The building also acknowledges its location between urban and suburban Washington, overlooking Rock Creek Park. The design splits the building mass diagonally in half, opening a glass-covered atrium to reveal a view from the Brazilian Embassy buildings and Whitehaven Street to the gardens of Dumbarton Oaks. A formal entry plaza is oriented to Massachusetts Avenue, recognizing that street's importance as one of L'Enfant's boulevards.

9. Brazilian Chancery
3000 Massachusetts Avenue, N.W.
Olaro de Campos *1973*

Many Latin American architects were schooled in European and American modernism, but in translation to their own nations and cultures added an exuberance unseen in the stark work of the Bauhaus. A fondness for bending reality by using boldly sculptural forms gives their buildings a distinct grandeur, exemplified in Brazil's capital city of Brasilia.

This building is firmly in the tradition of Latin-American modernism. It is elegantly simple in concept, a box upon a pedestal, but dramatic in exe-

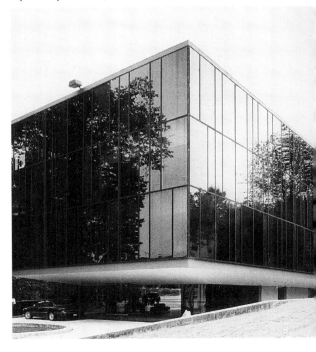

cution, a dark mass hovering on a seemingly weightless base. In the serene, green-trimmed setting of Embassy Row the building is a remarkable piece of sculpture.

10. Embassy of Denmark
3200 Whitehaven Street, N.W.
Vilhelm Lauritzen *1960*

The estate setting overlooking the Dumbarton Oaks gardens imparts instant dignity to this building. The simple composition of linked pavilions sits atop the hill with an air of repose.

The two-story white marble pavilions are linked by a single-story, recessed breezeway. The distinctness of the pavilions is emphasized by frames of white marble that enclose each one. Within these frames the building's horizontal massing is emphasized by the rectilinear patterns of the facade. The glass facades are broken into various patterns by vertical and horizontal elements, marble panels, and windowframes, thus creating patterns that complement each other from pavilion to pavilion.

11. Khalil Gibran Memorial Garden
Massachusetts Avenue, N.W. (west of 30th Street)
Helmuth Obata Kassebaum (Mary Ann Lasch) *1993*

After approval from Congress, a site search that included 13 locations, and review by a multitude of local and federal agencies, the design of this memorial must have seemed easy.

The Khalil Gibran Memorial Foundation wanted not only to memorialize the poet, but recognize his ideas and philosophy. The designer's concept was to introduce Gibran at the garden's

entrance but move the visitor beyond the man to his ideas in a peaceful, contemplative setting. On entering the garden, the visitor passes over a bridge to a small paved area with a sculpture of Gibran. From there a circular path, a reference to Gibran's ideas of harmony and unity, leads to a terrace paved in a traditional Lebanese pattern and furnished with benches carved with quotations from the poet's work. A grove of cedars of Lebanon terminates the sight line through the garden.

The garden's distance from the street, its canopy of mature trees, complementary plantings, and bubbling fountains create a peaceful mood.

12. Embassy of Finland
3301 Massachusetts Avenue, N.W.
Mikko Heikkinen, Marku Komonen *1994*

This embassy was conceived as a reticent building; on completion it will appear as a green hedge. The building is organized as a series of transparent planes that emphasize the surrounding natural landscape, which includes the mature, wooded grounds of Normanstone Park to the rear of the

site. The first plane is a gridded bronze screen. The screen stands free of the building to serve as a support frame for climbing vines, intended to modulate the climate and place the building naturally on its wooded site.

The second screen is the building's central axis, a rectangular atrium around which offices and conference rooms are arranged. The stairs, rooms, and catwalks are suspended in this space, referring to the structure of the bronze screen out front.

The third screen, the glass rear wall of the main reception hall, is visible from the central hall. Directly against these windows are the tall trees of the park, echoing the green screen out front. The building's materials—green, striated copper sheathing and translucent green glass block—have a natural, weathered appearance that reflects changing light patterns and extends the textures of the surrounding woods.

Sandwiched by nature, this building defers to its site in an elegant and inventive way.

13. Washington National Cathedral
Massachusetts and Wisconsin Avenues, N.W.
Vaughan-Bodley *1907–1990*

The National Cathedral takes its poignancy and power from the appropriateness of the Gothic style to express religious faith, from the sheer beauty of its composition and details, and from the dislocation of an Old World style in the contemporary New World. The cathedral has a weight lent by time. It took generations to build in an era when few of our buildings even last a generation.

Within the framework of peaked spires and soaring columns that seem to reach to heaven, the cathedral weaves local and recent history into its decoration and detail. President Wilson

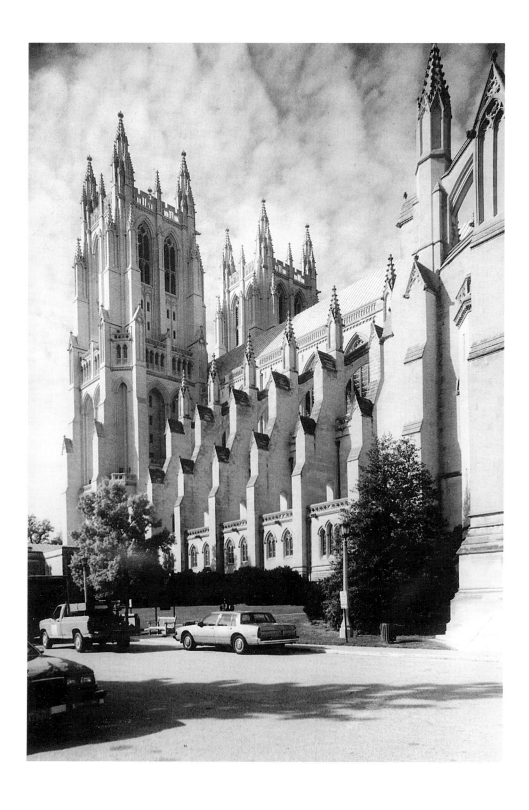

is buried in the nave, our founding president is commemorated in the Washington Bay and the Apollo moon launch is marked by a stained glass window that incorporates a piece of moon rock.

The choice of the Gothic style in 1905 was the result of a three-to-two vote of the building committee. Daniel Burnham and Charles Follen McKim, powerhouses of the McMillan Commission who advocated a neoclassical building, were voted down. The building committee went to the source for Gothic design and hired an English architect, Henry Vaughan, to collaborate with American George Bodley. Their design is modeled on the 14th-century English Gothic style, with a tripartite front, two-aisled nave, curved apse, and a tower over the crossing. With each generation a new supervising architect brought their plan closer to completion. Despite rumblings of modernism, the Gothic style persisted.

The building was topped out in 1990 with the placement of the last finial on the tower. Although medieval in its form, in its details and mission the cathedral remains a relevant and vital touchstone for Washington and the nation.

14. Republic of Germany Chancery
4645 Reservoir Road, N.W.
Egon Eiermann *1964*

This building is so finely sited and executed that it has a timeless elegance, without pretension or bombast. It is placed perpendicular to the road and the hill that rises above it, so that it does not overpower this neighborhood of single-family homes. Rather than taking its presence from a broad facade along the street, it is fronted by a gently sloping, curved drive that sets it on a

platform. The entry drive creates a dynamic approach that sequentially reveals the building.

The siting emphasizes the building's planes, which seem to slide out of the hill. The facade, articulated by four layered grids, also reflects the concept of planes; brown wooden windowframes make up the walls of the building, which is capped by a gray steel structural frame that supports gridded catwalks. Brown fascia boards act as sunscreens, and the entire building is covered with a thin white metal frame that extends beyond it to further emphasize sliding planes.

The entire site is carefully landscaped and detailed to create a unified image. A separate gatehouse uses the same motifs on a smaller scale, and scored concrete retaining walls pick up the linear patterns of the building's grids.

15. Republic of Germany Ambassador's Residence
1800 Foxhall Road, N.W.
O. M. Ungers *1994*

At first glance this residence seems very different from its embassy, but they are similar in many ways. Both use their sites and the nature of their materials to create simple but dramatic structures.

Eiermann designed the embassy to slide out of its hill with a dynamic sense of movement. His student, Ungers, designed the residence to sit square on its site, a temple capping a hilltop. It is a classical image that refers to Washington and the capital's own references to the democracy of ancient Greece.

The choice and arrangement of materials reinforce the temple image. The buff stone exterior is created by a series of rectilinear piers that march across the facade like a temple's columns. The central space of the house is a barrel-vaulted reception room topped with a gable roof, another temple reference. At the same time, the stone contributes to the building's solid feeling just as the steel frames of the embassy form a light and flexible cage.

The classical references continue through the interior. A formal entrance leads to a central reception hall, flanked by smaller sitting and dining rooms. The central hall, like the rest of the house, is detailed with patterns of squares in the floor, wall, ceilings, and windows. The repeated, yet varied patterns tie together a building of meticulous craftsmanship. The central hall's most spectacular feature is the view at its eastern end. The vista of the

Potomac seems to inhabit the room as much as any painting or sculpture.

The architect's concept, "that familiar forms and styles of architectural history can be well blended to form a modern, rational configuration," has been elegantly expressed by this official residence that refers to classical predecessors and a modern neighbor.

16. Mount Vernon College Florence Hollis Hand Chapel
Hartman-Cox Architects *1970*

In 1968 Hartman-Cox completed a master plan for this wooded campus in a residential neighborhood and later built the gatehouse at W Street, a dormitory hall, and this chapel. The brick chapel is designed in a modernist mode, abstracting shapes and images to a graphic result that relates to the site. The building is sited across a ravine to afford views and to keep a small streambed clear.

The chapel's entrance is at the top of a slope, perched at the side of a service road behind a small entry plaza. From there a sloping roof sweeps down the hill. On the building's high side, stepped brick and slate pavilions create the facade.

The sloping roof not only echoes the site, but creates a dramatically formed and lit space on the interior.

17. Mount Vernon College Pelham Dormitory
Hartman-Cox Architects *1971*

In early work, Hartman-Cox combined a graphic modernism with a fine sense of site and scale expressed in historically appropriate materials. This dormitory uses a device the firm also used in Georgetown at Dodge Center to

of structural supports as an aesthetic feature, that reflects the imagery of the exterior.

19. Foxhall Crescents
Foxhall Crescent Court, N.W.
Arthur Cotton Moore/Associates *1982*

Rather than the small English villages and American towns revered by neotraditional town planners, Arthur Cotton Moore took as his model for this housing development the grand residential crescents of London and Bath, an urbane building type that here creates a hybrid urbanism of single-family houses tightly defining the street.

The 26 houses on 25 acres of the former Nelson Rockefeller estate are each about 4,000 square feet and nearly fill their lots. The houses have convex and concave curved facades that edge the street. Low garden walls connect the front facades of adjacent houses and create a continuous wall along the street. Overscaled, mannerist details in brick and limestone mark the facade's windows, doors, and balustrades.

The effect is startling. The almost urban streetscape seems at odds with the two-car garages in the houses' front facades.

express a sloping site. Both buildings take a shape that is at once roof and wall, pierced by openings that catch light and shade.

The shape of both buildings echoes their sites. In this case the dormitory sits atop a steep hill, capping it by continuing its line. Triangular cutouts form balconies and windows, and create an overall pattern of shapes and shadows. Despite the dramatic profile, the building's materials, brick and slate, ease it into the more traditional campus and surrounding neighborhood.

18. St. Patrick's Episcopal Church
4780 Whitehaven Parkway, N.W.
Hartman-Cox Architects *1986*

Architecture magazine noted that this building looks as though its has "been standing at least half a century." The abstracted historicist work of Hartman-Cox has an immediate iconic quality.

Here the architects use the traditional ecclesiastical imagery of a simple chapel. Sloping roofs enclose the space, and the composition, in brick and brownstone, is punctuated by stepped gables and a modest bell tower. The whole is tucked into a wooded site and has a comfortable familiarity. A day school addition of more modern rectilinear forms is less prominent on the site.

The interior uses a graceful system

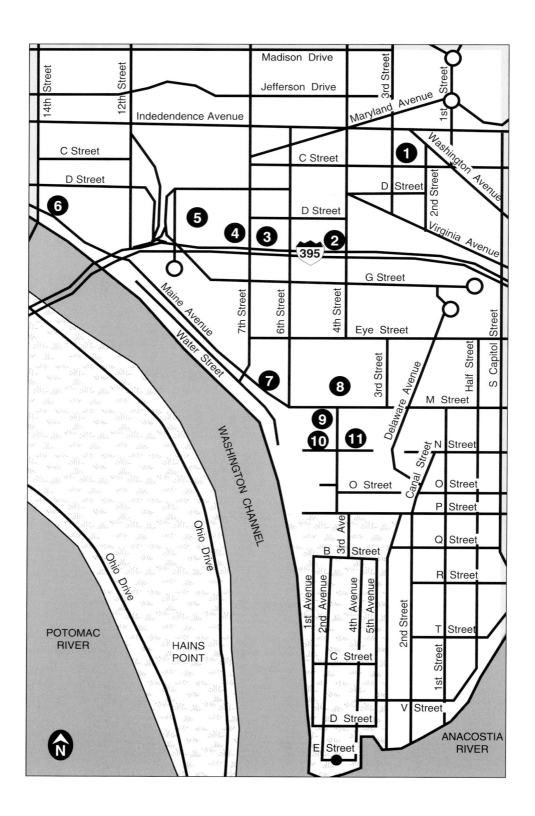

Southwest

"We need only here houses, cellars, kitchens, scholarly men, amiable women, and a few other such trifles to possess a perfect city. In a word, this is the best city in the world to live in - in the future."

GOUVERNEUR MORRIS, 1801

Like the earlier City Beautiful movement, American urban renewal of the 1940s and 1950s had grand designs for the city. City Beautiful planners used aesthetics to promote civic centers and grand promenades that seemed only incidently intended for real people; urban renewal had the authority of sociologists who identified urban pathologies caused by an inadequate environment. Designers of both movements simply found it easy and perhaps fun to sweep away history and create a new environment.

History in Southwest Washington had created an area isolated from the rest of the city by the Washington Canal (now Constitution Avenue), the Mall, and later by the B&O Railroad tracks. In the early 19th century the streets of this riverfront enclave were lined with the spacious homes of ship captains. As real estate values shifted the focus of development, Southwest became an area of warehouses and simple row houses. As the commercial riverfront declined, the area deteriorated into a slum of crowded, substandard housing.

In 1946, Congress authorized creation of the D.C. Redevelopment Land Agency to deal with the city's slums. In 1949, the National Housing Act provided the funding the agency needed. Two redevelopment approaches were proposed for Southwest. Elbert Peets thought that the area's red-brick row houses and apartment buildings had a valuable urban character and should be preserved. His plan was one of minimal intervention into the existing housing stock and street pattern that would have provided low- and moderate-income housing. Peets's approach has been rediscovered by contemporary planners who have embraced the economic, social, and aesthetic values of historic preservation.

Local architectural groups prepared a scheme that changed the area's street plan, preserving only Wheat Row and the Law House, some of the area's finest Federal Style residences. But in the 1950s razing the existing buildings and creating an entirely new environment seemed more progressive to architects and planners who saw social disease in the old buildings they pejoratively called slums.

The 550 acres bordered on the north by the Mall, on the south by the Washington Channel, and on the east by South Capitol Street were cleared in five sections. Developers made applications and proposals for redevelopment, and New York developer William Zeckendorf was chosen. He worked with modernists I. M. Pei and Harry Weese on a plan to rebuild the waterfront and create a neighborhood of town houses and apartments arranged along a central axis that ended with a shopping center. An office complex was proposed adjacent to the Mall. Given the expense and complexity of the entire project, sections were redesignated to other developers and Zeckendorf concentrated on the office complex, L'Enfant Plaza.

The resulting community created by urban renewal places some of the best and worst modern architecture in some the best and worst urban settings. The residential buildings run from banal to enchanting. Some are placed on intimate courtyards or have spectacular views, while others are hemmed in by public housing projects and freeways. Overall, the projects and their buildings are unrelated to each other and still isolated from the rest of the city. On close examination, the architecture of L'Enfant Plaza, the area's commercial centerpiece, reveals subtle variations of quality and finesse, but as a whole it is a windswept metaphor for urban anomie.

As noted by James Goode in *Best Addresses,* perhaps what is most striking about the Southwest urban renewal project is what was not built. The cultural facilities proposed for L'Enfant Plaza, the Ponte Vecchio—a bridge across the Washington Channel lined with shops and cafes designed by Cloethial Woodard Smith—and the national aquarium at the bridge's end on Hains Point all speak of a more complete and vital urban vision. ■

1. Hubert H. Humphrey Federal Office Building
Independence Avenue and 2nd and 3rd Streets, S.W.
Marcel Breuer *1976*

As in his building for the Department of Housing and Urban Development (see number 4), completed nearly a decade earlier, here Marcel Breuer uses bare concrete and the repetition of windows to build up a facade. The window's heavy frames become building blocks that create the larger block of the building. The structure is composed of four heavy concrete facades that appear to hang off the building, anchored by massive corner towers. Sloped concrete fins angle back toward the main block of the building, mimicking a pitched roofline.

Unlike the HUD Building, however, this building begins to respond to the street and ironically, by stepping into

line, loses the impact of heroic modernism. Sculptural expressiveness is swallowed into the streetscape. Although there is a degree of refinement to the detail and execution, the rough materials, empty plaza, and unvaried facade are uninviting. The building begins to fade into the background of bureaucratic buildings, and the viewer's eye is drawn to more exuberant structures along the Mall.

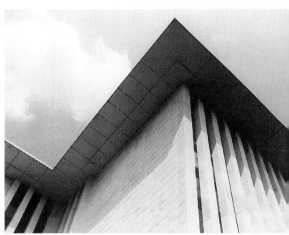

2. Design Center
4th and D Streets, S.W.
Keyes Condon Florance *1982, 1991*

This former refrigeration plant hidden next to railroad tracks is separate from the context of monumental and governmental Washington. Accordingly, the architects were able to concentrate on creating a glamorous warehouse for design and decorating showrooms.

The original brick warehouse was expanded with a crisp glass addition, and the two are tied together with a brick base that stands apart from the buildings like a screen. The brick base is punched with windows, and the glassy block of the addition rises from behind it. The glass curtain wall contrasts with the original brick building and is articulated with thin bands at every floor, while the top and base are articulated with heavier bands.

3. Nassif Building
Department of Transportation
7th Street between D and E Streets, S.W.
Edward Durell Stone *1969*

Some architectural forms are immutable and in Washington particu-

larly make eternal sense. This modernist interpretation of a classic temple form reduces it to a sculpted box, stripping away ornamental pediments and columns. Like Stone's other work, this building explores surfaces with patterns in white marble. The thin vertical window strips and the even thinner overhanging roof are hallmarks of this architect's work. But what might have been repose and elegance in a smaller building is ponderous when it covers an entire city block.

Like the buildings in the Federal Triangle, this building appears to be a solid block from the street facade but is in fact a donut shape arranged around a central courtyard punctuated by a dramatic fountain. But the building relates to the street in the severe manner of its modernist neighbors, without welcoming entrance features, even though its shape begins to reflect the street grid.

4. Department of Housing and Urban Development
7th and D Streets, S.W.
Marcel Breuer *1968*

Buildings send messages, and the one sent by this building may vary with

your point of view. Its repetitive facade may express the blank face of bureaucracy, or its dynamic sweeping shape may evoke a bold new frontier. The building, designed by a giant of modern architecture, epitomizes ideas central to the movement. The sculptural walls of bare concrete are lifted off the site on massive, angular pilotis. The curve of each wall expresses movement. The only details are the repetition of windows, the incised joints between concrete sections, and faint striations left by the formwork. This subtle and unvarying detail expresses the modernist's search for beauty in the repeated processes of the machine rather than the individuality of handwork. The building does not relate well to its site, but that, too, is a feature of modern architecture, which viewed the building as independent from its neighbors. The modern architect was also trying to build a new type of city and deliberately neglected old neighbors. That city was never built, and now the building sits amid cars and parking lots.

5. L'Enfant Plaza
10th Street and Independence Avenue, S.W.
I. M. Pei and Partners *1968*
Vlastimil Koubek *1973*

L'Enfant Plaza was intended to be the centerpiece of Southwest redevelopment; a mix of offices, hotel, shopping, and cultural facilities that would become a new urban gathering place. Instead, either because of program changes or a poverty of concept, it has a bleakness that has become symbolic of everything we dislike about modern architecture.

The Kennedy Center grabbed the cultural facility and the Ponte Vecchio proposed by Cloethial Woodard Smith, which would have linked L'Enfant Plaza to Hains Point via a shop- and cafe-lined footbridge, was abandoned.

PLAZAS

PLAZAS ARE DEFINING places in a city. As buildings enclose spaces and roads travel between them, the plaza breaks the routine of block and grid to draw and focus attention. A successful plaza appears to be a complex place, active with people and visually interesting.

Historically plazas have been used for emphasis. Rome's Piazza San Pietro dwarfs the human figure, but when the Pope addresses the faithful it is barely large enough. Napoleon called Piazza San Marco in Venice the drawing room of Europe, recognizing both its daily social life and its elegant furnishings. Whether we are awed by their size or enveloped by their intimacy, plazas make points about power and leisure.

In 1961, New York City adopted incentive zoning that allowed developers ten additional square feet of commercial space for every one foot of plaza provided on site. It was a popular concept picked up by designers and planners in other cities. While European plazas are enticing breaks in the urban fabric, these New World plazas are forecourts to office buildings. The resulting proliferation of plazas—fully 20 acres in Manhattan— diluted their impact and led urban observer William H. Whyte to study the characteristics of successful plazas. Interviews, time-lapse photography, hypotheses, and analyses led Whyte to conclusions that he called "staggeringly obvious."

Successful plazas have characteristics based less on aesthetics than on human nature and comfort zones. We like to see other people. It is comfortable to be alone in a crowd. Both Farragut and McPherson squares in downtown are crowded at noon, with

What remains are four peach-colored buildings arranged around a plaza off the center axis of 10th Street, which connects the complex to Independence Avenue. The buildings are grouped along the plaza's western edge, removing traffic from the square. The plaza has refined detailing and a repose that looks good in photographs, but its centerless space, vast scale, and low walls are off-putting for pedestrians.

A close look at the buildings reveals that they are not all the same. Pei designed the plaza's plan and the buildings on the north and south sides. Their articulated forms and textured concrete possess a warmth found in few other brutalist buildings. In contrast with the east and west buildings, by Vlastimil Koubek, the refinement of their detail and color is evident.

6. The Portals
14th Street and Maryland Avenue, S.W.
The Weihe Partnership *1991*

Built more than a generation after most of the Southwest neighborhood, this building returns to historical images incorporating architectural details to impart weight and formality. Next to its smooth modernist neighbors, its arches, domes, and elaborate details seem to leap and jump, calling out for attention. Even though the designers chose an architectural style that may seem more friendly, the complex makes the same urban design mistakes as its earlier modern neighbors by omitting walkable links with the rest of the city and by accommodating few activity-generating uses in its plazas or along its streetfronts.

lunchers squeezing onto benches and overflowing onto the grass.

Plazas should have flexible seating, walls that double as benches, and even chairs that can be moved. One of Washington's newest plazas, Market Square, is ringed with low walls and planting beds at a comfortable height and width to sit on. It is also free seating, as an alternative to the cafe seating of Market Square's restaurants. But food is also an important feature of plazas. People linger at cafes and become a lively part of the scenery. Even hot dog vendors are a clue to urban animation. A hot dog cart is always set up at the corner of 17th Street and New York Avenue, across the street from the Corcoran Museum of Art and the Old Executive Office Building, not at the empty plaza just two blocks north.

Good plazas also modulate the climate with trees and water. While the flat expanse of Freedom Plaza is best for organized events, it does not draw casual lingerers and lunchers. They are next door in the cool and shady glade of Pershing Park.

Finally, Whyte noted that plazas must be visibly and physically linked to the street. An inviting view and wide, broad steps draw people in from the sidewalk. Even though the south side of Pershing Park walls itself off from Pennsylvania Avenue traffic, on the north it is at grade and connects with the Willard Hotel.

Whyte's analysis is simple and right; we prove it every day by our own behavior. But it is often overlooked by designers making a grand statement or planners hoping to generate identity and activity from bricks and mortar. While the concrete constructions of a city are important, it is people that endow them with meaning.

7. Arena Stage
6th and M Streets, S.W.
Harry Weese *1961*

In its architecture and urban design, this building has few of the characteristics we associate with a theater, even after a generation of modern architects have stripped buildings of their evocative details. There is no marquee, let alone extravagant volutes or curlicues to signal entertainment and relaxation. Like a good modern building, it expresses its function, housing a theater in the round in an octagonal form. Its urban design, which places it on a lawn, does not generate the cafes and costume shops that often cluster in a city's theater district. Like other contemporary architecture in Southwest it is a fine building that departed from all the urban norms, losing the opportunity to create a neighborhood of physical and social interaction.

8. Town Center Plaza
3rd, 6th, M and I Streets, S.W.
I. M. Pei and Partners *1962*

This project combines apartment towers above a two-story office and retail complex intended to be the focus of the Southwest community. Instead the

complex seems particularly cold, surrounded as it is by parking lots and sandwiched between roads, without the softening effect of the riverfront.

The most notable feature of the Town Center apartment buildings is their glassy facades, which are created by bringing the windows flush with the building's skin. Perhaps when the building was designed this seemed a radical and fresh choice for residential buildings, but now they look like any speculative office building in any city.

The shopping center is a more typically suburban form. The storefronts sit behind a streetfront parking lot. The two-story building is set up on pilotis, creating a dark arcade for shops beneath a reflective glass second story. Together the two stories create a particularly repelling facade.

Consistent with the urban renewal approach taken in Southwest, no attempt was made to retain the characteristics of the older city, and this center looks as if it belongs in the suburbs.

9. Tiber Island
4th and M Streets, S.W.
Keyes, Lethbridge and Condon *1965*

Like other Southwest urban renewal projects, Tiber Island combines town houses with apartments. Also like neighboring projects, it creates many small, wonderful, private spaces unexpected in the city, but relates poorly to the streetscape. The concrete apartment house set up on a glass base abuts the street, and the town houses are behind it, perpendicular to the street, oriented to private courtyards. Underground parking has created opportunity for extensive gardens and landscaping, but also placed a raised, concrete paving stone plaza at the project's center. It is a barren space that blocks view and access to the river.

11. River Park
N Street, S.W.
Charles Goodman *1963*

This town house and apartment development, designed as a demonstration project for Reynolds Aluminum, is unique in its shape and materials. The shining metal roofs of repeated barrel vaults roll down the street with the friendliness of a toy train. The lunettes, or arched ends, of the vaults are filled with glass, and the facades of both the town houses and apartments are detailed with aluminum screens. The tall apartment building is placed in the center of the site and the town houses run along the sidewalk, creating a human-scaled streetscape enlivened by the comings and goings through town house front doors. As in other Southwest residential projects, the internal spaces modulate in a clear hierarchy from public to private, but overall, the project does not make links with adjacent projects to create a physically integrated neighborhood.

10. Harbour Square
500 N Street, S.W.
Cloethiel Woodard Smith *1963*

This building shows how wonderful modern architecture can be. The architect used scale, materials, and details to express the domestic use of these buildings and sited them to catch river views and to create defined spaces that vary between public and private.

The buildings are grouped around three quadrangles and include 448 apartments and 17 town houses. Gardens, paths, and fountains punctuate outdoor spaces exceptional in urban living. The buildings retain a inviting crispness.

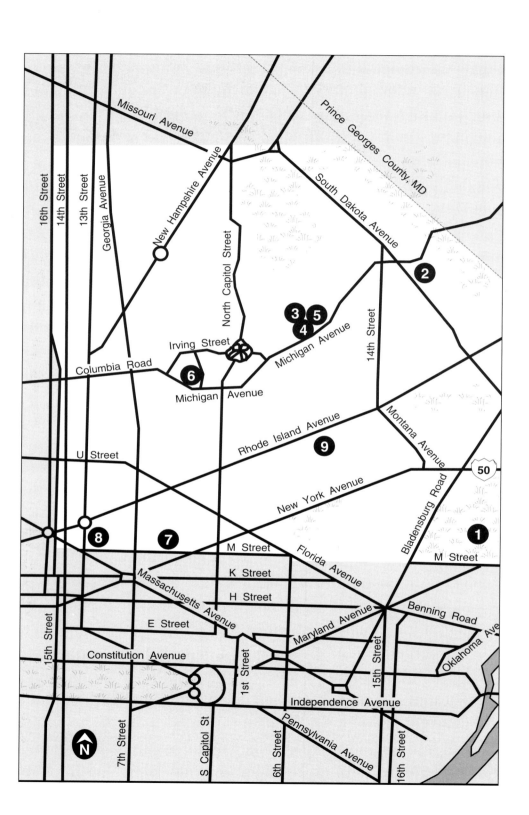

Rest of the District

Three things are to be looked to in a building: that it stand on the right spot; that it be securely founded; that it be successfully executed.

J. W. von Goethe, 1808

For most of the nation and the world Washington is the nexus between the Capitol and the White House, and its offshoots into the embassies, mansions, and offices of Northwest. But beyond the insatiable scrutiny received by the Capitol and the White House is a hidden Washington, off the tourist trail, but with its own treasures, like the McMillan Reservoir, the Le Droit Park neighborhood, and the National Arboretum. The intrepid explorer will find a different city beyond the monumental core, an area of beauty and stillness, of vibrant communities and forgotten blocks.

The focus of development—commercial and residential buildings downtown and around the Capitol and the White House—has left whole quarters of the city untouched. While neglect can sometimes preserve historic artifacts, sooner or later a new generation must come to understand and restore their value. In a sprawling city like Washington, though, many neighborhoods wait for their saviors, and neglect meanwhile means shabby playgrounds, cracked sidewalks, and boarded-up buildings.

But punctuating Washington's outer neighborhoods are civic uses of incredible scale and variety. Early plans for the city set aside large tracts of land in the city's northeast quarter for institutional uses. Some of these hospitals, cemeteries, and universities have grown into sprawling complexes.

These buildings, an eclectic group, are integral to the character and activity of their communities, but, scattered through outer neighborhoods of Washington, they are sometimes overlooked. They represent the evolution of institutions and architectural styles over time, and the depth and variety of communities that contribute to the city. ∎

1. Capitol Columns
United States National Arboretum
3501 New York Avenue, N.E.
Russell Page/EDAW, Inc. *1990*

The Capitol Columns rise on their hill
as a ghostly frame, neither ruin nor
shelter. Their reassemblage is a story of
patriotism and perseverance.

The columns were designed by
Benjamin Latrobe in 1806 to form the
Capitol's east portico and were seen
through to completion by Charles
Bulfinch. The columns predate the
Capitol dome and are formed of sandstone quarried in Aquia, Virginia, and
floated up the Potomac. The columns'
capitals are based on an ancient
Roman design; each one took a
stonecarver six months to complete.
Over the years they served as a backdrop for presidential inaugurations,
from Andrew Jackson's to Dwight
Eisenhower's. When the east portico
was dismantled in a 1958 renovation,
the columns were placed in storage,
first at the Capitol power plant and
later at the Botanical Gardens nursery
on the banks of the Anacostia River.
But preservationists immediately began
lobbying Congress to put them on display.

From their ignominious resting
place in a muddy streambank, the
columns have been resurrected to
frame a plaza that echoes the shape of
the east portico. As many as 50 coats
of paint were removed from the
columns, which were then pinned
together. Their dramatic silhouette at
the top of a grassy slope is emphasized
by a mirroring view in a reflecting
pool. Marble steps once used in the
Senate wing pave the plaza and form a
staircase down the slope to the pool.

The columns are a monument to
nothing but themselves, a sort of disembodied history, but their form and
placement combine to create a moving
and impressive construction.

2. Hospital for Sick Children
1731 Bunker Hill Road, N.E.
Wyeth and Sullivan *1929*
Vosbeck-Vosbeck and Associates *1968*
Weinstein Associates/Herbert Cohen
and Associates *1992*

The service of this hospital has
changed over time and so has its architecture. Originally an escape to fresh
air for city children, its cottage–like
buildings were reminiscent of farmhouses and reflected the site's bucolic
location and purpose. The Norman-
style, steeply gabled farmhouse–type
buildings are typical of the eclectic
designs of the time, which ranged from
stockbroker chateaus to ocean
liner–esque office buildings.

As the hospital provided more particular and specialized medical care for
children well enough to leave a hospital but too ill to go home, its architectural additions became more
institutional—though still like a friendly
elementary school. The first addition is
a series of pavilions that take their
architectural variety not from historical

ornament or mimicry, but from their arrangement of shape and texture.

The most recent addition combines a bit of history and a bit of modernism to create a building that defines its own place and time. Like a child's favorite blanket, the building is richly patterned and flows in and out of the arms of the two existing buildings. Set into a hilly lawn, it peaks up to the residential neighborhood and wraps behind the farmhouse-like original and the 1960s addition. A gabled gate between the original and this addition defines the space and links the buildings. A sweeping, curved pavilion at the corner punctuates the facade with an asymmetrical hierarchy, balancing the gateway and the original.

The building's back face is composed of long, stepped screens, alternating curved and straight facades. Brick patterning sweeps across the building, defining facades, floors, and windows. The addition's patterns and massing define and outline space, linking building styles separated by generations.

3. Catholic University
Edward M. Crough Center for
Architectural Studies
John V. Yanik and Vlastimil Koubek
1990

The long barrel vault of the building, topped by a crown, is a bold shape that provides an element of drama to this renovated gymnasium. The building is clad in a synthetic stucco surface that gives it a uniform appearance emphasizing its simple shed shape. The entrance is marked by a pergola, short, freestanding towers on either side, and a pyramidal roof flanked by two wings. The formal entrance is further marked by an allée of trees. The side of the

building is artfully connected to the site with a gateway of colored decorative structural pieces that extends from the side entrance into a hilly lawn, creating a more informal space.

4. Catholic University
Columbia School of Law
Florance Echbaum Esocoff King *1994*

Unlike the architecture school next door, which gives a new use to an old building and makes the best of an awkward site, the law school of Catholic University extends the campus and creates its own environment.

The university invited four firms to participate in a design charette, an open design process to explore alternative arrangements of uses and buildings. This firm best met the university's goals and was chosen to design a five-acre parcel which included the law school.

The gable-roofed buildings are placed to create a courtyard. The buildings are an arrangement of double sheds, half drums, pergolas, towers, and gables that house an underground parking garage, a student center, a reading room and library, and classrooms and courtrooms for mock trials.

While the site arrangement extends and defines the campus by linking the new buildings with views to the Basilica of the National Shrine of the Immaculate Conception, the building's style also relates to existing campus buildings. They are covered in a patterned brick in shades of gray and buff. These colors and the texture created by the patterning echo the rough finish and mottled gray of the campus's Gothic-style buildings.

5. Catholic University
Hannan Hall
Perkins and Will *1987*

Campus buildings are often designed and built to convey the seriousness of scholarly pursuits. Ivy-covered halls speak with a legitimacy that comes with time. Other new buildings on the Catholic University campus use this language. The patterned brick buildings of the law school are arranged around a classic quadrangle and even a renovated gymnasium is given a new facade marked with formal landscaping.

In contrast, the front facade of this building looks like a suburban interpretation of postmodernism, a boxy mass articulated with grouped windows and decorative round medallions applied to

the surface. The rear facade rises out of the hill and takes a different attitude. It looks like a retro space-age factory with silver, rocket-shaped spires at the top and long, vertical projecting tubes interspersed with glass block. Unlike other campus buildings, this building virtually ignores its context to perch dramatically, if awkwardly, on its hill.

6. Children's Hospital National Medical Center
111 Michigan Avenue, N.W.
Leo A. Daly *1972*

This complex of linked buildings was completed in an era when architects used unornamented material and shape to create a building's form. It was also an age of rising oil prices, and energy efficiency was an important goal as well. Here, canted exterior windows create a sandwich of buffering air between interior windows. Floor upon floor of these glass sandwiches create an idiosyncratic facade that rises like a glassy fortress above its park setting. A beneficial side effect of the facade design is patient rooms flooded with natural light and views, promoters of recovery and high morale.

While modern architects railed against ornament for the sake of

ornament, modernism taken to its extreme seems to produce idiosyncrasy for its own sake.

7. Metropolitan Community Church
474 Ridge Street, N.W.
Suzanne Reatig *1993*

This building demonstrates that good architecture comes not from expensive materials and rich ornament but from an elegant ordering of shapes and spaces to their site and purpose. Using the same building materials as a fast-food restaurant—split-face block, glass, and steel framing—the architect has created a building that transcends its materials to bring image and meaning to a community.

The Ridge Street facade is a wall of pinkish split-face block broken by a series of doors and windows that open it and create a lively composition. The door is set in a broad, low arch with a column-like drum at its center. An inset steel beam continues the line of the arch across the facade. Small square windows are ranged beneath it and larger windows run across the top of the facade. The corner is marked at the second story with a window and doorway behind a shallow grate.

The solidity of this facade increases the impact of the glass barrel-vaulted sanctuary around the corner on 5th Street. It rises like a transparent, taut bubble above the solid base. The modern reliance on geometric shape to give form to a building has been combined with a material—glass—to give meaning as well. Rather than images of saints or the Trinity behind the altar, the architect here has offered instead a direct view to heaven.

oriented to a Metro station and, as the building's focal point, punctuates the intersection.

The taut tile skin that wraps the building provides a distinctive facade and highlights the site configuration, marking a transition between a Metro station and a residential neighborhood. The cutouts of the stepped roofline, which further emphasize the building's surface, are echoed in the stepped pattern of windows on the first floor. The sleek shape is a simple but distinctive marker, in scale with its neighborhood.

10. Franklin D. Reeves Center of Municipal Affairs
2000 14th Street, N.W.
VVKR, Devereaux & Purnell, Robert Traynham Coles *1986*

This municipal building is named for a prominent African-American citizen of the District. Reeves was the first black member of the Democratic National Committee, served as an advisor to John F. Kennedy, and was a professor at Howard University. The Center is designed to bring city services out to this neighborhood. It shares the concrete slab and piloti construction of many downtown buildings but assembles them in a lively way.

Floors are marked by rectangular slabs of pinkish concrete. Windows are inset behind screening concrete grid and the pilotis that rise through the facade. The corner is marked with a gabled glass and polished steel pavilion, whose structure echoes the grid pattern of the facade. The building's windows are also framed in polished steel.

One of the building's most successful features is its ground floor retail and service uses that respond to the neighborhood and commerical character of 14th Street.

8. Logan Park Apartments
1245 13th Street, N.W.
Arthur Cotton Moore/Associates *1981*

Arthur Cotton Moore has always used bold strokes in his work. Within the rectilinear strictures of modernism he inserts curves, movement, and color. His most visible work, Georgetown's Washington Harbour, piles curve atop arc to make a building that virtually vibrates.

This apartment building is a more retrained assemblage. Across the facade, bulging bays and shallow arches are tied together with a sweep of supergraphic polychromy.

The individual entrances of street-level offices and apartments, which enliven the building edge, add human scale and provide an urbane touch.

9. Perpetual Savings Bank Branch
Rhode Island Avenue and 8th Place, N.E.
Keyes Condon Florance *1981*

The sharp corner of this site is a shape that occurs often in Washington as diagonal boulevards intersect with the grid of local streets. Here the corner is

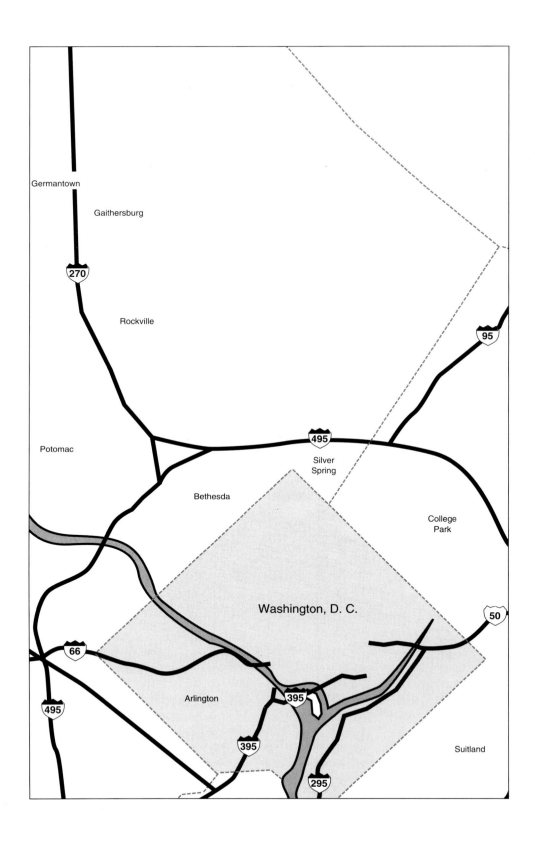

Maryland

Architecture is worth great attention. As we double our numbers every twenty years, we must double our houses...and it is desirable to introduce taste into an art which shows so much.

THOMAS JEFFERSON

Washington's Maryland suburbs, Montgomery County and Prince George's County, were carved out of colonial land grants. Their farms fed a growing metropolis, and both later attracted suburban development directed by joint water, sewer, park, and planning agencies. But their location relative to the District of Columbia and development decisions made by their local governments led to different patterns of community.

While country club developers were drawn to the rolling piedmont landscape of Montgomery, Northeast Washington's industrial development followed rail lines out to the flat terrain of Prince George's County. Small lot zoning in Prince George's encouraged industrial workers to settle there. Established a century ago, that pattern has only recently changed as headquarters and high tech development slowly move into Prince George's County. Montgomery County developed from a wealthy bedroom community for Washington into a regional and even national business and retail center. Large lot zoning invited wealthy homeowners. Large estates were eventually developed into high tech office campuses.

When Montgomery was formed out of Frederick County in 1776 its residents were tobacco farmers. By the mid-19th century soil depletion encouraged farmers to form an agricultural association to protect their interests. To speed their crops to market the association encouraged road improvements as well as the use of the C&O Canal and the increasingly accessible railroads that began to crisscross the county. After the Civil War the capital's expanding population followed the roads and rails to the "country," at first drawn by the resorts and Chautauquas at Glen Echo, Great Falls, and Rockville and later by suburban developments like Chevy Chase, built with large homes, tree-lined streets, parks, and clubhouses.

In 1883, the Civil Service Act made a job with the federal government secure work, and employees who came to Washington started families and stayed. Through the 1920s the political and population emphasis shifted from the farming county seat in Rockville, south to the newer suburbs. Political power moved with the population. In the 1920s two suburban agencies were formed, the Washington Suburban Sanitary Commission and the Maryland-National Capital Park and Planning Commission. The agencies' mandates were to control growth and to provide services like water, sewers, and parks, which were of little concern to independent farmers but were demanded by suburban settlers.

Between 1920 and 1930, the county's population grew from 35,000 to 50,000, a more than 40 percent increase in 10 years. During the 1930s, the county's federal employment buffered it from the effects of the Depression, and its population grew by 77 percent. By 1940, farming was a small part of the county economy.

Like most suburban areas, Montgomery County grew during the 1950s and 1960s. Highways opened up new areas to development, and, by the 1970s, condominiums had begun to sprout in cornfields. At the same time highways were spreading development out, the Metro system began refocusing the development pattern around its stations. Planners rethought the station areas, and what were once local shopping villages became major business centers attracting corporate headquarters. The new suburban downtowns were close to the District but far enough out to feel safe. They also offered less expensive commercial space.

The pattern of planned development supported by services that was set early in the century attracted wealthy residents to comfortable homes and professionals to white-collar government and research jobs. It has continued in contemporary redevelopment. ■

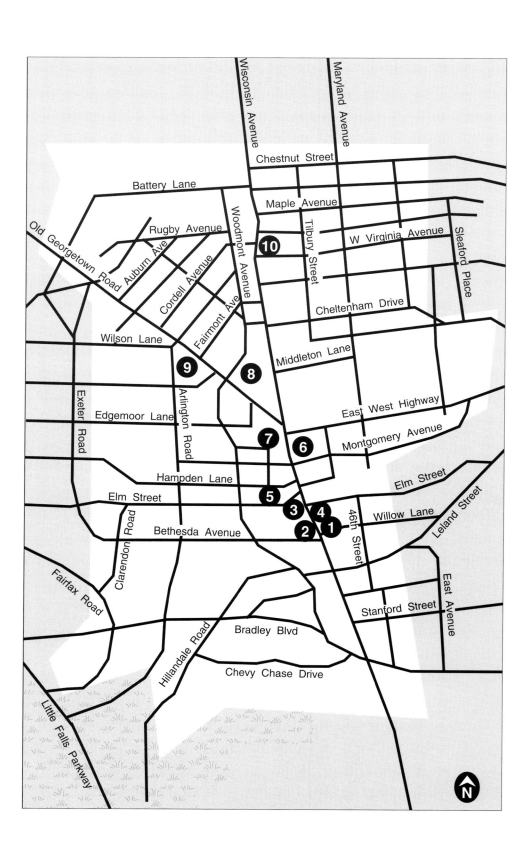

Bethesda

This mode of taking possession of and improving the whole district at first must leave to posterity a grand idea of the patriotic interest which prompted it.

PIERRE CHARLES L'ENFANT, *DESIGNING A FEDERAL CITY*

Bethesda, like other edge cities, draws on a regional office and retail market. But unlike most edge cities, it grew from mass transit-spurred development. Most edge cities across the country have sprouted on farmland around highway interchanges. Tysons Corner in Virginia, for example, redeveloped around three highways and the scale of its buildings and its development pattern are oriented to the car. Bethesda is the growth and regeneration of an existing town center at a Metro station. Bethesda and Tysons are both regional commercial centers, but they look very different. In Tysons buildings are set back from the road, surrounded by parking lots; in Bethesda buildings hug the street and parking is underground, on the street, or in decks. Despite sidewalks, walking is difficult and sometimes dangerous in Tysons Corner; in Bethesda it is easier to walk. Retail uses in Tysons Corner are gathered in malls or are large regional services, such as car dealerships or chain restaurants. The smaller sites and lower overhead in Bethesda encourage individual entrepreneurs.

Bethesda developed in the early 1800s around a store and tollbooth on the Rockville-Washington turnpike. The community was named after a nearby meeting house. The small crossroads became a gathering place for the surrounding tobacco plantations and later became a starting point for westbound settlers, memorialized by the Madonna of the Trails statue, one of 12 that mark the settlers' route.

In the late 1800s, the railroad and then streetcars began to traverse Montgomery County. While rail connected farmers to their markets quickly, the streetcar brought suburban settlers out from the city. Bethesda followed the pattern, established in the 1920s, of suburban development planned around services, and farms were subdivided for comfortable suburban homes.

In the 1930s, what is now a vestige of the county's rural past settled in Bethesda. The Farm Women's Market was built in 1934 as a self-help response to the economic hardships of the Depression. The small clapboard building and the flowers and vegetables sold there contrast with the banks and offices of contemporary Bethesda. Also in the 1930s and 1940s the National Institutes of Health, Naval Medical Hospital, David Taylor Research Facility, and the Defense Mapping Agency all settled in the Bethesda area, establishing a base of steady, professional employment.

By the 1950s, Bethesda's farms had been replaced by houses surrounding a local shopping area clustered at the intersection of Wisconsin Avenue, Old Georgetown Road, and East West Highway. Many of the 20th century commercial buildings in Bethesda were covered with a gray and tan quarried stone and had Tudor-inspired detailing. A few are visible today, but the majority have made way for growth driven by the expansion of the Metro system.

Metro planning began in the early 1970s. As well as creating new focal points for development, Metro's planners located stations at existing commercial centers. In Bethesda, redevelopment plans recommended larger commercial and residential buildings on sites arranged along the existing pedestrian-scaled street pattern. Metro accelerated development patterns that had been established over decades, bringing more luxury housing and corporate offices to the new high-rise center.

County planners responded to Metro with a rigorous plan designed to protect the surrounding residential neighborhoods with buffering parks and public facilities, while focusing dense development around the Metro station. Once the county established new zoning standards to accommodate urban uses, the plan focused the tallest buildings directly adjacent to Metro. Development stepped down in scale as distance from the Metro station increased.

In the early 1980s, planners embarked on an ambitious plan to guide future development. Developers could choose either the "standard method" of development, with defined zoning requirements, or the "optional method" of development, which increased density in exchange for amenities and greater county control over design elements. Planners organized what came to be known as the "beauty pageant," in which projects were judged and those that ranked high enough were allowed to proceed. Planners sought the creation of housing, a pedestrian environment, and amenities such as public art, brick sidewalks, and landscaped plazas.

As built, these amenities contribute to an interesting visual environment but one that sometimes functions awkwardly, requiring connections across bridges, through tunnels, and along redundant and out-of-the-way midblock paths. These elements were created with good intentions, but it often seems that the purpose was to create a laboratory of urban design techniques rather than to allow the community to evolve over time.

The final judge of their value must be the shoppers, employees, and residents who use them every day.

Ironically, the most active areas of downtown are the Arlington Road shopping area and the Woodmont Triangle restaurant area, which are adjacent to the new development. The redevelopment of these areas was delayed in the planning process, but the expanded market provided by increased development just a few blocks away generated new vitality. The relatively inexpensive properties with access to Metro became attractive to individual entrepreneurs who established unique restaurants and shops. The two areas are filled with shoppers and diners meeting friends who do not seem to mind the lack of brick sidewalks and street furniture so beloved by urban designers. They are drawn by the convenience and variety of shops and restaurants.

While the architecture and urban design of the Bethesda central business district is sometimes ungainly, the efforts and experiments have helped it develop with some character in its evolution from small town to edge city. The existing pedestrian scale has helped foster shops and restaurants. The area's lively new activities force a reevaluation of suburbia. ∎

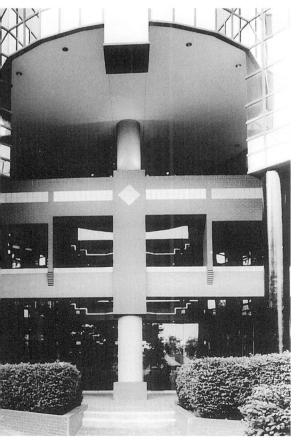

1. Gateway Building
7201 Wisconsin Avenue
Ward-Hale Associates/EDAW, Inc.
1986

Bethesda's southern entrance is clearly signaled by a change from the wooded, green edge of the Columbia Country Club into a streetscape of shops and offices. But four blocks later the planners have defined a gateway, so here sits the Gateway Building. To fulfill its role in the urban context, this building emphatically opens up with a plaza at the corner of Wisconsin Avenue and Willow Street. The mosaic pattern of colored brick that enlivens the lower facade of the building continues onto the sidewalk and is intended to represent a map of Bethesda. Above, mirrored and black glass, orange and blue brick all compete to provide visual interest.

This barroom brawl tumbles out onto the corner above a glass sculpture and a small outdoor amphitheater. The mosaic, the sculpture, and the small amphitheater were accepted as amenities, and intended as a gathering place, but instead force pedestrians out to the street edge. Residents regularly joke about holding poetry readings here over the roar of Wisconsin Avenue traffic.

While the building facade is hyper-active and the amenities awkward, the amount of wasted open space is merci-fully small, and the building frames the major corridor of Wisconsin Avenue.

2. Artery Headquarters Building
7200 Wisconsin Avenue
CHK Architects and Planners/EDAW, Inc. *1987*

Completing the downtown southern gateway defined by planners, the Artery Building connects an older and a newer building to each other and to the transformed streetscape of Bethesda. The building's main tower recedes, allowing an elegantly designed and lushly planted plaza to envelope the corner. This gateway is defined by a pergola and a corner-anchoring gazebo. These typically residential ele-ments, though delicate, are anything but residential in scale. The plaza gar-den's gracious steps, tactile sculpture, and intricate fountains along Bethesda Avenue invite exploration.

The architects and planners involved in this project point to the extraordinary combination of architec-ture and sculpture. Artists and archi-tects worked together from the project's conception to integrate art into the design of the building and plaza to cre-ate an interesting and pleasant urban environment.

3. Apex Building
7272 Wisconsin Avenue
Oldham and Seltz *1989*

Polished granite, metal trim, and lay-ered massing give this building an oddly glittery facade for a suburban downtown. But despite the high level of finish, this was not one of Bethesda's "beauty pageant" buildings; it was built under the standard method of develop-ment. Its tall retail facades, overhanging floors, and a deep corner plaza appear to make this building loom over the sidewalk. With the Gateway and Artery buildings, the Apex forms a trio that tries to provide sculptural and ornamental interest without relying on historicist themes.

The retail facades along Wisconsin Avenue may be the building's most successful aspect. The tall windows abutting the sidewalk give shopkeepers the access and visibility they need to succeed. The multiscreen movie theater, even with its awkward entrance, has added an entertainment dimension to what was strictly an office district.

A lost opportunity is the building's Elm Street facade. Instead of creating an active street edge to link the area's office and shopping districts across a sloping grade change, the imperatives of the theater create a blank facade.

4. Riggs Bank
7235 Wisconsin Avenue
John Blatteau Associates *1991*

This corner of Wisconsin Avenue and Elm Street seems to belong to an older Bethesda. This building's elegant classicism and incised detailing evoke the limestone neoclassicism of the 1920s and 1930s. That the building is a Riggs Bank—itself a Washington institution—completes the illusion.

With the advent of modernism, classicism appeared stodgy and out of date. But as the pendulum of taste swings, the eye tires of steel and glass, and a new generation of architects is returning to the order, detail, and materials of classical architecture and adapting its formal attitude to modern uses. Purists might complain of faux classicism, but the relationship between the columns of Riggs and the concrete pilotis of the Gateway Building next door is pleasing. The bank also gives downtown Bethesda physical weight that otherwise almost disappears amid glass and metal.

With the streetscape improvements

and the Gateway Building's lush landscaping, this block is one of the most pleasant, if brief, walks in downtown Bethesda.

residences within walking distance from Metro are built into the building's western and northern flanks, and gently bring the building to the street, following the line of the hill.

This site represents a good application of urban design. A portion of an otherwise redundant midblock path system called the Discovery Trail passes between the larger and smaller buildings to create a shortcut through the long block that is not broken by a cross street.

6. Bethesda Crescent
7475 Wisconsin Avenue
Keyes Condon Florance *1988*

The designers of this building did not miss the opportunity to emphasize an important corner. A dramatic corner tower with a rooftop belvedere punctuates the center of downtown Bethesda. One of the central business district's best art amenities is the neon sculpture on the tower. It glows down Old Georgetown Road and creates an orienting landmark, though it has been mistaken for a corporate logo.

This building's corner tower is noticeably similar to the one on Republic Place (1987) in downtown Washington, by the same firm. A cynic might say that the designers were saving effort to make some money; a more generous observer might comment that they were developing a theme.

The base of the building continues the dark granite and vaguely Egyptian motif of the older bank next door. A disappointing feature is the plain, setback penthouse, which could have provided a much livelier cap.

One of the amenities this building provides is a tunnel under Wisconsin Avenue to the Metro station, reached through the building's lobby. As an

5. One Bethesda Center
8500 Hampden Lane
Oldham and Seltz *1986*

This building was designed with a careful awareness of its surroundings. The footprint is shaped to fit the site, reinforcing existing streets. A ziggurat profile steps the building down to meet a smaller neighbor. A smaller, secondary building covers the blank wall of a neighboring building to add visual interest and activity. Town house

urban form, pedestrian tunnels, like raised sidewalks, seem an easy (if expensive) solution to separate pedestrians from cars at difficult intersections. What may seem like an obvious engineering solution founders when faced with human irrationality; people do not like to leave an active street to walk through a dark tunnel, even though it may be safer and more direct. County police have been known to ticket determined street-crossers at this corner.

7. Bethesda Metro Center
Wisconsin Avenue at Old Georgetown Road and East West Highway
Benham Group *1985*

Metro Center is a complex of three buildings arranged around an open space intended to be the social and architectural centerpiece of downtown Bethesda. Instead, mundane architecture and awkward urban design

conspire to create a pass-through rather than a place where people linger. The plaza's primary feature is a hole blocked by a wall. The escalators to Metro descend through a large opening, breaking up the plaza. A large, horizontally oriented sculpture blocks the view beyond. The use that might generate activity, a fast-food court, is pulled well back from the street, out of sight of passersby.

Compare this with Union Station on Capitol Hill, a grand and active public space also oriented around transportation. Metro links are visible and accessible, but off to the side of the main hall. Most travelers pass through the area of shops and restaurants, perhaps stopping to pick up a magazine, a snack, or a last minute souvenir, mingling with shoppers and tourists. The resulting experience is enhanced by the grand Beaux-Arts architecture but not created solely by it. At Union Station, unlike Metro Plaza, design and activity are linked symbiotically.

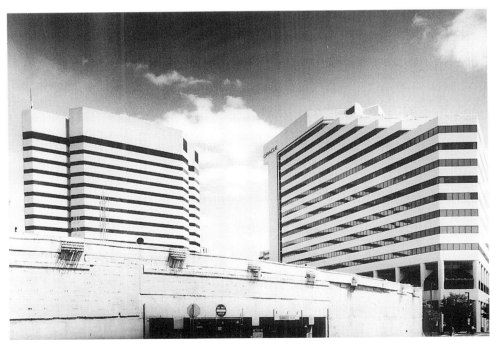

The strained design of this building goes to extraordinary lengths to create nothing. The apartment and office buildings of this project are linked by a plaza raised nearly two stories above street level. Its retail uses are further hidden from the street in a covered arcade. The Safeway supermarket, which would certainly generate activity, is tucked beneath the building with no relation to the plaza above.

The bloated office building, an elliptical prism intersecting a rectangular volume, does nothing to resolve the site's complex geometry. Only along one of its narrow edges—Wisconsin Avenue—does it reinforce the existing street edge.   The building is set so far back from Woodmont Avenue that it must be reached by a wall-like stairway. The opportunities to create a visual link between two major roads and to create a dramatic urban space connecting two roads and neighborhoods were lost.

It is also disappointing that the spectacular mosaics and friendly fountain of this plaza are hidden from street view. The project is eventually intended to be linked to Metro Center by a series of raised sidewalks and plazas, while perfectly good sidewalks are left untrod beneath.

9. Chevy Chase Garden Plaza
Arlington and Old Georgetown Roads
Leo A. Daly   *1988*

This project's massing is arranged in two separate buildings to accommodate a historic house on the site and to create a densely landscaped interior plaza. The visibility and seclusion of the plaza are carefully balanced to create a public space that feels private.

8. Bethesda Place
Woodmont Avenue between Wisconsin Avenue and Old Georgetown Road
Nelson-Salabes   *1990*

Ironically, this building placed first in the Bethesda developers' "beauty pageant." The plaza, the stepped profile of the main building, and the small scale of the secondary building must have appealed to the judges.

Unfortunately, the executed building is flawed. The deep red brick and matching mortar and the dark smoked glass make for a brooding presence on the street. The plaza's orientation to the street is awkward; shops have limited access and visibility from both the street and the interior plaza, their sources of potential customers. Even at its high visibility corner—the star-shaped intersection of Old Georgetown and Arlington Roads—the development hides behind a meager flowerbed and an unadorned facade, instead of offering a grand entrance, as is traditional on acute corners, to catch more foot traffic.

The plaza's garden is the gem of the project. Designed by the noted landscape architecture firm Oehme, van Sweden, and Associates, the profusion of meadowlike plants enveloping the old house creates a natural feeling in a hard-edged environment. The garden plaza's slate paving is a welcome counterpoint to all the red brick.

10. 8001 Wisconsin Avenue
Muse-Wiedeman *1990*

A curved brick facade defines this building's important corner at Wisconsin Avenue while focusing attention away from the residential neighborhood behind it. Open pavilions defined by metal framework add height but not bulk, and the punched windows emphasize the screen of the facade. When streetscape improvements recommended by the latest plan for the northern portion of Wisconsin Avenue are undertaken, this building will set the standard.

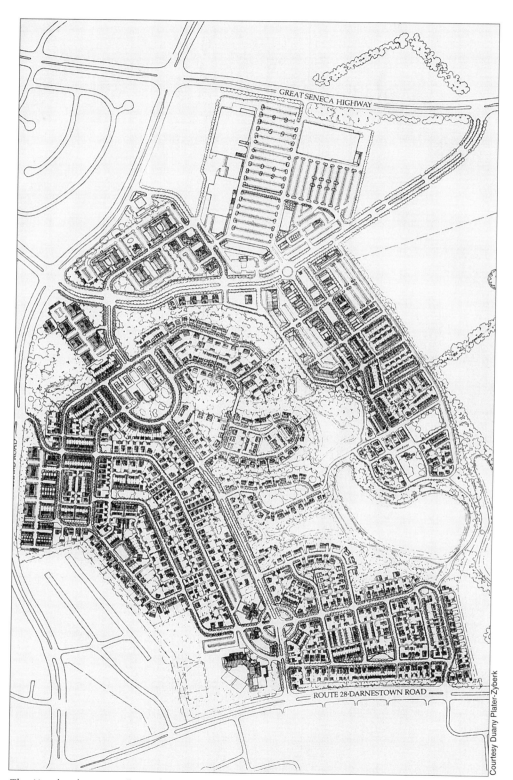

GREAT SENECA HIGHWAY

ROUTE 28-DARNESTOWN ROAD

Courtesy Duany Plater-Zyberk

The Kentlands map reflects the tenets of neo-traditional town planning. Natural features are incorporated into overall planning. Landscape and compatibly-scaled buildings line gridded streets that lead to clearly defined community centers.

Kentlands

Men, thinly scattered, make a shift, but a bad shift, without many things.
A smith is ten miles off; they'll do without a nail or staple. A tailor is far from
them; they'll sew their own clothes. It is being concentrated which
produces high convenience.

DR. JOHNSON

Everything old is new again, particularly in town planning. Two Miami-based architects, Andres Duany and Elizabeth Plater-Zyberk, have turned suburban subdivision into the noble profession of town building.

Development plans used to be drawn with circles defining vague areas of different land uses connected by sinuous arterial roads. By contrast, Duany and Plater-Zyberk carefully work out an interconnected pattern of streets lined with a variety of lot sizes in distinct neighborhoods. By incorporating layers of information from different viewpoints they strive to create a community that is visually complex and attractive, but that offers alternatives to total reliance on the car for work, school, and shopping. What is perhaps most astounding is that they achieve this using a one-page zoning ordinance in contrast to the hundreds of pages of legalese used by even the smallest municipalities.

In Montgomery County, the architects have teamed up with developer Joseph Alfandre to create Kentlands. The 352-acre community is built among the woods, lakes, and buildings of the original Kentlands farm.

Like other neotraditional towns designed by Duany and Plater-Zyberk, Kentlands was designed in a "charette" process, an intense period of work when landowners, architects, planners, local politicians, engineers, and residents were brought together to create a new community. Environmental, safety, marketing, and local historical information were incorporated into a plan that was tweaked and altered over two weeks, mimicking, in that short time period, the evolution of communities created over time by thousands of individual decisions. The layers of information and individual input are intended to create a more subtle and complex plan than a traditional subdivision.

One of the first, and highest, hurdles was convincing the city of Gaithersburg that the density and mix of uses in the neotraditional town, which could not be created under the city's zoning regulations, would not threaten public health, safety, or welfare. At one point, planners had to show that the narrower than standard Kentlands streets were still maneuverable for emergency vehicles by testing a new driver, on a snowy day, on a street blocked by a stalled car.

Planners also sought to create a community with true local flavor and looked at nearby communities for inspiration. From Washington they took the traffic circles of the L'Enfant plan. Dooryards, the small green gardens in front of town houses, were suggested by Georgetown.

They also found inspiration on the site. On the more than 350-acre farm, the original farm buildings were built in a tight group, creating intimate spaces, and even a small alley, barely 10 feet wide. The farmer found that this building arrangement was efficient for doing his work and left more land to farm. This efficiency and well-defined space were an example for Kentlands' designers.

Even though Kentlands exercises some design review, unlike many planned communities and suburbs governed by homeowners associations, it does not limit residents' choices of paint color. Again, the designers looked at Georgetown's painted town houses for inspiration. This kind of flexibility allows for idiosyncrasies of individual expression. Perhaps in a few years there will be a bright pink house which becomes a local landmark.

Another difference from most suburban developments which are only residential, is Kentlands' large regional shopping center. Despite the surrounding pedestrian-oriented community, many of its customers come by car. But the architects managed to avoid the worst characteristics of strip development. The large buildings are brought down to a pedestrian scale with columned facades and a pedestrian gateway marked with two-story towers. The buildings are oriented inward, rather than to the surrounding arterial roads. The space created by the buildings is now used for parking, but could be build out in a grid pattern, creating a more urban place.

Many communities threatened by new growth take the attitude that anything built degrades the natural environment. But our need to build and live in communities is undeniable. The builders of Kentlands are trying to build a community that enhances the natural and human environment. ∎

1. Rachel Carson Elementary School

98 Church Street
Duane, Elliot, Cahill, Mullineaux and
Mullineaux *1992*

This school is a departure from other
Montgomery County schools, the most
recent of which tend to look like shopping malls. This design returns to the
traditional iconography of civic architecture: columns, combined with a
friendly, home-like gable appropriate
for an elementary school. The columns
were a point of discussion in the
charette process, but once constructed
became so popular that they were also
incorporated into the design of the
Kentlands shopping center.

A small but significant battle was
fought with the county over the
school's name. During the charette
process it was called the Kentlands
Elementary School, recognizing the
important role it would play in the
community. The county, however,
wanted to keep that community link
ambiguous, to retain flexibility in
drawing school district lines designed
to maintain a socioeconomic balance
between schools. The "intractable
Montgomery County School Board,"
which insisted on a different name, is
memorialized on a plaque in front of
the school: a dishonor roll of members
who refused to recognize the spirit of
community instilled by the site's previous and current owners.

NEOTRADITIONAL TOWN PLANNING

MANY PEOPLE REMEMBER *walking down the street to buy a newspaper and running into a neighbor, chatting with acquaintances, and enjoying the seasonal changes in the gardens and homes along the way. Maybe you used to live in a place like that, or visited it on vacation, or even just saw it in a movie. Welcome back to the neotraditional town.*

Suburbs were intended as places of respite. Their salubrious breezes would blow over individual lots next to compatible neighbors. But the urban exodus that left downtowns abandoned re-created urban pressures in the suburbs. Isolated amid congestion, suburbs are full of chauffeuring and commuting families. The leisurely life of country clubs and scout troops has been replaced by an endless web of car trips from home to school, to store, to work, and back home again.

Some developers and designers have returned to the pattern and function of towns, villages, and small com-munities developed over time before the car became an indispensable appendage.. Their goal is to lessen our dependence on the car, freeing up our time and space for more neighborly interactions. They want to create places with a depth of experience, with the idiosyncrasies of communities developed over years by thousands of individual decisions.

Andres Duany and Elizabeth Plater-Zyberk, the designers of Kentlands, have founded an architecture and planning firm that has codified and successfully marketed this concept to developers. They have established a set of principles for neotraditional town building based on their observations of historical communities. Their concepts have been adopted in greater or lesser detail by many planning firms and agencies around the country.

They begin with a master plan showing the routes and hierarchy of the town's streets, the variety and rela-

tionship of building types, and the public spaces and buildings. The community's layout is carefully related to the site's physical and historical character. Old buildings on the site are reused, and features such as hills, tree stands, and lakes become defining elements. This master plan shows much more detail than the usual development plan, which shows only general areas of development and primary streets.

The intersecting street and pedestrian network is laid out in a grid modified by the landscape. This does not mean that ruler-straight roads stretch to eternity without respite. It means that streets and paths are laid out in logical and memorable patterns that offer alternative routes between neighborhoods and commercial districts, rather than taking meandering curves and leading to countless cul-de-sacs.

Street section drawings illustrate the relationship of buildings, streets, sidewalks, landscaping, and parking, creating a visual image of the town that entices clients, planning boards, and potential buyers. Creating the town's visual image is also an opportunity to work out its scale. Buildings and lots are proportionate to the width of the streets they line, creating outdoor rooms with defined edges. Unlike the coarse density, setback, and lot coverage prescriptions of typical zoning, neotraditionalism focuses on specific building configurations, sizes, and locations that support the goals of the land use plan.

This regulating plan and a set of development codes identify building types and uses appropriate for each section of the town, creating a place of physical and social variety. Lot sizes are mixed and so are the buildings and activities that take place on them. What once may have been the wrong side of the tracks is now an affordable place for young families. What once may have been the flat above the grocery store is now a home office where Dad can keep an eye on the kids. This is all governed not by a thick volume of bylaws vetted by lawyers, but by a skeleton plan of general site design guidelines that allow for creativity and perhaps a little eccentricity.

Finally, public buildings and squares are set aside as essential elements of community. The buildings are flexible, accommodating whatever use the community wants: a town hall or a community theater. Public squares and parks lend elegance, definition, and a shared sense of responsibility and enjoyment. The careful balance of private and public, large and small, home and work, is an effort to create a community of options and depth.

Neotraditionalism and its effect on town planning are analogous to postmodernism and its effect on architecture. Each is trying to recapture positive characteristics wrung out of our communities since World War II by returning to old forms of town and building design. The images painted by neotraditionalists are charming, and their guidelines make sense, but there are also those who see them as facile solutions to complex problems.

Urbanists debate the effect of environment on behavior, but it is the hope of neotraditional town planners that people who live in a community where they can walk to work, meet their neighbors, and participate will really do all these things. But our lives are complicated; our responsibilities and interests range beyond the small universe of home. We are connected to the world by phone and fax. Perhaps we are responding to merely the idea of community and the illusion of a neotraditional town.

2. The Church of Jesus Christ of the Latter-Day Saints
Tschiffley Square Road
Reed Architects *1993*

This building uses traditional ecclesiastical architecture: a central block flanked by wings and topped by a steeple to send messages of community and worship. Placed on a slight hill at a central intersection, the building is a local landmark. The detail of beehives on the brick walls is a reference to the Mormon Church's Utah origins.

3. Kentlands Recreation Center
Tschiffley Square Road
Robert Orr and Associates *1993*

The Shingle Style, a uniquely American style associated with late 19th-century resort architecture, is an apt choice for a community recreation center. The style's sloping roofline, which creates deep eaves over multipaned windows, bespeaks ease and leisure. The details of this building are well executed and seem to be generated by the style and the site, rather than applied.

4. Kentlands Square Shopping Center
Kentlands Boulevard
D.I. Architecture *1993*

The designers were reluctant to use columns here even though they were a successful feature of the Rachel Carson Elementary School, feeling that such imagery should be reserved for civic buildings. Of course, history is full of images to appropriate: the Greek marketplace, the stoa, was a columned arcade.

The design of this center departs from our contemporary idea of a shopping center. Its buildings are arranged to form a courtyard, now used for parking, but intended to be built out in a grid street pattern. The developer also resisted the temptation to orient the center to arterial roads and regional customers. Instead, the design makes safe and aesthetic pedestrian links to surrounding neighborhoods a design priority.

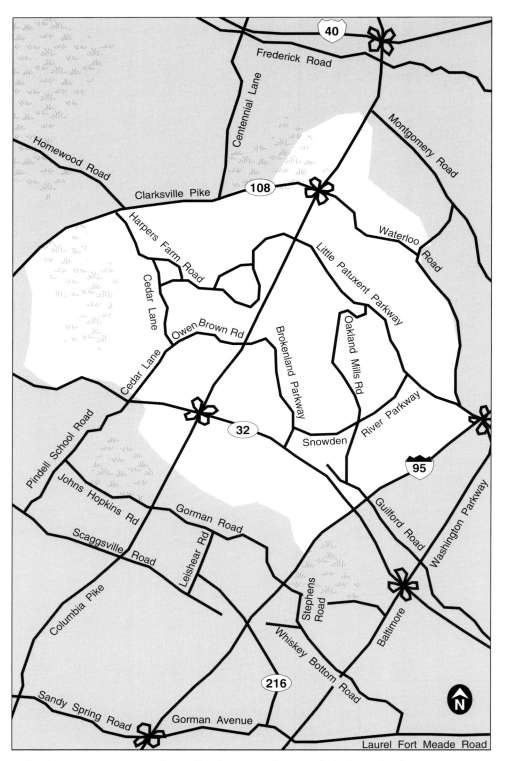

Columbia's centerpiece is "The Mall" whose storefronts include the Columbia Association. While twenty years ago planners might have viewed the mall as the future of community, planners today look to history for community patterns and function. Likewise, modern housing forms in Columbia have given way to neo–colonial and farm styles.

Columbia

No architecture can be truly noble which is not imperfect.

JOHN RUSKIN, *THE STONES OF VENICE*

L ike the New Deal bureaucrats who created the older Greenbelt, developer James Rouse called in experts to advise him on architecture, education, recreation, government, health, and religion when he envisioned Columbia in 1967. Along with the site layout and engineering plans required for any development, the experts developed goals such as "lifelong education" and "individual freedom." Rouse also added a dose of market reality. Columbia would have no safety net of public subsidy; it was a profit-driven venture.

The community's development and direction were to be informed by citizen participation, but first a community had to be built to attract residents. Columbia was not designed as a standard subdivision, but as nine residential villages, each centered on local shops. The villages have varied housing types and a full complement of recreational facilities. They were intended to create a social and ethnic mix for a community of people who wanted the variety of the city without its grit. The community's downtown is a shopping mall overlooking a lake and adjacent office buildings. Columbia, unlike Greenbelt, was intended not just as a bedroom community, but as a complete community. It includes offices, commercial uses, and a small industrial park.

Parts of Columbia look like a well-manicured office park. Buildings and neighborhoods are hidden behind berms and landscaping. Establishing personal landmarks takes time and keen observation. Walking in Columbia is not a way of life as it is in Kentlands, but one of many recreation alternatives. It does not challenge the traditional notion of a car-dependent lifestyle.

Like most new towns, Columbia became an enclave, separate from the surrounding farmland. After Rouse had acquired one-tenth of Howard County he had to convince the rural county to redefine its future to assure an increased population base and more urban development direction. From its first 1,000 residents in 1968, to 75,000 people and 53,000 jobs in 1980, Columbia has shifted the emphasis of metropolitan-area growth and grown into its concept.

The relentless social and physical planning that created Columbia has in some

New Towns

WE HAVE ALWAYS tried to re-create Eden, from the mythical city of Atlantis and fictional places like Erewhon, to short-lived but well-intentioned communities like Brook Farm and Oneida. Our new Edens strive to combine the virtues of city and country, with none of their vices.

At the turn of the century, Ebenezer Howard sought to create garden cities that placed industry amid farms and parks, as a healthful alternative to London's gritty slums. In America, during the Depression, Rexford Tugwell used the New Deal to build communities that would turn the economy around. Tugwell's Resettlement Administration proposed 25 towns. Eight were funded by Congress and three were built. Greenbelt, Maryland, was the most complete. The projects were intended to create jobs and provide housing. The communities would provide schools, recreation, and shopping. It was an ideal vision of townhouses amid woods, children safely walking to school, and wives welcoming their husbands home after the workday.

Although Greenbelt developed into a thriving community with loyal residents, it was an experiment that was not repeated after construction costs proved to be three times higher than market rates. After World War II, new government policies, VA loans, and a highway system supported returning GIs who moved their families to burgeoning suburbs. In the 1960s visionary developers James Rouse and Robert Simon reacted to the excesses of those suburbs by trying to transplant urban vitality into their new communities of Columbia and Reston. Even an in-town new town was attempted at Fort Lincoln in the District.

At heart, new towns seem to be an escape from something—from urban chaos and challenge—to communities that combine people and activities in a place the market would not otherwise bring together. Created by visionaries, these communities are intended as paradises of rational governance, equal opportunity, clean streets, and meaningful work. They are created by people who are part missionary and part developer.

New towns share a concern for form, in the belief that it will affect people's behavior. Just as the teeming slum bred depravity, the new town's parks and plazas will foster a healthy community; proximity to nature will breed a noble race. Form is governed by regulations, limiting the appropriate paint colors for houses or creating a cemetery where gravestones do not protrude above the ground. The controlled form of new towns denies the messy character of life and communities. Even death is subsumed into the landscape by cemeteries without headstones.

New towns seek to combine people and activities in a way that market forces might not. Adults can live and work in the same community. Children attend integrated schools. Shops and recreation are all at hand. But in today's electronic and mobile world, our links are not based solely on physical proximity. Our community extends to scattered school friends and family; our loyalties are to careers, hobbies, and ethnic and religious groups.

New towns place high value on a natural setting—development surrounded by parks and paths. Arterial roads are edged with greenery and signs are placed unobtrusively in landscaped berms. The lack of man-made landmarks combined with a plethora of like-sounding names— Sunrise Valley, Sunset Hills—require the nose of a woodsman to navigate successfully.

New towns seek to incorporate culture in the community, from Chinese restaurants to local theater. But, while new towns may create the opportunity for mixing people and activities, they also limit it through rules and regulations. By smoothing the rough spots no mountains are created.

Another characteristic new towns share is the difficulty of funding and constructing them. Initially land is often amassed by hidden buyers to keep land values low. Local zoning codes must be changed to allow new levels of density and mixes of uses. The upfront costs for acquisition, construction, and infrastructure are high. It is difficult to meet these costs without sales revenues or property taxes.

New towns are a reaction to their times. Ebenezer Howard was trying to escape an overcrowded, unhealthy city; Kentlands is a reaction to time and land-wasting suburban sprawl. But the creation of new towns is a modern notion. Believing that the problems of social inequity, urban blight, health, and economics can be solved by creating a new, previously untried community form may seem naive, but it is also forward-looking and hopeful. Like a good modernist, the new town builder leaves the past behind, seeing only its errors, and moves into uncharted territory.

But it does not end there. Kentlands is a postmodern new town. Like modernists, its designers believe a new form of community can change our lives, but they look to the past for older forms that have worked for generations.

In America, a land built on so many dreams, from 40 acres and a mule to streets paved with gold, we will no doubt continue to search for Eden.

ways created a sterile environment, with community life centered on a mall and a tasteful physical landscape that offers no jarring surprises, but no landmarks either. Most recently, Columbia has completed a cemetery, making it literally a cradle-to-grave community. In order to maintain a natural appearance, the cemetery's design standards call for markers that do not protrude above the slope of the land. Some may feel that this drive to neaten up life and death is paternalistic, but it has produced a profit for developers and high property values for loyal residents. ■

Notable Buildings

1. Howard Hughes Medical Institute
4000 Jones Bridge Road
Hillier Group
1993

The campus setting has become a popular sales image for the most mundane of suburban office parks, where it usually means more than one building, some landscaping, and a stormwater retention pond. But here at the headquarters for the world's largest private medical foundation, the idea of a self-contained, detached campus is well suited to the program in which scientists take up short-term residence to share ideas. Even though the institute is not a public facility, the stone walls, landscaping, and brick buildings peeking through the trees lend a depth and visual variety to the suburban landscape.

The L-shaped campus is made up of residential buildings clustered at the end of the long leg, followed by common areas—a theater, meeting rooms,

lounges, recreation rooms, and dining halls. The institute's ceremonial entrance and larger administrative areas occupy the corner, and offices fill out the short leg of the L. This arrangement allows self-sufficiency and privacy for both visiting researchers and permanent staff, yet allows each to meet in the common areas. The buildings and their arrangement create a series of public and private spaces suited to their uses. The dormitories are residentially scaled and detailed, two-story, brick, gable-roofed buildings arranged around a tree-lined green. Conference and meeting spaces are arranged overlooking a terraced hill and pond. Offices are grouped in a tighter cluster around a small courtyard.

The overwhelming feature of this campus is the landscaping. The buildings seem to have been here for decades since mature hardwoods come right up to the windows. Buildings and landscape are visually connected by views through and to the buildings. The buildings are physically connected by interior and exterior paths and spaces where people can meet and gather. These paths meander through the site, inviting visitors to explore. The attention to detail is thorough, yet allows the natural site to take precedence. A graceful ornamental pool that is the focal point of the composition serves the same purpose as every mandated, unattractive puddle in the suburbs— retaining stormwater.

The building's detailing and materials suit the campus image. Brick walls, stone detailing, multipaned and shaped windows vaguely recall Thomas Jefferson's University of Virginia. The Arts and Crafts style of the finishes makes one think of Berkeley or the California where Hughes made his money. This campus, from its plan to its details, is a graceful composition of buildings and spaces.

2. Mormon Temple
9400 Stony Brook
Emil B. Fetzer *1974*

Nearly 800,000 people toured the Mormon Temple when it opened after a six-year construction period at a cost of $15 million. The temple is now open only to Mormons, but its six marble towers topped with golden spires rise above the Beltway, making it a landmark for all. The Angel Moroni flies atop the tallest spire, higher than the Washington Monument. As nonmembers learn at the Visitors Center, which offers a tour and video, the church is heavy in symbolism. The temple's white marble facing indicates purity and enlightenment, and members pass over a bridge to enter the temple, leaving their worldly cares behind as they enter the Lord's house.

For many in the Washington area, the temple lodges in their consciousness as roadside architecture. Its scale, color, and shape are nothing if not eye-catching.

3. COMSAT Laboratories
I-270 North
Cesar Pelli/DMJM *1969*

The COMSAT building is truly a machine in the garden. The facade's dull white aluminum panels and clear and bronze-tinted glass broken by aluminum mullions glint in the sun against a cool green rural backdrop. Pelli intended his design to be clearly a "man-made object placed within a natural area." Despite this seeming incongruity, the building harmonizes with the surrounding rural landscape. Its

long horizontal profile fits into the rolling grounds, while its clean lines and hard surface are a pleasing contrast to the greenery.

Pelli is noted for exploring the skin of a building and the ways in which structural detailing and subtle variations in the wall system can produce dramatic variety in a building's profile. Here, glass and aluminum wall panels fit together as a tight, flush skin. Window arrangements vary from individual panes for workspaces to continuous bands for corridors; clear glass reveals the building's inner life. Finally, the skin is not sheared off at the roof but curls to meet it, emphasizing the tautness of the exterior.

COMSAT is an early work, but it is a precursor to Pelli's designs at New York's Museum of Modern Art and World Financial Center. At the museum, Pelli enlivens moribund modernism by giving shape and articulation to a sleek, flat tower. The buildings of the financial center avoid the excesses of postmodernism by slightly varied proportions of stone and glass in subtly stepped and receding facades to create evocative profiles.

COMSAT is organized as a series of spaces along a central spine, a theme that Pelli has explored in other work. The spine not only provides access to laboratories and defines courtyards, but serves as a central meeting space, the building's main street.

4. International Association of Machinists and Aerospace Workers Headquarters
9000 Machinists Place
Upper Marlboro, Maryland
Boggs Group *1993*

In Washington, metaphor in architecture is not only for monuments. This union headquarters is an expression of the work of the union's members—shaping metal into everything from gears to airplanes. The vertical trusses, metal sunscreens, and steel honeycomb panels that are the dominant features of the facade are crisp, uncomplicated, and utilitarian. The way these components and the carefully detailed building skin interlock suggests a large machine set in the landscape.

The building has a cruciform plan, and its tall, beautifully detailed granite walls frame barrel-vaulted skylights. The office floors are extended beyond this cross to fill out a rough rectangle. But the human hand is evident as well. The building is organized on two grids, one at a slight angle to the other, creating a bit of handcrafted uncertainty.

A close look at the facade will reveal that the elaborate machinelike elements are not so much of the building as on the building. This approach is expressive of an architectural trend of the late 1980s and early 1990s to utilize modernist elements in a decorative, picturesque and sometimes evocative way. Here, "techno" elements are feverishly applied to the outside of a well-executed but fairly ordinary building. Unlike International Style buildings whose straightforward simplicity alluded to the machine and its coming influence on society, this building is a celebration of its occupants' craft.

5. WSSC Water Infiltration Plant
River Road (access from canal towpath at Swain's Lock)
Paul D. Spreiregen *1982*

Modern architecture is often faulted for being cold and impersonal. When coupled with the strictly practical demands of factories and utilities, its subtle, unornamented lines can be brutal. But in this water infiltration plant, function has created an elegant form.

The concrete bridge and abutments are shaped in concrete artfully marked with the grain of its wooden molds. The molds were spaced to create vertical striations, a pattern that is echoed in the slight spacing of the concrete panels. The opened spaces give glimpses to the canal and river.

Most significantly, this design returns a public utility to the public domain in the tradition of WPA bridges and Victorian pumphouses. The abutment creates a plaza and viewing tower off the towpath with information about the canal and its high water marks.

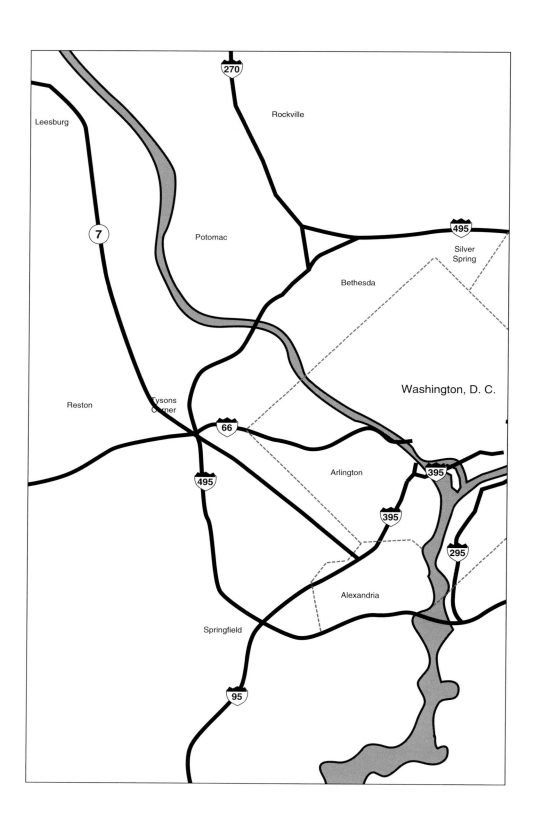

Virginia

A man and what he loves and builds have but a day and then disappear.

GEORGE MACAULAY TREVELYAN, 1937

The landscape of suburban Virginia has evolved from rolling green farmland to often barely rolling traffic. As the federal government has grown beyond the District's borders, the Virginia suburbs have grown. Small, rural communities have been absorbed into the powerful orbit of the capital. The once busy port of Alexandria and the former dairy and grain farms of Fairfax and Loudoun counties now take their wealth and vitality from their proximity to Washington, D.C.

War has always spurred growth in Washington. The District's population in 1850 was 50,000. By 1870, following the Civil War, it had grown to 132,000. That growth was also felt in the surrounding communities. But the most rapid and noticeable change came in the 20th century, after two world wars. During and after each war, the influx of workers to serve the war effort increased the demand for office space and housing. In the 1960s and 1970s, Washington's consistently strong economy generated more jobs throughout the region. Old communities were revitalized, and new communities were built. As the automobile shortened distances, cows were replaced by commuters and country crossroads became regional centers.

In Virginia, two forces converged to create the suburban landscape. The first was the federal government's move to decentralize its facilities in areas outside the District. One of the first agencies to move outside the district was the Department of Defense, which relocated to Arlington, Virginia, in the newly built Pentagon in 1940. The CIA later followed to Langley. As does any business, the federal government was seeking cheaper land and more space, but decentralization was further spurred by the fear that the capital could be a target in a nuclear war. As in communities all over the country, the Federal Highway Act funded the construction

A second force in shaping Northern Virginia, the area included in metropolitan Washington, was the outlook of local and state governments in a largely rural state. The Dillon Rule, which divides the responsibilities of state and local government, sets limits on local government initiative in land-use regulation. Virginia's small towns and farms flourished with minimal government services. The small and self-sufficient population placed limited demands on roads and schools. Farmers did not expect garbage pick-up or snow removal. As Northern Virginia's suburban population grew, however, so did the demand for services. The three-acre "farmette" gave only the illusion of rural life. The need to invest in public services was evident, but often beyond the means of formerly rural counties that had relied on the state. As a result, homeowner associations flourished to pick up the slack. Parks and recreation facilities were accessible to paying members of the community. Some groups went so far as to regulate paint colors and have spent time in court fighting the placement of a basketball hoop. In suburban communities around the nation homeowner associations have become de facto governments that limit change with both good and bad results.

Furthermore, the Dillon Rule allows local governments to do only those things which they are specifically empowered to do by the state government. So, while in Virginia zoning is established as a legitimate use of the police power protecting public health, safety, and welfare, any innovative techniques used by a local government to finance, time, or regulate development must be approved by the state legislature. For Northern Virginia, this often means that urban areas with complex problems must convince a legislature trying to balance the demands of rural and urban communities. As an alternative, the local government turns to the private developer to build infrastructure in exchange for the right to develop. Unfortunately, the road goes where it is best for the developer,   or parks are limited by covenant only to residents or employees of a development. And when the real estate market bottoms out, parks and roads simply are not built.

Elements of Virginia's patrician colonial landscape still exist in the delicate details of Old Town Alexandria row houses, or in the carefully manicured farms of Loudoun County, but they are sometimes lost in a disorderly landscape of rapid growth. Today suburban Virginia is an area of sprawling suburbs dotted with older communities trying to preserve their identity amid redevelopment pressure, new communities built to   idealistic goals, and outlying farms whose days are perhaps limited. The new buildings and communities reflect different responses to the pattern of suburbia and also reflect an adaptation of traditional town planning   patterns to new locations and technologies. ■

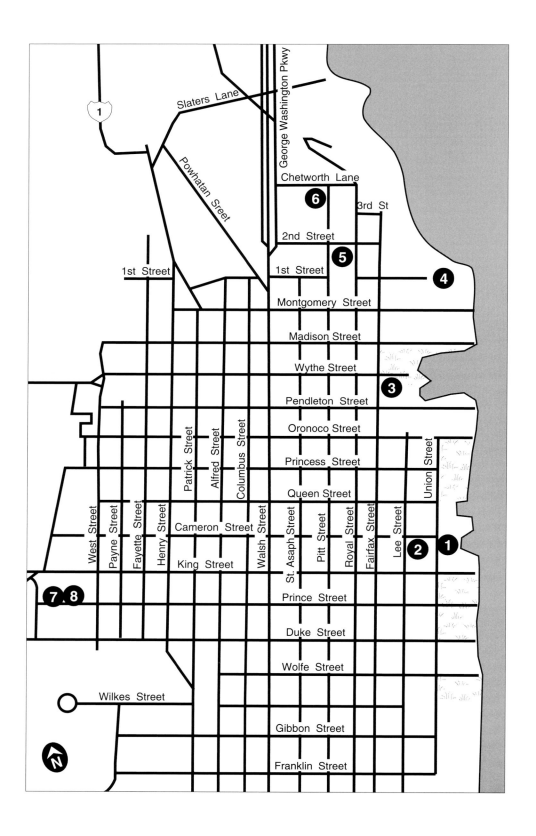

Alexandria

*A chaste plan sufficiently capacious and convenient for a period not
too remote, but one to which we may reasonably look forward, would meet my
idea in the Capital...*

GEORGE WASHINTON, IN A LETTER TO DAVID STUART, COMMISSIONER OF
THE DISTRICT OF COLUMBIA, 1792

Alexandria was established by an act of the Virginia General
Assembly in 1749. The city was a busy port through the 18th century, shipping tobacco to England and later linking the capital region with the Ohio
River Valley via the Chesapeake and Ohio Canal. In 1801, Alexandria was
included in the area of the federal city, but a prohibition on public buildings in Virginia limited development to commercial and residential uses. In
1846, the city was returned to the State of Virginia. Alexandria was seeking
a more hospitable business climate, which it felt Virginia could provide
and, in return, Virginia added two proslavery members to its assembly.
After retrocession, Alexandria experienced a building boom that lasted
until the Civil War.

By the end of the 19th century, the Southern Railroad and the
Richmond, Fredericksburg, and Potomac Railroad lines shifted growth
to the city's western edge, and the waterfront's piers and warehouses
drifted into obsolescence. But as early as the 1920s the restoration of Old
Town began, focused on the city's many historic houses. Today Old Town,
with its traditional urban grid, walkable streetscape, and mix of uses
and buildings, sets the pattern for new development in Alexandria.
Underneath the gewgaws and souvenirs, Alexandria exhibits the basics
of civilized urban life.

As technology changes, so do the profiles of our communities.
Alexandria was a thriving port well before the federal district was established. Its river transportation made it a crossroads for goods and people.
But as railroads made the waterfront obsolete the focus and character of
development changed. Air travel later made the railroads obsolete, and
both the waterfront and railyards were left behind. Neglect of the archaic
infrastructure has preserved valuable waterfront land and acres of rail yards
in the midst of a congested city.

With vision and flexibility, these reserves created by obsolescence can be made into new communities combining the special features of urbanity with the ease and space of modern construction. At the same time, they can absorb development pressures on the popular historic core. Redevelopment along the riverfront and around King Street Metro station is based on the lessons of city building that make Old Town so appealing and may create areas of similar, lasting value.

The Waterfront

Alexandria's working waterfront of the 1990s is made up of high-tech, service-oriented businesses and new housing. Both use the water for prestige and amenity, not for access and transportation.

Alexandria's traditional grid pattern has weathered time and adapted to contemporary demands. In Old Town, the grid pattern creates a distinct part of the city with blocks fronted by single-bay houses, rows of town houses, and large single homes. The pattern and architecture retain the appeal of variety and elegance. Residents can walk to a variety of shops, perhaps even to work.

It has been a challenge, however, to integrate parking into the old city fabric. Parked cars of residents and visitors line the streets and, ironically, create an effective traffic buffer for pedestrians. With money and creativity the cars are worked into site design of new projects, either underground or in the center of the block.

The redevelopment of Alexandria's waterfront has continued the grid pattern on a larger scale; the formerly industrial lots can accommodate larger contemporary buildings and the cars that go with them. The commercial architecture along the city's waterfront is as undistinguished as that along K Street but, arrayed along the Potomac with spreading views and the changing light and sky of the waterfront, and linked by a series of trails and parks, the buildings create a luxurious urban environment decorated with sculpture and wrapped in landscaping.

New housing developers have followed the successful pattern of the past by building town houses that create a streetfront environment and private internal spaces. Brick is the material of choice and, except for occasional high-rise and garden apartments, neocolonial town houses in neat square blocks are the standard. All built at one time, they have none of the rough and tumble individuality of Old Town, and their condominium associations preclude odd paint colors and personal windowbox expressions.

King Street

Focusing development at Metro stops has been a policy in Virginia as in Maryland. In Alexandria, the King Street Metro station was placed about one-half mile west of U.S. Route 1, creating a new downtown of offices, stores, and housing, away from the historic waterfront.

stores, and housing, away from the historic waterfront.

Outside the historic district, the scale and architecture of King Street changes from the fine-grained detail of colonial and Victorian architecture to the larger scale of contemporary architecture. Like its historic neighbors, the new construction defines the street edge and creates an interesting pedestrian environment by building along the sidewalk. Old Town uses have also continued along King Street, creating a mixed streetscape of restaurants, specialty shops, and offices.

At the King Street Metro station new development is oriented toward Duke Street. The future mixed-use Carlyle neighborhood will be connected to Metro and commuter rail on King Street. The Carlyle neighborhood is a long-term plan to rescale and redevelop an area of suburban, car-oriented development and old industrial uses to a traditional urban grid, lined with buildings and public squares. Developers propose higher densities on the 75-acre parcel, including market-rate housing and various urban-style amenities, including a performing arts center. The King Street Station is the first completed part of this new neighborhood. ■

1. Torpedo Factory
105 North Union Street
architect unknown *1918*
Keyes Condon Florance *1983*

This building is a transformation of guns into butter. Construction of the cast-concrete building began after Armistice Day, and the factory operated through World War II making torpedo shell cases and other types of munitions. At its peak of production, the complex expanded to 10 buildings. After the war the federal government used the remaining four buildings for storage until 1969, when the City of

Alexandria bought them for $1.5 million.

After reviewing a number of redevelopment proposals, the city approved the use of the two smallest buildings as an arts center. The artists association, which formed to operate the center, used the city's $140,000 renovation fund to build interior studio walls, expand the plumbing and electrical services, and paint. The volunteer group eventually removed 40 truckloads of debris from the building.

In 1988 a wider renovation was completed, which created a mixed-use complex of residences, offices, shops, and restaurants. A full complement of public infrastructure, including docks, parks, and plazas, combine with the Arts Center to attract more than 850,000 visitors each year.

sidewalk, without the gardens and courtyards of the more residential parts of the city. The development is set on a first-floor parking garage behind a brick screen, and its other facades are articulated with individual front doors, stepped porches, or bay windows, depending on the character of the street they face.

This dense urban housing turns in on itself, away from the intensity of this urban environment, while creating a vivacious facade with stringcourses, gable roofs, decorative insets, and other eye-catching details.

3. Edward F. Carlough Plaza
601 North Fairfax Street
H. D. Nottingham—Robert Ingram
1986

This building is different from others along the Alexandria waterfront. Rather than copying K Street architecture or decorating itself with neocolonial ornament, the building recognizes its freestanding site and creates a sculptural presence.

The brown brick street facade is set above the sidewalk on a landscaped podium. The facade appears as a thin veneer, punched by small square windows, curved around a corner, lifting

2. Torpedo Factory Condominiums
125 North Lee Street
102–160 North Union Street
Metcalf and Associates *1984*

As with other new housing in and near Old Town, this development picks up on contextual clues. In this area of former industrial structures, the building is a single large mass, built right to the

up at the entrance and stepped to follow the building's sloped roof. The riverfront facade is composed of sloped solar panels sheathed in dark gray-green metal panels, also punched with square windows. Pipe rails complete an appearance that echoes the former and existing waterfront industrial uses.

Although the brown skin is a dull finish, the building finds its way to incorporate energy efficiency, the sheet metal work of its tenant, and a unique aesthetic position.

4. Canal Center Plaza
North Fairfax and 1st Streets
CHK Architects and Planners/M. Paul Friedberg & Partners *1986*

These office buildings were the first new construction along the riverfront and helped begin the area's revitalization and transformation of the riverfront from industrial uses to office uses. Their architecture is strictly K Street. Bands of brick alternate with dark glass ribbon

or punched windows. The buildings are lifted off the ground with pilotis and overhang a retail first floor. It is their spectacular waterfront location that distinguishes them.

The buildings are shifted into parallelograms to catch river views and sit around a courtyard behind the linear riverfront park and railroad tracks. A stepped fountain and sculpture garden lead to a riverfront walk. The sculpture is composed of fragments of seemingly ancient monuments which add an interesting layer of time to the project. It seems that as the river flows past, it has eroded to reveal pieces of a former city.

The sensitive riverfront siting that incorporates park and building has created a new community of buildings and people, both office workers and residents. New development has created new markets, and the older one-story, light industrial buildings in the vicinity have been renovated into luncheonettes, dry cleaners, and copy shops.

6. Pitt Street Center
1240–1250 Pitt Street
Rust Orling and Neal *1988*

5. Watergate of Alexandria
North Pitt and 2nd Streets
Smith and Williams *1974*

This megablock development breaks
down its scale and size by arranging a
variety of two- and three-story town
houses around paths and courtyards.
From the street, the brick, stucco, and
clapboard facades are in scale with
neighboring town houses, and colonial
details fit into the area's ambience. At
great expense, parking has been placed
underground.

Despite this careful contextualism,
the project is still less a part of the
community than a private enclave.
There are no paths or views through
the block, and the megablock breaks
up the gridded street pattern.

Other new housing development in
this part of Alexandria follows a similar
pattern of historically contextual buildings constructed on a larger scale than
their individual lot counterparts in Old
Town. Overall, they have created a
new neighborhood of mixed housing
and office uses.

This building, on the outer edge of the
waterfront neighborhood, evokes old
photos of cities where marvelously
ornate and stately buildings stood alone
amidst dirt streets and empty lots. The
building's neighbors include an auto
repair shop, an empty lot, and some
garden apartments.

The postmodern building uses both
the colonial and Victorian details of
Alexandria's architecture, but blows
them up to a huge scale. The two
facades of the L-shaped building define
a walled courtyard. The voussoirs of
their huge arched entrances are oversized and alternate between red brick
and white precast concrete. Both
entrances are topped with large round
windows that continue the alternating
pattern. A clock tower and large precast concrete balls at the entry gate add
Victorian references. The sloped roof,
split-face block watertable, and raised
basement give the building a colonial
feel.

By both simplifying and exaggerat-
ing historical details, the building
makes local references, but carves out
its own space and time.

7. King Street Station
Duke Street and Diagonal Road
Florance Eichbaum Esocoff King *1993*

Alexandria's urban fabric gives this
community its distinct character. The
narrow grid streets are tightly woven
with row houses, detatched single family homes, and their gardens. The
weave is looser at the edges where
larger projects are neatly finished with
parks and plazas along the riverfront.

The tight weave begins to unravel at
the community's western edge, where it
meets train yards and highways. This
project begins to restitch the fabric by
using buildings to define outdooor
space as well as enclose indoor space.

The complex of buildings fills a
block. Their different materials, decoration, and size distinguish the project's
different components. The buildings are
arranged to define the outer street edge
and to create a central plaza lined with
shops and restaurants that is reached
through a series of axes. Along
Diagonal Road the hotel's buff brick is
vaguely Art Deco, marked with towers
and barrel-shaped bays, capped by a
checkerboard cornice. Along Reinekers

Road the office building is raised above
a retail first floor and sheathed in brick
with burgundy accents.

The most dramatic facade is along
King Street. The buff brick building is
ranged in a hemicycle around a plaza
and drive, and fronted by a single-story
shed-roofed structure that echoes the
building's curve. It seems oddly oriented now, facing a strip shopping center across a busy road, but it will
eventually anchor the Carlyle neighborhood being built in Alexandria's traditional grid pattern.

8. 1555 King Street
Anderson Pace *1988*

Another careful stitch in Alexandria's
urban fabric, this new building neatly
fills its spot on the street. By meeting
the neighboring setbacks and using
brick, the building responds to the
established urban context.

Above the retail floor the building
steps back behind a porch level to
lessen its impact on the street, while
providing the leasable space that makes
reconstruction feasible.

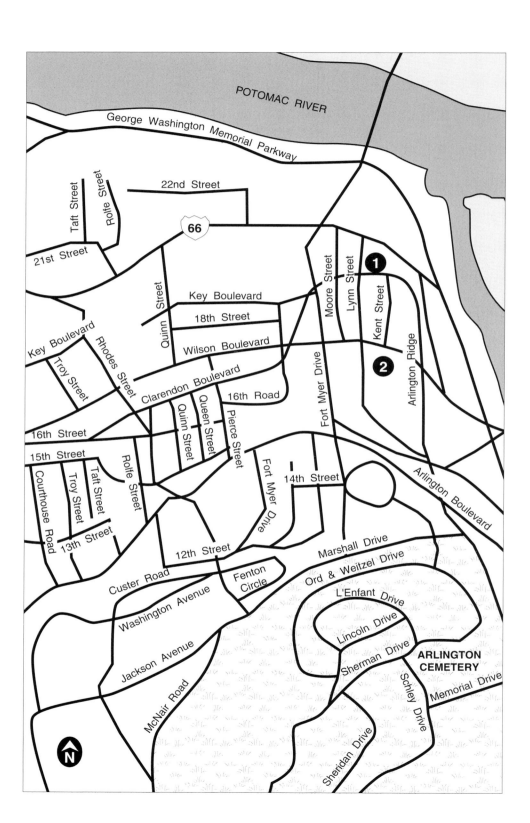

Rosslyn

Rome, if built at all, must be built in a day.

Marcus Cato

Rome was not built in one day.

John Heywood, Proverbs, 1546

Economics is a straightforward master, using resources in the manner most expedient. Rosslyn was laid out shortly after the Civil War, and was a transportation terminal for land and river traffic, connected with Georgetown over the C&O Canal's Aqueduct Bridge. Rosslyn's waterfront location became, and was until recently, an area of light industry and warehouses, oil storage tanks, and retail uses. Transportation by river and later by highways provided quick access to downtown Washington.

Viewed from Georgetown across the period lamp-festooned Key Bridge, Rosslyn looks European, like the completely modern districts built just outside the historic centers of continental cities after World War II. These districts are uncomfortable and barely livable, but they absorb

267

contemporary development while saving the historic center from intrusions. So it is with Rosslyn. Its tidy—if ugly and boring—clump of office towers and hotels takes development pressure off Georgetown and Washington's monumental core.

In the 1960s Rosslyn began its transition into an office center, still taking advantage of its waterfront views and proximity to downtown. Between 1960 and 1970, 27 major buildings were built. Rosslyn was reconstructed at a time when the designer's hand was almost impossible to detect in the sameness of modern architecture. At the same time, the planner's hand was evident everywhere in complicated traffic patterns and other urban systems, like raised sidewalks. Pleasing and functional patterns of city building that had worked for centuries were set aside for a grandiose plan. In Rosslyn, the result is an awkward, nowhere neighborhood of bland buildings that have become fortresses separating the pedestrian from the auto.

"Every principal highway which serves the region passes through Rosslyn or can be reached within minutes." This boosterish statement in the Rosslyn Station Area Plan sums up the essence of contemporary Rosslyn—a neighborhood so fractured by freeways that pedestrians, for their own safety, are routed through skywalks that barely connect buildings. The system's approach, seemed so rational on paper—separating conflicting uses—has created an alienating environment.

New planning efforts include the creation of a Main Street-type focus for development lined with ground-level retail, "project monumentation" (translation: vapid pieces of public art that no one likes or understands), a series of linked plazas, and a riverfront overlook. These planning goals recognize the essence of a successful urban environment—an accretion of activity that creates character in an adaptable space—and are a move away from the inflexible structure—freeways and skywalks—that have branded Rosslyn.

Today's planners have to live with the expensive fabric created 20 years ago, so the skywalks stay. Architects force their buildings into odd gyrations, using shape or detail to grab a view or punch out a piece of skyline. ■

1. USA Today Towers
1100 Wilson Boulevard
Hellmuth, Obata, Kassebaum (Davis Buckley) *1977*

Until recently, the buildings that made up modern Rosslyn sprouted with little regard to the Potomac River. Rectangular towers, they faced all directions equally. That changed with the USA Today Towers. The building's two towers were designed to work on a narrow, hilly site and to accommodate the path of Nash Street. Their siting, perpendicular to the river, defines a Rosslyn skyline without blocking views to Washington.

The buildings dominate the Rosslyn skyline. Originally designed as 16 stories, they were raised to 32 stories by a

transfer of development rights from another site. While neighboring buildings squat in their dark glass and earth-tone precast panels, these buildings shimmer with a silvery aluminum and glass curtain wall. The ribbon windows follow the building's soft curves, reflecting patterns of light across the length of the facade. While these ribbon windows could have been ultra-dark and mullion-less, they are grayish blue, are broken by mullions, and have the added detail of an operable sash.

By relying on a defining shape and elegant detailing rather than decoration of the moment, the architect has created a building with a timeless image.

2. Potomac Tower
1001 Wilson Boulevard
Pei Cobb Freed and Partners *1988*

This office building at Rosslyn's Potomac shore is a gentle curve of mul-tihued glass rising in steps to two glass finials. Like most buildings of the 1980s, this one bursts out of the plain box of its predecessors. Following an approach Pei's firm calls "complementary fragmentation," the design uses

varied materials, shapes, and colors on the building's facades to relate it to neighboring buildings and the site, while reducing its apparent bulk. The building is sensitive to its riverfront site and its details are carefully modulated; no move is so bold that it overwhelms the whole composition.

The building's facade is banded with concrete and glass, and curves to follow the shoreline. The concrete panels are lightly tinted and scored to emphasize horizontal lines. The facade rises to twin lanterns, lit in the evening, which add a depth and variety to the Rosslyn skyline. The central glass and concrete facade is flanked by setback wings of precast concrete that read as separate buildings. As with all Pei buildings, geometrical forms and fine detail combine to create a high finish.

The building also takes advantage of views to Georgetown and downtown Washington. It begins to address Rosslyn as a place, and not an office dumping ground.

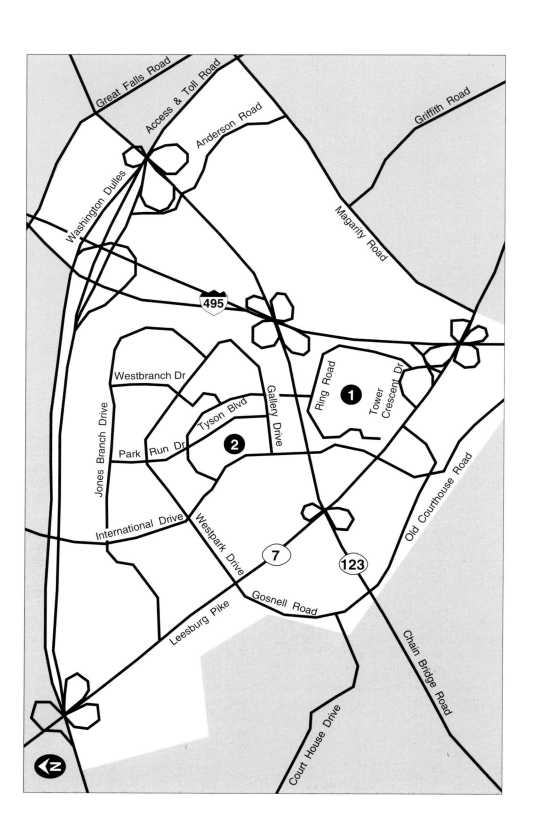

Tysons Corner

The fine arts are five in number, to wit: painting, sculpture, poetry, music, architecture–whose main branch is confectionary.

Marie–Antoine Careme

Until little more than a generation ago, Tysons Corner was a rural crossroads where locals gathered at a feed store or a beer joint. It was surrounded by apple orchards and dairy farms and was far enough from the District of Columbia to be "the country." As suburban development spread, the area was farmed for a different crop: gravel. The gravel pits and the grading that went along with them changed the profile of the land and set the stage for a new era.

The development of Tysons Corner has been portrayed as a battle between greed and good, the powerful and the powerless, old ways and new ways. Value judgments aside, forces of individual vision and larger societal changes combined to radically alter the old farms and rolling hills to a new environment criss-crossed by highways, spotted with buildings in parking lots, and offering hospitals and headquarters.

The first new houses were built in Tysons after World War II; they were seen as a sign of prosperity by locals who had toughed out the Depression and World War II rationing. In 1964, the Capitol Beltway opened and increased access between suburban settlements in Maryland and Virginia, while bypassing the District. With the construction of the Dulles Toll Road and the upgrading of Routes 7 and 123, Tysons Corner became a regional center rather than just a country crossroads.

The area's location between the District and Dulles International Airport and its ready highway access began to draw offices and high-tech businesses. The businesses were attractive and generated jobs and taxes—just what a growing suburban community would want.

Tysons grew during the 1970s and 1980s following the edge-city pattern, which is supported by the economics of land development. Land costs are low enough, at least initially, to spread buildings out, separated

EDGE CITIES

MOST PEOPLE WORK in a technoburb, or shop in a service city, or go to dinner and a movie in superburbia. At the very least, they probably drive through a peripheral center once a day without even realizing it. These weird terms are the coinage of planners and urbanists grappling with what Joel Garreau, a Washington Post reporter, calls edge cities and describes in a book by the same name.

Edge cities are concentrations of office and retail development usually built at the freeway edges of a metropolitan area. As downtown land became scarce and expensive and its buildings grew outmoded and difficult to reach by car, businesses sought new suburban locations that were closer to highways and airports, within easy reach of a large and educated labor pool, and where land was abundant and relatively cheap. Edge cities sprang up from what, only a decade or so before, had been cornfields or a country crossroads.

The overwhelming physical characteristic of edge cities is that they are built at a car scale. That scale creates a faster and larger environment than downtown's pedestrian scale. The car scale dictates every detail of edge-city construction. The architecture of edge-city buildings is designed to be noticed at highway speeds—exaggerated cornice lines, two- and three-story porticos, multiple corners of folded glass—creating a kind of supergraphic architecture. The buildings are set in parking lots and surrounded by manicured landscaping, fountains, and plazas. Miles of marble foyers and truckloads of brick pavers contribute to a "class A" environment that reads high rent. The extremes of size and luxury are necessary to define a new

environment that cannot rely on the historical shorthand used in downtowns to send messages about safety and class.

Socially, edge cities function differently from downtown. Rather than bumping into a friend or colleague on the sidewalk, one is more likely to bump a stranger's fender during the lunchtime rush hour. The scale of an edge city makes us dependent on our cars. Even though sidewalks are everywhere, they lead nowhere and no one walks. An edge city is also an agglomeration of private spaces. There is no room or reason for courthouse steps or public gardens in edge cities, which are built strictly to the bottom line. Parks and plazas are provided as amenities, required by local planners and used by developers to attract tenants who can pay higher rents. While a shopping mall or office building plaza might seem like a great place to gather signatures for a petition or watch an impromptu performance, just try it and watch security swoop out of nowhere.

For the most part, planners and architects who cut their teeth on Italian piazzas do not like edge cities, but these communities are the undeniable future. Behind the steering wheel or at a sidewalk cafe, people are people. They like to gather and watch and participate and will find ways to do it regardless of the built environment's hospitality. Rather than lamenting downtown we should seek to create it anew.

by surface parking lots; underground or structured lots are too expensive to build.   Highway proximity dictates commercial uses—either office or light industrial, and eventually, retail malls. Without a resident or voting population, Tysons Corner grew as a political nonentity, an area that generated taxes but could take development without upsetting residents.

The buildings that make up Tysons Corner are designed to catch the attention of drivers passing by at 60 miles per hour. The three white stair towers of the National Automobile Dealers Association loom over Route 7 like space-age silos. The gigantic moon gate on the facade of the Tycon Courthouse has earned it the name of the Toilet Bowl Building.

Eventually, Tysons took on a life of its own, becoming an archetypal edge city, a surrogate downtown—thousands of square feet of offices and shopping malls, generating traffic and tax revenue. It was a place without a center, but for sheer size and variety it has become a tourist destination in its own right.

Most recently, consultants have been hired and competitions have been held for ideas on how to retrofit Tysons Corner to create community. Plans have proposed everything from more residents and a ring road, to a "Ponte Vecchio" connecting isolated office buildings. Developers and urbanists debate whether Tysons and edge cities are good or bad, dead or alive, but they all agree that edge cities are evolving, and like any unfinished work, they have rough edges. ■

1. Tycon Towers
8000 Towers Crescent Drive
Philip Johnson *1987*

As a self-admitted "whore" of architecture, Philip Johnson must occasionally turn a few tricks, and this building is one of them.

The building is an odd hybrid—a modern glass curtain wall screened with engaged brick columns running nearly twelve stories between a brick base and cornice. Grouped, freestanding columns in the center of the building rise from an arched portico and are topped with doubled brick arches. The color and composition remind some people of a giant shopping bag. Johnson explores the motif of columns screening a glass wall more subtly and successfully at One Franklin Square in downtown Washington.

The building's unwieldy scale

comes from its location along a high-way and the need to be visible and memorable to passersby. Also to accommodate the car, the building is backed up by a parking garage from which most people enter the building through the back door. Yet Johnson also uses the architectural iconography of a more traditional urban building: a formal front door behind a landscaped lawn complete with front stairs and flower beds. No one will ever walk up those stairs, and as they march across the lawn they are as decorative and useless as a man's necktie on his shirt-front. Johnson has ignored the realities of car-dependant suburbs and applied traditional architectural forms at a such a huge scale that they become foolish.

2. Tysons II Galleria
Route 123 and International Drive
Hellmuth Obata Kassebaum *1988*

While this project's architecture is unexceptional, the development is an archetype of edge-city development. Built on a reclaimed gravel pit, the site is inching its way toward highest and best use, from woods to farmland, to surface mining, and now real estate development, including retail, office, and hotel facilities.

The designers and developers have specified and built high-quality infra-structure and broad, sweeping roads, equipped with coordinated light posts and signs and landscaped with flower beds. When complete, 30 percent of the site will remain open space.

The buildings are what real estate agents call signature sites: big buildings with large, flexible floor plans that make big architectural statements. The mall department stores have a shared theme of a broad arched entry, and the hotel is topped by a gabled roof. The patterns are reminiscent of some histor-ical past—Louis Sullivan or Georgian mansions—but carry only a faint scent of the original's meaning.

Like much edge-city development the complex floats loosely in space and time. Its physical environment leaves no sharp images in memory, but is an amorphous mass of winding roads and parking lots. Its architecture is neither an accurate recreation of the past, nor a challenging future aesthetic.

MALL VS. MAIN STREET

SOME ELEMENTS OF architecture and urbanism have developed out of our physical nature. Our eyes can see only so far and we can cover only so much ground on foot; both simple and complex transactions require physical presence. Television has extended our vision, the car has expanded our step, and the computer has linked us to the world, but our physical environments are still shaped to meet our physical limits.

The world's oldest settlements were arranged to create either market or ceremonial main streets. The Aztec pyramids, the Greek stoa, the Roman fora are all primary spaces of community interaction shaped by buildings. These ancient forms were repeated in Europe and colonial America at varying levels of grandeur and purpose.

The arrangement of buildings along a street made sense for a walking citizenry, and shopkeepers took advantage of their pace and proximity to create signs and storefronts to catch their attention. Our natural wish to gather and meet our neighbors created the Main Street of myth and reality.

Every American community has had a main street—skirting a common, running alongside railroad tracks or a river, anchored by a depot or bridge. Along the street are varying certainties: old houses that have been turned into shops or offices; a gathering place for the local sages, maybe a coffee shop, street corner, or garage; a civic use such as a post office or city hall. Main Street's form and uses served pedestrians, horses, and carriages, and adapted to streetcars and automobiles. What many main streets could not adapt to was the shopping mall. New stores in a new environment with free parking were too much for Main Street.

Ironically, the mall simply took the form of Main Street—buildings arranged to create a space—and placed it in the middle of a parking lot. Eventually the mall was covered and climate controlled, expanding its uses to include events and entertainment.

But the mall is only a facsimile, not true community. The mall is a controlled environment designed to generate consumption. A path through the mall takes you past as many storefronts as possible. Music, views, and even smells are choreographed to entice a person to spend more time and more money. But the mall represents only one aspect of community: commerce. There is no place for governance, education, or worship. Even charity is kept at bay. Some malls refused to allow the Salvation Army's Christmas bell-ringers on their property until first lady Barbara Bush made a pointed shopping trip and donated for the cameras.

There is no challenge, surprise, or serendipity in a mall. Main Street, on the other hand, has a depth of history and purpose. The environment it creates may not be cohesive, but it is one that we can change and use according to our desires.

Reston's sinuous roads create enclave of houses segregated by the streets that lead to no single center. Each neighborhood has its own center and services. Reston's attitude of secluded naturalism is even apparent its selection of map design.

Reston

Which of you, intending to build a tower, sitteth not down first, and counteth the cost, whether he have sufficient to finish it?

LUKE, 14.28

From its earliest days, the land that is now Reston was envisioned as community. This part of the land grant to Lord Fairfax was farmed for many years, but as early as 1790 a community was formed: Ash Grove.

In 1886, the land was sold to Dr. William Whiele, whose dream was to develop a town on this former dairy farm. Roads were laid out, lakes were dug, and buildings were constructed. But before the community was established, Whiele died. The land was sold to a gentleman farmer, A. Smith Bowman, who kept his eye on the future. He continued to farm, but when it was clear that Prohibition would be lifted, he built a distillery and turned an old hotel building into a clubhouse and dance hall.

After World War II, metropolitan Washington began developing into suburban communities. Bowman's farm soon sat amid an international airport, a shopping mall, and freeways. Again moving with the times, he created a master plan for a town of 30,000 that included single-family homes and commercial and industrial districts amidst parks and bridle trails. Sewering problems and the lack of a suitable zoning ordinance in the Fairfax County Code scuttled the plan.

In 1960, the land was sold to Robert E. Simon (whose initials would form the community's name), a New York developer who envisioned a community combining the natural beauty of a rural environment with the variety and excitement of midtown Manhattan. He persuaded Fairfax County to amend the existing two-acre-lot zoning to allow construction of his community. In return, the county required a low-density buffer on Reston's eastern edge and 10 acres of parkland for every 1,000 residents.

Simon, like most new town developers, set forth goals for the community that went beyond making a profit. He wanted to offer a choice of leisure opportunities and a range of housing styles and prices. He believed that individual dignity should be the focal point for all planning. Reston was to be a place where people could live, work, and find a variety of cultural and commercial facilities in place, and where structural and natural beauty would be fostered. The final goal was for Reston to be a financial success.

After financial difficulties brought on by the project's large scale, Simon ceded management to Gulf Oil Company in exchange for a $15 million loan. Mobil Land Development Company later acquired control. The Reston Land Corporation is now bringing Simon's vision into the future with the development of Reston Town Center.

Today Reston is a mature community with residents of 20 years or more. Like every community, it is evolving. Home rule, commercial development, and other issues of community change are given close attention by residents who are committed to the Reston way of life. ∎

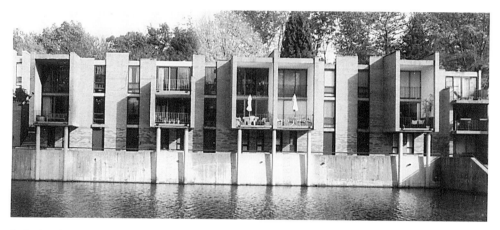

1. Lake Anne
North Shore Drive
Whittlesey and Conklin *1964*

Lake Anne was the first of Reston's seven village centers to be constructed. It was intended to provide convenience shopping but also to be a center of community life. It was also unlike anything anyone had ever seen in the suburbs or in most American cities.

The lake itself was created from a hollow in the land. The village around it was modeled on that architectural favorite, the Campo, or central square in Siena, Italy. Both are well-defined spaces created by tightly placed buildings. At Lake Anne Village, apartments

above shops are arranged in a semicircle around a plaza that fronts the lake. The village is further marked by a highrise apartment building, Heron House. The outer edge of the village center abuts a parking lot, an abrupt notice that Reston is not Siena.

Lake Anne is charming. Its buildings are sited, scaled, and detailed to create visual interest and pleasant spaces. On a fine day parents bring their children to feed the ducks, neighbors meet at the stores, and people linger at the outdoor restaurants. From within, the plaza at the center seems a modern interpretation of a medieval square—a sudden opening in the dense fabric of a town. Unfortunately, immediately outside the walls of this carefully scaled space are parking lots and bucolic suburbia. The village center is hidden and lacks the sheer density of people needed to activate this type of new urban space. It remains, however, a symbol of all that Reston strives to be.

2. Waterview Cluster
North Shore Drive
Chloethiel Woodard Smith *1965*

Reston's planners and designers experimented with planning notation and community signage in the conscious realization that they were building something new. They also, of course, experimented with architecture.

These 90 town houses dispensed with the typical suburban pattern of separate houses with front and back yards. Each home instead is sited to take best advantage of the surrounding woods and water views. The houses also provide outdoor access, some with exterior spiral staircases right into the waters of Lake Anne.

The attention to detail in these buildings and their thoughtful siting has created a development that is dense, but that offers a real variety of building profiles and experiences, rather than mere repetition. On a warm, sunny day when a resident can take to the water on a raft with a magazine and a cool drink, the appeal of Lake Anne and the houses in the Waterview Cluster is obvious.

3. Hickory Cluster
Maple Ridge Road
Charles Goodman *1964*

The first residents of Reston had a pioneer spirit; they were willing to experiment with community and with

architecture. The Hickory Cluster, a series of attached town houses, some arranged in straight rows and others stepped around plazas, look neither urban nor suburban, but some kind of happy combination.

The buildings lack the clapboard walls, gabled roofs, and fanlight front doors of typical suburban homes. Instead the structural elements, concrete lintels, brick and stucco walls, windows, and balcony railings recede and project to create alternating rectilinear patterns. As with the best buildings in Reston, they are sited to emphasize entry into the cluster, to take advantage of views, and to balance private and public spaces.

4. Reston Town Center
Reston Parkway and Market Street
RTKL Associates, Inc. *1990*

In planning Reston, a large commercial and community center was envisioned at the outset, but the concept needed a population and an economic base to make it a reality.

In the early 1960s, when Reston was planned and designed, its architects and developers sought new forms of community. Since then, designers

have returned to traditional community and building forms. Reston Town Center and the surrounding villages of Reston present an encapsulated lesson in community design over the last few decades.

In contrast to the sinuous roads, landscaped paths, and wood-sided buildings tucked into hills and valleys of Reston's early villages, the town center is constructed along a straight axis, its sidewalks are lined with brick and precast concrete buildings oriented to a central cross point marked by a fountain. Reston Town Center has taken the form of a traditional main street and altered it to meet current economic demands. Reston's main street is surrounded not by a grid of streets lined with more buildings, but by parking lots (intended eventually to be built out). It is lined with shops, even a movie theater, but the civic uses— library, police, and hospital—are in the next neighborhood and not easily accessible by pedestrians.

In fact, Reston Town Center is more like a mall without a roof than a main street. Like a mall, it is privately owned and a designed shopping experience under single management that supplies advertising, maintenance, and security. The main street of the past was a sometimes unpredictable place created by individuals coming together. Unlike a traditional main street, the streets and sidewalks of Reston Town Center are private property. Events must be cleared by a screening committee. The owners of Reston Town Center understand the special character of community in Reston and have sought to create both a civic space and an appealing shopping environment.

Reston Town Center is a perfectly painted picture, the picture of community as we wish it could be: festivals, sidewalk cafes, and balloons. It has none of the melancholy of time or loneliness. It floats in time and space as a discrete object, connected to history only by slim threads of imaged details.

The Art Decoesque theater marquee speaks of Saturday matinees, but inside it is a multiplex.

Planned expansion of Town Center includes high-density residential uses located adjacent to the Dulles Toll Road to increase the feasibility of future public transit. Expansion plans also include regional retailers—large stores with comprehensive inventories. This would be a departure from the small-scale, walkable urban street profile that fits with the image created in Town Center. Reston Land Corporation feels this use is a market niche that will make Town Center economically stronger and a design challenge they are up to.

5. Pavilion at Fountain Square
Reston Town Center
RTKL *1993*

The pavilion's site, at the centerpiece of Town Center's main street, was intended as a gallery to house art on loan from museums, but the concept presented architectural and operational problems. Reston Town Center developers scheduled entertainment programs, like concerts and seasonal ice skating, as a temporary way to enliven the space. The events proved so popular that the developers shifted their concept and decided to continue the events and permanently house the programs.

The designers had to create a permanent, year-round structure but without the visual weight of a building. It also had to accommodate an ice rink, yet have acceptable acoustics for concerts. The building is a delicate combination of steel, glass, and fabric. The result is a pavilion reminiscent of London's Crystal Palace, winter gardens (elegant greenhouses) and even a market shed. As Benjamin Forgey wrote— perhaps the highest compliment from an urbanist—"It belongs."

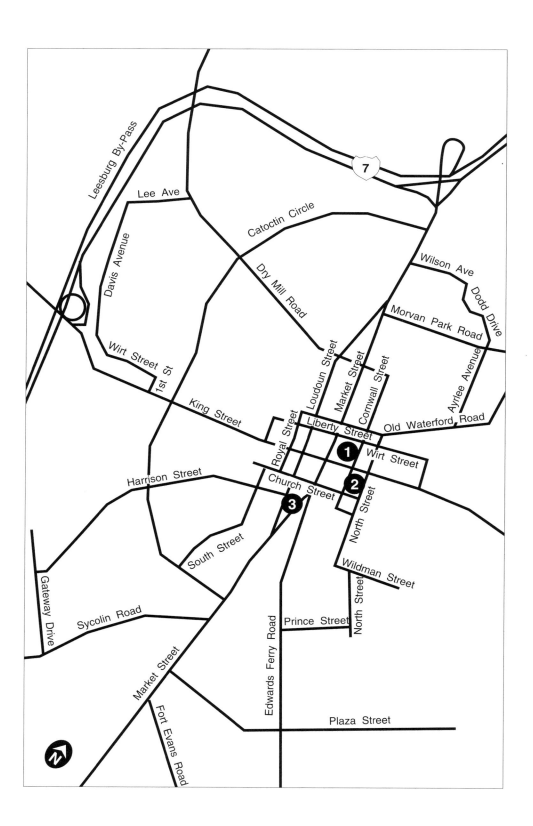

Leesburg

*If we are to save our cities, and restore to American public life the sense of
shared experience, trust, and common purpose that seem to be draining
out of it, the quality of public design has got to be made a public issue because it
is a political fact.*

SENATOR DANIEL PATRICK MOYNIIHAN, ARCHITECTURAL RECORD, DECEMBER 1967

Settlers from Pennsylvania and New York came to Loudoun County
in the 1720s, establishing farms and small villages. Leesburg, at the intersection of the Old Ridge Road, crossing the Blue Ridge (now Route 7), and
the north-south Carolina Road (now Route 15), was well located to
become a market center and county seat. The town was chartered by the
Virginia General Assembly in 1758 and the first courthouse was built there
in 1761. The original town, which has since annexed land to cover 11
square miles, was 60 acres divided into 70 lots.

The railroad arrived from Alexandria in the 1840s, further solidifying
the town's role as a market center. The Washington and Old Dominion
rail line is now a 45-mile long bicycle and hiking trail stretching from the
District to the Piedmont.

Throughout history Leesburg has played its small role. Local farmers
contracted with General Washington to feed Revolutionary troops, a local
manor house sheltered the Constitution and Declaration of Independence
during the War of 1812, and a Civil War battle was fought on bluffs overlooking the Potomac. Leesburg was the sleepy center of a rural community and a charming getaway for the rich and mighty in nearby D.C. The
guide at Oatlands, a 19th-century Classical Revival mansion surrounded
by tiered formal gardens, recounts tales of Franklin Delano Roosevelt dri-
ving out from the White House on an occasional hot summer afternoon.

By the 1950s, however, Leesburg had been absorbed into the metropolitan economy. The Federal Aviation Administration settled there, and,
as development spread west through Fairfax, Loudoun County's roads and
subdivisions stretched east to meet it.

The historic core of Leesburg with its pre-Revolutionary and colonial
buildings was placed in the National Register of Historic Places in 1970.

The charming town center is surrounded by a moat of partially leased strip shopping centers and their parking lots. Although the pattern of development has changed over time, the town is still a market and local government center. Even as population in the county shifts to the more suburban east, and office parks sprout along Route 7, Leesburg retains its historic role as the focal point of community. ∎

1. Town Hall
25 West Market Street
Hanno Weber and Associates *1993*

In 1987 the Town of Leesburg held a design competition for a new town hall. The site, a former gas station, is in the middle of the block, between Loudoun and Market Streets. This modest and hidden location contrasts with the more traditionally sited County Office Building and Courthouse on a central, green public square, marked by a fence and surrounded by war memorials. The Town Hall site is a slot in a block, rather than a formal site distinct from mercantile buildings.

The modesty of the site is compounded by the architect's decision to pull the building back from the sidewalk and Market Street, behind a small plaza. Although it distinguishes the Town Hall from its neighbors, the effect is quiet and contemplative, more colle-

giate than civic.

The competition program also required the design to accommodate a parking garage in the center of the block. Although the garage makes an airy, open connection to a green plaza behind the Town Hall, it presents a blank facade among Loudoun Street's shopfronts, and dominates the interior of the block, which was once an open and easy shortcut for pedestrians.

In a small historic town center like Leesburg's, scale is everything. The parking garage, though graceful in its connections, overpowers the Town Hall. Instead of making the Town Hall just another slot of building, it might have been placed in the center of the block, higher than the street, in a complementary relationship to the County Courthouse. Alternatively, placing the Town Hall on the streetfront would have maintained the integrity of a building edge along the sidewalk, but

that effect is lost by pulling the building back behind the courtyard along Market Street and the blank garage face along Loudoun Street.

2. Loudoun County Offices
18 North King Street
Kamstra, Dickerson and Associates
1976

For many years the Loudoun County Offices were housed in an old resort hotel on the edge of the courthouse green. The two-story, wood-frame building eventually became unsafe and was lost by demolition through neglect. When the county chose to rebuild a new office building on the same site, the design had to meet with the approval of Leesburg's Board of Architectural Review. Many of the conservative board members thought that the new building should look like an antebellum mansion, complete with white columns. Rather than ersatz history, the architects wisely created a design sensitive to the site and the town's surrounding historic buildings. A local lobbying effort convinced the town council of the building's merits, which were later recognized with a number of awards.

The two-story building edges the courthouse green, providing a subtle

background for the historic courthouse, which remains central on the site. The building's street edge is the brick facade and sloping metal roof of the supervisors' auditorium, in scale with the neighboring mercantile and residential buildings. The offices are behind an arcade on the ground floor and are set back on the second floor mimicking the design of the old hotel porches and creating a covered space from which county offices are visible and accessible. A covered shortcut runs between the auditorium and the offices. Both the building's brick color and roof pitch were chosen by sampling the brick and roof slopes of neighboring buildings and finding a compatible tone.

The building's historic links are further emphasized by the inclusion of a piece of Loudoun Castle, brought from England by the Countess of Loudoun, who visited for the Bicentennial.

3. Mighty Midget
217 Market Street, SE
architect unknown *circa 1946*

This odd building is, in its small way, representative of American vernacular architecture. Vernacular styles use local materials, shaped by the craftsman's hand to meet an immediate demand. They are buildings of both common sense and whimsy. Mighty Midget exhibits a little of both.

Cobbled together from the fuselage of a B-29 bomber, and serving quick meals to a loyal clientele, it represents technological and social change: a world in which old airplane parts are handier than wood clapboards and a quick hot dog is a satisfying lunch. A *Washington Post* writer described this local landmark as looking like a "space-age outhouse."

Notable Buildings

1. Pope-Leighey House
Mount Vernon Parkway and U.S. Route 1 (at Woodlawn Plantation)
Frank Lloyd Wright *1940*

Wright not only designed custom buildings like Fallingwater and the Guggenheim Museum for wealthy clients, but also applied his genius to the construction of housing for the common man. Rather than build "another little imitation of a mansion," Wright developed the Usonian house. This concept for mass-produced housing was based on principles of construction, organization, and decoration that could make home building cheaper and faster, but still create unique homes.

The Pope-Leighey house was originally built in Falls Church and moved to the grounds of Woodlawn Plantation in 1965 when it was threatened by the construction of U.S. Route 66. The house is constructed of interlocking panels of sandwiched plywood on a slab floor warmed with "gravity heat," two construction techniques pioneered by Wright for the Usonian house. The

house also features familiar Wrightian design motifs. Its low, overhanging eaves enclose interlocking wings of the building. The horizontal lines created by the sandwiched plywood facade contrast with the strong vertical patterns created by grouped windows and doors.

In *The Natural House* Wright described the Usonian concept as reflecting the spirit of democracy, "the individual integrated and free in an environment of his own...." It was a comment directed, perhaps, at the monolithic sameness in the work of his International Style contemporaries. Ironically, the construction industry and popular tastes have swept aside the housing ideas of both Wright and the modernists. The suburbs have been filled with the little mansions so derided by modern architects.

2. Hollin Hills
off Fort Hunt Road, Alexandria
Charles M. Goodman *1950*

After World War II, Washington and the rest of the country underwent a suburban explosion. Acres of farmland and woods were developed to build housing for veterans and their young families. While many suburban developments were miniature versions of the local historic vernacular, from Mount Vernon to a Cape Cod saltbox stamped out on flat, curved streets, Hollin Hills was an attempt to use the natural environment in both siting and designing houses.

The neighborhood's hills were neither graded nor stripped of their trees, creating small house lots, but ones that have privacy and views. Flat roofs, rectilinear and interlocking buildings, and glass walls are combined in various patterns to create nearly 500 houses out of a standard palette that offers variations for site and personal taste. Residents speak fondly of comfortable homes that are cool in the summer and warm in the winter, filled with sunlight slanting through glass walls.

Charles Goodman is a Washington architect who was instrumental in introducing contemporary housing styles to the metropolitan area. His designs have been built as well in Reston and in Wheaton, Maryland.

3. Dulles International Airport
Dulles Access Road, Chantilly
Eero Saarinen and Associates *1962*

On a flat plain at the foot of the Blue Ridge, about 30 miles outside of Washington, stands Dulles Airport. Built three decades ago, it is one of the greatest buildings of 20th-century Washington and one of the best in America. The airport is a dramatic expression of flight in a concrete catenary that Saarinen described as "the best thing I have done."

Passengers enter the airport along a sweeping curve of parkway that offers constantly changing views. The thrusting peristyle of the terminal dominates, anchored by the futuristic tower beyond. It is an especially stunning sight at night. Despite the building's modernity, it has a classical symmetry and repose accentuated by the fact that the visitor circles around it in order to reach it.

Along with a beautiful structure, Saarinen introduced operational inno-

vations to airport design. Rather than bringing the airplane to the passengers, he brought the passengers to the airplane, via shuttle buses that could connect directly to the planes and gates. Freed of loading and unloading aircraft, the terminal could be compact. Saarinen's terminal sits on a raised podium that allows vehicular traffic to be separated into three levels.

Dulles was designed for international jet traffic in 1960, and is struggling to adapt to the regional hub systems of the 1980s and 1990s. But over time little development has occurred to diminish the terminal's presence. Airports typically grow by grafting concrete megastructures onto an existing terminal or adding new buildings. Dulles's dynamic beauty and purity of form would be destroyed by careless additions just as a classical temple would. Expanded gate facilities have been added in the middle of the airfield, away from the terminal.

Unlike a classical temple, Saarinen's form can be expanded, and plans are underway to do so. Some of Saarinen's innovations, the shuttle buses and the mechanical schedule board, will be lost in the renovation, but the original terminal will be marked by a subtle change in building

4. Immanuel Presbyterian Church
123 Saville Road, McLean
Hartman-Cox Architects *1980*

The firm of Hartman-Cox is known for combining historical vernacular with a modern attitude. This church is an example of the architects' deftness in creating a defining form. By mirroring a simple farmhouse that serves as a parish house and connecting it with a covered walk the design creates a courtyard focused on two linden trees. At the same time it creates a new form and site for the church.

The gabled, barnlike new building is a singularly appropriate form for a church, and an apt local reference. It is not an overpowering single mass, but rather is brought into scale with the farmhouse by a series of stepped gables. The building's courtyard facade is a light-filled grid of windows, while its outer facade is a solid face of linear board-and-batten walls. The gable roof on this side is enlivened by alternating dormers.

Many contemporary churches opt for strangely shaped roofs inspired by Le Corbusier's master work of ecclesiastical modernism, Notre Dame de Ronchamps. Here the architects have returned to a simple but expressive form that is elegantly sited and

detailed. The whole composition is one that is pleasing and functional. It creates a convivial yet calm space.

5. Center for Innovative Technology
2214 Rock Hill Road
Arquitectonica *1988*

The architects here have created a singularly exciting building, not only in its appearance, but in its function as well. This startling building is bold by Washington's conservative design standards. It stands apart from its mediocre neighbors lining the Dulles Toll Road. Such innovation does not come easy; it is also one of Washington's least popular new buildings.

From the toll road, the CIT's randomly patterned sloping glass walls and oddly raked roof emerge from the trees, giving drivers a teasing, only partial glimpse of the building. It is approached from a curving drive that sweeps around the building, offering more at each bend. The building's base is a black, caged podium that houses

parking. From that, two glass buildings emerge, the sloped tower visible from the toll road and a lower pavilion clad in similarly patterned glass skin. The two are connected by a curved pavilion of clear glass and bold white window frames.

The building's seemingly odd configuration creates unique links with the site. The inverted slope of the glass tower reflects the thick surrounding woodland, emphasizing the natural environment.

Most exciting is the approach to the building. From the curving drive a direct ramp leads through the parking podium to its landscaped roof, which is a formal entrance plaza. No cars are visible on the site; they are neatly tucked into the parking podium on which the building sits. The architects have recognized that this building will be reached by car and have designed an approach that is best appreciated from the dynamic view of the driver. This organization allows the CIT to be a compact, refined object in a relatively unspoiled landscape.

Others have addressed the sprawling, auto-oriented suburbs by looking backward and trying to instill urbanism in the suburbs. Arquitectonica has designed a building that works with the modern suburb without perpetuating its typical use of land.

6. National Airport North Terminal
George Washington Parkway
Cesar Pelli *1996 (projected)*

Pelli cut his teeth on airport design, working in Saarinen's office on the design of Dulles Airport. In his work since then Pelli has explored patterns of linear organization that are eminently suitable for an airport terminal. Planning for National Airport began in

Photo credit: Cesar Pelli

1938, and the airport was operating fully by 1941, after armies of WPA workers had completed its curved terminal with glass windows overlooking the runways. In 1942, the WPA Guide to Washington noted that cab fare from the airport to downtown was 60 cents and that a sightseeing blimp moored at the airport was part of the Washington skyline. As the suburbs grew conflicts over the noise generated by flight paths grew also, but despite repeated attempts to move or close the airport, its convenience to downtown keeps it open.

The new terminal will provide a more direct Metro link and will house 35 gates along a 1,200-foot-long concourse. As at Dulles, arrivals and departures are separated on different levels. A central level—the main concourse—is designed as a retail street and will connect to the existing Metro station. The focus of the main concourse will be a vaulted glass-domed roof supported by steel columns and aluminum mullions. This open and glassy space is intended to be a dramatic gateway to the capital.

Houses

Light, God's eldest daughter, is a principal beauty in a building.

THOMAS FULLER, 1608–1661

The vast majority of us will never live in an architect-designed house, unless perhaps we live in public housing, or find ourselves enjoying the fortune left by a rich uncle. The custom house for the wealthy client who acts as a patron is where many architects work out themes and ideas that might be otherwise limited by the bottom line of a cautious corporate client.

Modern houses represent a shift from the static conception of a building as a box cut out with utilitarian openings—doors and windows—and decorated for our delight, to a conception of architecture and building as movement in space. Modern space is an unadorned arrangement of light and dark, void and solid, which has to be moved through to be appreciated.

This shift of concept was made possible by new technologies and by social changes. Steel-reinforced concrete, elevators, autos, airplanes, and more informal family life supported by appliances rather than servants, created new physical possibilities and new residential demands. Just as our first view of the earth from the Apollo space shot shifted the sense of humankind's responsibilities to our planet, modern architects' new ability to mold and move through spaces expanded their notion of society and its form. As our interpretation of the world changes, so does our art.

The architect's new concept of a house as a cohesive whole rather than an accretion of details evoking a historic era allows site and function to be generative of form. For example, the breezeway is a functional aspect of southern homes, allowing air to circulate in a hot climate. In a house by Peter Forbes shown in this chapter, this function was the basis of form in the way a dentil, molding, or material could not have been.

Private houses were the vehicles through which modern architects explored and solidified their concepts. Mies van der Rohe's Barcelona Pavilion was based on earlier house sketches. Le Corbusier's Villa Savoye was designed as a prototype for mass reproduction, literally set above the ground, distinct from the landscape, as an expression of an idea. The open plans of Frank Lloyd Wright's prairie houses fundamentally changed our concept of home from the hierarchical spaces of the Victorian era to a building filled with light and air. Walter Gropius's own home in Lincoln, Massachusetts, became a literal and figurative mecca for students of modern architecture.

At its small scale, an individual house becomes the sketch for larger projects to come. At the beginning of both the modern and postmodern movements, large businesses and institutions were not yet willing to invest in these new styles as expressions of corporate goals and ideals. Each generation of pioneering architects relies on wealthy and sophisticated clients who can afford to be patrons.

These houses by no means reflect the average or standard in American housing. They are outstanding buildings, the places where concepts that will shape our larger world are formed. ■

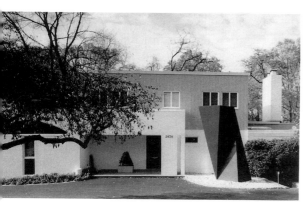

1. English House
Hechinger House
Walter Gropius *1950*

These two houses on adjacent lots reflect the austere modernism of Walter Gropius. Rather than dramatic cantilevers and intersections of masonry and glass used by his colleagues, Gropius here used a simple box shape.

Gropius is most noted for his leadership of the Bauhaus school and movement, from which a generation of artists, architects, and designers would change the way we viewed the world. They abandoned classical motifs and romantic elaboration and built an aesthetic based on the reality of the machine age. As a refugee from Nazi Germany, Gropius settled at Harvard University, where he threw out the precepts of the Beaux-Arts and founded The Architects Collaborative, a still active firm.

These houses exhibit many of the themes of modern architecture established by the Bauhaus. The simple box shape with a flat roof abandons the typical image of a house as a cozy gabled cottage and creates a rational building. The houses' taut skin is created by placing boards on edge, without the traditional batten to mark the seam and seal the joint. (Hugh Newell Jacobsen later used the same technique in the Dreier-Barton House, although the seams there are etched to create a

subtle vertical pattern.) The box is articulated by a series of voids and solids
that create windows, doors, and decks.

Later additions have altered their
exterior appearances somewhat, yet
these are among the first modern
houses in Washington. By one of the
movement's founders, they are the real
thing.

2. Ferris House
Charles Goodman *1956*

As with many modern buildings, this
house is a machine in the garden. The
house's glassy walls and boxy shape set
it apart, and it literally stands alone,
connected to the hillside by a bridge,
rather than settling into the slope.
Landscaping was kept as natural as
possible to preserve the separateness.

Despite being distinct from its surroundings, the house opens gracefully
to the site's natural landscape. A
retaining wall runs from the house
along the driveway, a light reminder of
the line between the natural and built
environment. The main features of the
house are not elaborate cornice lines or
a formal facade, but square and rectangular glass panels that frame views to
the outside and which, from the outside, contrast pleasingly with the solidity and natural forms of the trees and
woods.

Charles Goodman's primarily residential work, from subdivisions to cus-
tom-designed houses, was influential in
introducing a livable modern architecture to the Washington area. His buildings combine themes of modern
architecture—glass walls, rectilinear
detailing, flat roofs, open plans, and
complex, interlocking massing—with a
sensitive siting that capitalizes on views
and privacy.

3. Robert L. Wright House
Frank Lloyd Wright *1958*

The architecture of Frank Lloyd Wright
is completely individual. Independent
of any historical movement, it remains
a strong influence. His work is
described by architectural writer
Leonardo Benevolo as "an architecture
which has precise needs in space,
while living in a mythical, imaginary
sphere of time."

Beginning with the mailbox at the
very edge of the site, there is no mistaking that this house, designed for one
of the architect's sons, is a Frank Lloyd
Wright house. Each small detail of the
design, from landscaping to windowframes, is marked with his unique
style of decoration—here triangles and
semicircles— creating a complete environment.

From the street, Wright controls
movement through the site. The sloping driveway hides the house from
immediate view, and its curve sweeps
visitors through the site and into the
sinuous lines of the house. Even a tree
cutout, slightly off-center, is elliptical,
echoing the house's shape. Terraces

and paths surrounding the house intersect at points that highlight striking
views of it.

Nothing about the design reads
house: its elliptical shape, concrete
block walls, and lancet and screened
windows are not the usual icons of
home, but its scale and attitude mark it
as domestic.

The focal point of the house's front
facade is a tower with lancet windows.
The tower widens at the bottom and is
engaged in a sweep of curved fascia
that notches and comes to a point at
either end. The building's concrete
block lightens as it moves up the
facade toward the deep wooden eave,
first in a strip of windows above eye
level. Just beneath the eave, a block
screen alternates with glass. Where the
tower and curve meet, a notched space
creates a protected door entrance.
While the front facade is dense and
protected, the rear facade is open.
Glass walls give views of the surrounding woods, and decks project outside.

Wright, who used circles as decorative elements in early work, explored
circular building forms later in his
career at this house and in the V. C.
Morris Gift Shop (1948), in a Phoenix
house for another of his sons (David K.
Wright House, 1950), in the
Guggenheim Museum (1956), and in
the Marin County Civic Center (1957).

4. Krieger-Katinas House
Marcel Breuer *1959*

This rectilinear house exhibits many
typical qualities of modern architecture: an open plan, glass walls, nontra-
ditional materials, and shapes and lines
that move through the house, uniting it
as a single design.

Also like many modern homes, this
house is carefully sited. Tucked into the

side of a slope, the house sits above its
neighbors, achieving both privacy and
views. Rather than using the hill as a
podium or platform, the house seems
to extend out of the slope.

Interestingly, this sensitivity to site is
not evident in Breuer's commercial
work. His most noted building, the
Whitney Museum of Modern Art, is a
dramatic tour de force of overhanging
stepped tiers, unlike anything in the
Manhattan streetscape. His work for
the federal government in Washington,
the Housing and Urban Development
and Hubert H. Humphrey office buildings, take no notice of their classical
neighbors and persist in a modernist
ethic that is almost brutal.

The house is bounded by brick side
walls that reach out into the yard,
defining space and uniting the inside
and outside, so visible through glass
walls. Interior rooms are detailed with
warm materials: a wood-and-cane
screen divides the living and dining
rooms. (While head of the furniture
design section at the Bauhaus, the
architect used cane to create the nearly
ubiquitous Breuer chair.) A tongue-in-
groove wooden ceiling runs the length
of both rooms, which are paved with
irregular pieces of bluestone. Despite
what may seem austere spaces, the

warm materials and light that flood the house make it warm in the winter. In the summer, many of the glass walls slide, opening the house to outside patios.

As with many residents of modern homes, the owners here struggle with aging appliances and finishes. Many materials cannot be replaced since they are no longer available. Colors, the placement of new doors and windows, even installing a microwave are carefully considered in light of what the architect and original owners might have intended.

5. Slayton House
I. M. Pei and Associates *1962*

This house on a small city lot relies on strong geometries for its impact, is filled with dramatic natural light, and has meticulously crafted details for an elegant finish. As in his larger-scale work, here Pei uses concrete in the barrel vaults that define the house.

The house is composed of three linked concrete barrel vaults, resting on brick piers and side walls. The ends of the barrel vaults are completely filled with glass. The front facade is screened from the street by a high brick wall that encloses a garden. The strong shapes of the vaults are not typically domestic, but they are well scaled to the neighborhood, creating a welcoming and compatible neighbor.

The building sits formally on its site, the glass-walled vaults coming to rest lightly on a thin base of concrete. The house is set on its sloping site to create a split level plan that places bedrooms on the lower level and the main living spaces on the higher level. Rooms at both levels are at either end of the house, separated by a service spine, to take advantage of views and light. Pei further emphasizes the geometry of the barrel vault by insetting a skylight that dramatically lights a flight of stairs, almost as if it were a proscenium stage.

The clean lines and sophisticated profile of this house work well on its site, but also create a comfortable home cushioned by its walled garden from the surrounding city.

6. Cafritz House
Hugh Newell Jacobsen *1965*

Although Hugh Jacobsen is undoubt-
edly a modern architect in his use of
light to define forms and arrangement
of open spaces to create a building, a
property owner can entrust a historic
building to him. His fine appreciation
of line updates a building in effective
ways, highlighting historical detail by
throwing it into relief.

In this Italianate row house,
Jacobsen opened the windows by
lengthening them and replacing the
horizontal panes with long vertical
panes. The deep black reveals of the
windows emphasize the width of the
wall and the weight of the window.
Although the new windows are vertically divided, the crossing mullions are
so thin as to be almost unnoticeable.
While clearly changing the facade, the
windows are set in carefully, maintaining their width, not crossing cornice
lines or stringcourses, and keeping the

slightly curved window tops of the
Italiante style. Jacobsen's alterations
work with the elongated graceful spirit
of Italianate houses, which emphasize
window openings with heavy frames.

To further maintain the spirit of the
street, the most drastic changes were
reserved for the rear facade, where the
long windows are repeated in varying
sizes and arrangements to express a
base, piano nobile, and upper story.

7. Tempchin House
Charles Moore *1967*

Charles Moore's influence on residential design stemmed from the ideas he
expressed in *The Place of Houses,* and
from his work at Sea Ranch, a beach-
front condominium community in
California. In this work he explores the
forms houses can take in response to
their sites, climates, neighborhoods,
and residents.

Moore was an influential postmodern architect whose later work ques-
tioned the universality of modern
architecture and introduced historical
and regional elements, sometimes in a
very playful way. His Piazza d'Italia in
New Orleans was one of a few projects
in the mid-1970s that reintroduced

classical and figurative detailing. In his work at Sea Ranch he took a modernist approach to form and combined it with natural materials that would weather in the sea air. Its sloped roofs and wood clapboards created a new domestic form copied in residential developments across the country.

In this house, Moore begins to refer to regional and historical styles: the farmhouses of the area and Palladian villas, which are tied to outlying dependencies either by arcades or landscaping. But in no way does he follow their historical detail. The house is informed by their spirit.

In *The Place of Houses,* Moore addresses room arrangement options. One option is a house organized along a single axis. In the Tempchin House a central spine changes from hallway to arcade as it moves through the house linking it with the carport. The pattern and arrangement of rooms is a personal expression of family and lifestyle.

8. Brown House
Richard Neutra *1968*
Cass and Associates *1993*

On a spectacular site overlooking a park, this house, like many modern homes, makes use of glass walls meeting planes of stone and white stucco to shape spaces defined by light.

Much of Richard Neutra's work was built in California, where cantilevered, planar white walls became a signature of his work. While at Smith College the owner of this house studied architectural history with Henry-Russell Hitchcock, who, with Philip Johnson, wrote the seminal work, *The International Style.* The owners later sought out Neutra and looked at three Washington sites with him.

Neutra's talent for siting buildings in a natural setting was nurtured during an apprenticeship with Frank Lloyd Wright and explored in his later work. He found this sloping site both chal-

lenging and intriguing. It had been used informally as a dump. Wooded and secluded, it overlooks Rock Creek Park yet is just blocks away from busy urban streets.

The relationship of a building to the land is central to our perception of that building. A Georgian mansion sits formally and orders the surrounding landscape by its presence. Many modern homes link themselves more organically with nature, sometimes literally inviting it in, as with the stream that runs through Wright's masterpiece house, Fallingwater. This house, which is quite distinct from its surroundings, grows from the hill as a natural extension, inviting outside in through glass. The house is composed of interlocking walls that visibly rest on each other, sometimes to spectacular effect where masonry meets glass.

9. Kreeger House
Philip Johnson *1969*

The Foxhall area of Washington is one of estates on wooded sites tucked into hills and valleys and buffered from the rest of the city by Glover Archbold Park. With each generation, many of the grand estates in the neocolonial, Georgian Revival, and Tudor Revival styles have turned over either to subdivisions or embassies.

David Lloyd Kreeger, founder of GEICO, commissioned this house to make a home for the very personal collection of Impressionist, post-Impressionist, and African art that he and his wife had assembled. The building was designed as a house, but with all the features of an art gallery. It is at once a backdrop and a commanding presence.

Johnson used a simple but classic

form, the groin vault, to create a series of open and closed pavilions that frame spaces and views. The shallow domes top two-story pavilions grouped around a one-story entrance that is defined by a panel of white travertine and a dark recessed doorway. The arched windows tucked under the shallow vaults are screened with dark metal louvers. This treatment is reminiscent of Johnson's work at the Boston Public Library. While on different scales, the library and the Kreeger House share an elegant simplicity generated by strong forms and fine finishes.

The house is composed of a series of spaces and shapes. The shallow arch of the groin-vaulted domes is the central theme, enhanced by the round drums supporting railings that double as benches, the squares of the building's travertine cladding and paving blocks, and the rectangles of piers, cross beams, windows, window louvers, and railings. The composition flows from walled to open spaces, with the shallow arches billowing above, and ends in a pool court walled with a travertine arcade that echoes the shallow arches of the vaults.

The building is arranged in modular units of 22 feet, used both vertically and horizontally. On the interior, full-height spaces alternate with half-height rooms, varying the degree of formality and intimacy. As with the exteriors, the interiors are finished with materials not usually associated with domestic buildings. A large entry loggia, an inner courtyard, and connected rooms are designed to accommodate circulation. Travertine and carpeted walls provide a background for the art collection.

Here, Johnson has achieved a serene classical elegance without the ornate details of capitals and columns. One looks with an almost voyeuristic eye, wondering how a person could live in a place where domestic images seem to have been set aside to create a home for art. This house museum is intensely personal and unique, as is the collection it houses.

10. Residence
Hartman-Cox *1969*

Unlike other modern or contemporary houses, this house departs from a firm modernist tenet. While the massing is anything but traditional, the house gently incorporates traditional domestic forms and scale to create a hybrid. It is this integrating approach that has helped make Hartman-Cox such a successful Washington firm. They are consummate contextualists who can work in just the right amount of history to please the client, the neighbors, and the public taste.

The house's most notable feature is its asymmetrical massing, facing away from busy streets. Unlike that of a traditional house, the floor plan is not a single enclosed shape but a series of spaces that creates a notched floor plan. The long slopes of the shed roofs build up to a central point. The board-and-batten siding and wooden roof shingles of this house are traditional domestic details, but ones that have been used elsewhere by the firm. The Immanuel Church in McLean is sided with board and batten, and the dramatic, sloping roof of the chapel at Mount Vernon College shapes that building. This house, within its traditional skin, focuses inward, creating its own environment, distinct from the street.

The combination of architecture and siting results in a house that is compatible with its neighbors, but that meets the demands to create privacy on a difficult site.

11. Dreier-Barton House
Hugh Newell Jacobsen *1977*

This spare and elegant house is composed of four offset gabled pavilions sheathed in vertical boards separated by thin spaces, creating a pattern reminiscent of board and batten. The house gains its impact from the use of traditional forms stripped to their essential. The arrangement of distinct pavilions, a theme explored in other Jacobsen works, has a graphic effect that, combined with the pure white skin, makes the house seem almost like a piece of intricately folded origami.

The house sits on a podium-like deck that steps to the ground in front of the house and floats out over the slope of the back. The podium lifts the house off the ground, emphasizing the house's pure form. On the interior, pavilions organize and separate uses, distinguishing between public and private space. Each pavilion has a distinct position marked by views and purpose in the overall composition.

The current owner's experience with historic preservation has led her to approach the house, which had deteriorated, with an eye for detail and verity. Siding and shingles have been carefully replaced and flashing added as subtly as possible so as not to take away from the house's crisp lines. The owner has also worked with carpenters who were able to replicate the high level of craftsmanship needed to retain the integrity of the house. Changes and repairs were approached as if this was a landmark of the future, which it is.

large, reflecting the cost of lots in this desirable neighborhood, which demand using every inch available.

The shape of this house is formed by its roughly triangular site. At street level a sweep of gray clapboard is broken for entrances. As the facade rises, the house opens into two masses topped with chimneys and separated by a bridge. The taut clapboard skin is broken by windows on the upper level. Moore acted as a design consultant on this house and, typical of his work, he makes historical allusions in a completely contemporary context.

12. Verleger House
Moore Grover Harper   *1983*

Charles Moore was a peripatetic architect teaching and practicing architecture across the country. His first firm, MLTW, designed Sea Ranch, which became a prototype for contemporary residential design. He founded Moore Grover Harper—now Centerbrook Architects—in 1975, while teaching at Yale. He left the theorizing to others and pursued instead the creation of architecture that expressed his views.

This house is in a neighborhood of extraordinary houses including Hillwood, Marjorie Merriwether Post's mansion, which boasts not only the main house but a re-created Russian dacha, and an Adirondack-style cabin. Neighborhood houses include some well-settled neocolonials, but also a range of modern houses. Early International Style houses in the neighborhood are modestly sized and hang their rectilinear masses off the hills sloping down to Rock Creek Park. The houses of the 1970s and 1980s reflect aesthetic standards of their times, from dramatically sloped roofs and glassy walls, to more traditional re-creations of Shingle Style and Queen Anne houses. The most recent houses are

13. Residence
Cesar Pelli   *1989*

Pelli began his career in the office of Eero Saarinen, the architect of Dulles Airport, and made his name designing corporate headquarters. Until this commission, he had worked only on conceptual residential projects for exhibitions. For the Venice Biennale he proposed a house organized along a central spine with pavilions that could be added or taken away. Pelli also used the center spine as an organizing feature in Maryland's Comsat building (see chapter 8).

The concept of a central spine is the basis for this house. The clients worked with Pelli on a model of the site and house, shifting, adding, and subtracting pavilions to create the desired result and, in the process, completely exploring his Biennale concept.

The central gallery has been described as a street connecting all parts of the house. Like the central hall of a traditional house it is an organizing center. Pelli uses residential materials—brick, slate, and stucco—as well as residential motifs, like hipped and gabled roofs, arranged in a new way to reexamine the concept and function of a house.

distinctly different from the neighboring tall rectangular town houses. Instead its massing is reminiscent of a carriage house in a mews.

Ironically, nearly 50 years after Capitol Hill's notorious alley dwellings were razed by urban renewal, this alley house is a luxury.

14. Residence
Davis Buckley *1993*

Infill construction in an urban historic district is among the most challenging of architectural projects. Any proposal brings out the bureaucrats with their regulations, the neighborhood die-hards unwilling to accept change, and the historians who focus their attention on the detail of a window. Rarely is there an advocate for modern architecture, for an approach that is sensitive to context but daring in outlook.

Rather than plugging a building into its streetfront slot, the architect here redefined the urban environment by creating a streetside garden marked with a pergola that leads to a hidden house in the alley behind. Building a small pergola that covered only a fraction of the streetfront lot allowed construction to the lot lines on the alley site. The house's single-story, compressed silica block walls enclose two interior courtyards—one with a fountain, the other around a lap pool. French doors open to the courtyards. The shape and plan of the house are

15. Residence
Peter Forbes *1993*

This subdivision was originally built in the 1930s with simple houses. Since then, many of the small, brick homes have been redeveloped, and the street is now a delightful pastiche of styles.

The redevelopment of this one-and-a-half-story house retained three original brick walls and the chimney. The old house was oriented to the street. The new house is oriented to a desired view and is built between the old walls, creating a shift of 10 degrees between the old and new structures.

The long, two-story, front-gabled building is flanked on either side by two single-story, attached ells between the new building and the old walls. One ell is an entry and the other is a kitchen overlooking a courtyard. The new building's sides and roof are wrapped in sheet metal and the front is almost entirely glass. The house is stunning and unlike any other on the street, but it is comfortably domestic in scale and residential in reference.

The architect sees this as a southern house; both the central spine and side spaces are like open breezeways allowing air and light to flow through the house. The idea of the breezeway, in Charleston-style houses, became a generative concept that gives the house an overall shape and attitude. The house is not precisely like historic southern houses, but takes its spirit from them.

16. Knight House
Mark McInturf *1994*

This house is the result of an ongoing collaboration between architect and client. The first project was the renovation of an in-town house; the second, a newly constructed vacation house in the Shenandoah foothills. This third project, a newly constructed in-town house makes architectural references to its predecessors.

As in his other work, the designer uses shapes and materials that are not traditional to residential design to create a building that nonetheless reads house. The building is organized in two distinct masses, a rectangular box sheathed in black seamed metal and an arched roof over a glassy volume. The two spaces are divided diagonally through the center of the house by a line of concrete columns leading to a reflecting pool. The materials and colors, the same corrugated metal used in the vacation house, burnt red metal work, deep orange window frames and blue-green slate are not jarring but a richly varied palette.

The two parts of the house are linked by a front door and portico oriented to the suburban street behind a driveway, like its more traditional neighbors. Also, as in his other work, the designer responds to the site, in this case suburban. On either side of the site are houses by Charles Goodman. His houses are assemblages of wood and glass designed to shelter while opening to their natural surroundings. All three share views to Rock Creek Park, and the Knight House echoes the window pattern of its two neighbors.

Further Reading

Goode, James M. *Best Addresses.* Washington, D.C.: Smithsonian Press, 1988.

Highsmith, Carol M. and Ted Landphair. *Pennsylvania Avenue: America's Main Street.* Washington, D.C.: American Institute of Architects Press, 1988.

Longstreth, Richard, ed. T*he Mall in Washington 1791–1991.* Washington, D.C.: National Gallery of Art, University Press of New England, 1991.

Reps, John W. Washington on View, *The Nation's Capital Since 1790.* Chapel Hill: University of North Carolina Press, 1991.

Scott, Pamela and Antoinette Lee. *Buildings of the District of Columbia.* New York: Oxford University Press, 1993.

Weeks, Christopher, *AIA Guide to the Architecture of Washington, D.C.* Third Edition, Baltimore: Johns Hopkins University Press, 1994

Index